EXPECTATION

D1607620

Also by Jean-Luc Nancy and published
by Fordham University Press

Expectation

PHILOSOPHY, LITERATURE

JEAN-LUC NANCY

Translated by
ROBERT BONONNO

Texts compiled with the assistance of
GINETTE MICHAUD

FORDHAM UNIVERSITY PRESS
New York   2018

This book was originally published in French as Jean-Luc Nancy, *Demande: Philosophie, littérature*, Copyright © Éditions Galilée, 2015. Five texts from *Demande*—"Faire, la poésie," "Compter avec la poésie. Entretien avec Pierre Alferi," "Il dit," "Péan pour Aphrodite," and "Vox clamans in deserto"—are not included in the present volume but appear in English in Jean-Luc Nancy, *Multiple Arts: The Muses* II, ed. Simon Sparks (Stanford: Stanford University Press, 2006).

The translations of "Noli Me Frangere," "Exergues," and "Psyche" first appeared in Jean-Luc Nancy, *The Birth to Presence*, copyright © 1993 by the Board of Trustees of the Leland Stanford Jr. University. All rights reserved. Reprinted by permission of the publisher, Stanford University Press, sup.org.

Ouvrage publié avec le concours du Ministère français chargé de la Culture–Centre National du Livre.

This work has been published with the assistance of the French Ministry of Culture–National Center for the Book.

Visit us online at www.fordhampress.com.

Library of Congress Cataloging-in-Publication Data available online at http://catalog.loc.gov.

Printed in the United States of America

20 19 18   5 4 3 2 1

First edition

CONTENTS

EXPECTATION: PREFACE TO THE ENGLISH-LANGUAGE EDITION

As is often the case, my title is not easy to translate. Nothing is easy in any transla-
tion, and Robert Bononno knows very well the many and great difficulties he has
encountered in this text—unexpected, of course, and unwanted (especially in some
texts written in the 1970s with the wit and joking taste of the time). That is why
I start this preface writing an English of my own in order to lighten his work and
to help the reader laugh.[1]

The French title is "*Demande*." In English, "demand" resonates with
much greater imperiousness or exigency than in French. A *demande* is a
request and can even be a kind of prayer, supplication, or entreaty. Colored
by psychoanalysis, it resonates like a "demand for love,"[2] which is quite
distinct from both need and desire. The *demande* waits, hopes, wishes.
Desire advances, rises, and moves forward.

"Expectation" responds better to what "*Demande*" says to me in French.
Philosophy and literature are in need of one another: not because they
desire something of the other but as a "demand for love" or, at least, for
encounter and sharing. Moreover, expectations are not symmetrical and in
that sense I need to correct my introductory "Coda" somewhat. Philosophy expects more than literature because philosophy is experienced
through suffering and is required to have a sense, whereas literature continues to defy sense. From this point of view, the "expectational" affect is
much stronger in philosophy. On the other hand, literature expects to
make sense while defying demonstrative and argumentative regimes. It
doesn't want to be merely decorative or entertaining.

Philosophy does indeed hope to achieve the freedom of the narrative or
myth, which no concept can touch. Literature would like to elide or elude
the concept so that sense might be more strongly felt. Their division is a
division of sense itself. The division that forms what we call "sense": from
the outset, the word itself names its own division, its fissure, its opening.

But I have to stop here, for I'm beginning to rewrite the entire book . . .
or a different one.

"Wet the Ropes!": Poetics of Sense, from Paul Valéry to Jean-Luc Nancy

Jean-Michel Rabaté

This compilation of essays and poems by one of today's most distinguished philosophers is a *summa poetica*. *Expectation* provides a non-systematic corpus of poetics that is both retrospective and prospective. In a classically philological mode, Nancy is attentive to the genealogy of terms such as *aiodos*, *parodos*, and *muthos*; at times, more experimental explorations pave the way for the creation of new forms valid for the twenty-first century. The texts collected in *Expectation* were written over a period of thirty-five years and thus offer multiple pathways for investigating, inchoatively— that is, in a gesture that is always new and always to be repeated—the loaded, enigmatic, and tantalizing interactions between poetic form and abstract thought.

In terms of the concepts deployed in the following pages, we encounter here an original dialogue between "Philosophy" as such and "Literature" as such. For the first time, however, Nancy takes his stand both as a philosopher and as a poet facing these abstractions. It is not uncommon to see philosophers doubling as novelists or playwrights (one can think of Jean-Paul Sartre, Maurice Blanchot, William Gass, or Alain Badiou) but rare to see thinkers who are primarily philosophers succeed in the production of poetry. The names of Coleridge, Hölderlin, and Hopkins come to mind, but their meditations limited themselves to issues of aesthetics. In the French tradition, only Paul Valéry comes to mind; it is not a coincidence that he plays an important role for Nancy.

In the dialogue between philosophy and literature, no doubt an ancient dialogue fraught with suspicion and leading to attempts at reciprocal containment, the two domains appear less as enemies than rival neighbors; they act as sparring partners, each attempting to stare the other down. Taking as his point of departure a German Romanticism marked by the parting of ways between Hegel and Hölderlin, whereby Hegel, the systematic thinker, let his friend, the poet, Hölderlin explore the night of myth, tragedy, and lyricism on his own, Jean-Luc Nancy offers his own version of the age-old confrontation.

Nancy accomplishes this by exploring a venerable tradition that goes back to Homer, Heraclitus, Plato, and Aristotle, and includes Schlegel, Novalis, Heidegger, and Blanchot, not to mention the numerous contemporary French poets with whom he has been interacting for decades. This is why Nancy can resort to old tricks in this tight interaction, one of them being the conceit of "wetting the ropes." The expression was used by Valéry to explain how inspiration came back to him when he was struggling to complete one of his major poems, the 1917 "La Jeune Parque" (often translated as "The Young Fate"), a long and obscure poem rewritten as "La Jeune Carpe" ("The Young Carp") in *Expectation*.

In "The Prince and the Young Fate," an essay published in *Variété*, Valéry explains that after having spent his youth writing poetry, he decided to abandon poetic writing as a waste of time. He would devote his energy to science, philosophy, and other intellectual pursuits. Later, the longing to make music with rhyming words returned, especially after he heard the recitatives from Gluck's 1767 opera, *Alceste*. Valéry accumulated a mass of notes (five hundred different layers of text have been found), all evoking a young woman's inner monologue, but despaired of introducing any order. One day, exhausted and frustrated by his literary labors, he sat down in an empty café and started reading a newspaper, focusing upon a review of Rachel's career. The famous actress, who died in 1858, was much admired by a German prince, who was in love with her. The prince talked with the journalist, who quoted him in his evocation of her gestures and intonations, providing a detailed analysis of her vocal range during her extraordinary performances. The eloquent description of the actor's mannerisms served as a trigger for Valéry. His inspiration was renewed; a method, a structure, and a style were found for "The Young Fate."

To make his meaning clearer, Valéry compared the chance discovery of this article with an event that took place in Rome in September 1586, when Pope Sixtus V planned to erect an Egyptian obelisk in the middle of Saint Peter's square. He hired the architect Domenico Fontana, who gathered a small army of 800 men, 140 horses, and 40 cranes to transport and raise the imposing mass of red granite. The pope had ordered, under pain of death, that no one should speak during the operation. As the obelisk was being lifted, the hemp ropes that held it loosened and the granite blocks of the obelisk began dangling halfway, threatening to fall back and crush the onlookers. At this juncture, someone disobeyed the order to keep silent and shouted: "Wet the ropes! Wet the ropes!" This person knew that when one wets new hemp ropes, they shrink immediately. Water was poured, which allowed the ropes to tighten around the stone blocks. Once they were pulled tight together, the blocks fell into place at the desired spot, to everyone's relief. Valéry concludes: ". . . an idea set the stone upright."[1] Later, the poet wanted to verify that the incident had not been random or subjective. He mentioned it to his friend Pierre Louÿs, his mentor in poetry after the death of Mallarmé. With a grin, Louÿs pulled out the article on Rachel that he himself had covered with annotations in red ink.

The anecdote of the Vatican obelisk has been recounted many times, always with diverging interpretations. At times, it is an Italian sailor who is mentioned as screaming "Acqua alle funi!" or "Acqua alle corne!" At times, it is a British sailor who passes by and screams in English: "Wet the ropes!" Some believe that the water prevented the ropes from burning, given the friction with the granite; others thought that wetting the hemp provided slack instead of tightening. In all versions, however, the screaming individual is first condemned for having broken the silence and then handsomely rewarded by the pope. One could take this story as a cultural metaphor and follow its transformations the way Hans Blumemberg has done when he analyzed the successive versions of the story of Thales's fall into a well when he was gazing at the stars.[2] Here, for Valéry at least, this would testify to the power of an "idea" over matter.

Can this incident be called an "idea"? It was a sudden flash of insight conveyed to overwhelmed workers by a specialist in ropes. If it was a sailor, and why not an English sailor, it was at least someone who "knew the ropes," to use an idiom deriving either from the language of seafaring or from the vocabulary of theatrical machines. The useful tip thrown in at the last moment by a specialist suddenly corrected a flawed apparatus made up of cranes, horses, and men. The shout of "wet the ropes" fixed things by a sudden tightening that was both verbal and ideal. It was more than ideal, for this "idea" had rendered an erection possible. No reader of Valéry, especially of "The Young Fate," with its teeming serpents, can disregard the florid sexual imagery of many passages. Moreover, in the Roman anecdote, the action was made possible by the intervention of the feminine substance of water—which also happens when the young Fate hesitates between earth, sea, and sun, allegorizing the drama of self-consciousness and unconscious eroticism that Valéry's poem displays.

The only point not in dispute in the accounts from Rome in 1586 was that the performative utterance of the command "Wet the ropes!" had been felicitous: it was immediately obeyed with positive results. The anecdote can turn into an allegory, almost a witticism, if not straightway a *Witz*. The statement that served as a motto for the author of "The Young Fate," a poem that inspired Nancy as we will see, confirms that Valéry was interested in architecture and technology. Like Leonardo da Vinci, Valéry was awed by scientific miracles that make stones stand, iron wings fly, and electricity convey information. However, "wet the ropes!" has a homely ring. The forceful injunction had been heard by Nancy when he decided to rewrite the poem with radical modifications. "Wet the ropes!" is not far from the witty spoonerism that inverts the name of "*la Jeune Parque*" into a vulgar "*jeune carpe.*" The lovely and forlorn young Fate has been metamorphosed into the "queen of rivers," here also a smelly fish caught up in the stale and rotting waters of a lake.

> What sinister décor the asylum of a carp
> Slips beneath the oblique procession of my days!
> And what forbidden laugh is revealed by the contours
> Of this fleeting and sluggish life that limits itself
> With a monotone skin and a dismal rule . . .
> Every moment abandons me to the detailed pattern
> Of the number of the scale, with the scale entwined.

(See "The Young Carp" in this collection.)

In a further twist on the ropes used by the pope's architect, these ropes turn into the threads of life spun by the first Parca, whose name was Nona in Latin, and Clotho in Greek. Nona would spin the thread of life of all humans from her distaff onto her spindle; because her name called up "the ninth one" (*nona*), she was associated with pregnancy. Pregnant women would invoke her name in Rome, which may have something to do with Nancy's choice of a different title in English: *Expectation* is also a text about giving birth, or more precisely about expectant mothers—and perhaps fathers. *Expectation* stages a courtship between philosophy and literature that has never been presented with such wit, grace, and finesse. What's more, this intense courtship leads to a marriage blessed with specific off-spring: Nancy's book offers both an epithalamium and a pregnant poetics, a poetics of awakening and emergence—poetics as obstetrics ushering in new "senses" in and of the world, plus strong and luminescent poems never seen in English before. Precocious chords indeed:

> O Fate! . . . your intimate fragrance enthralls me
> When, within your ambit, I detect the furtive presence
> Of man, incessantly shaped by your fingers
> From a branch of hemp in which his destiny slept,
> Fine frail fiber and too precocious cord.

(See "The Young Carp" in this collection.)

Nancy's version is faithful to what inspired Valéry in the first place, a rewriting in the feminine of Mallarmé's *Prelude to the Afternoon of a Faun*, a re-twining of diverse strands of mythical or pastoral lore; in both poems, heady insinuations of auto-eroticism recur, as in this excerpt. The Young Fate feels her breasts swell and expects them to be kissed by the wind and whoever comes upon her, almost regretting that she cannot kiss herself. Much like Freud's generic baby who discovers ecstatic thumb-sucking, she wonders aloud, "A shame I can't kiss myself."[3] This narcissistic wish recurs in the last text of *Expectation*, "Let him kiss me with his mouth's kisses," a truly modernist rewrite of Louise Labé's famous sonnet XVIII, "Baise m'encor."[4] For the carp, as for the Fate, a reflexive question recurs: Is one kissing one's lips at the same time that one kisses someone else's lips?

> Gift of mercy
> Where all mouths are joined
> Kiss and kiss one another
> Touch and touch one another.

> > "The Young Carp"

The *parque/carpe* spoonerism soon discloses a more learned witticism in which one could discern a Romantic *Witz*. The witty reversal of the consonants /p/ and /c/ has a function other than ironic disruption, for any reader aware of Latin tags will recognize a submerged echo of *carpe diem* in the irreverent title of "*La Jeune Carpe*." Horace famously wrote in his Ode:

> . . . sapias, vina liques, et spatio brevi
> spem longam reseces. Dum loquimur, fugerit invida
> aetas: carpe diem, quam minimum credula postero.

A literal translation might be: "May you acquire wisdom and work on your wines; because of brief life, sever any long-term hope. As we speak, enviously a lifetime has fled. Seize the day and have little trust in the future." We will have to read "The Young Carp" as Nancy's serious parody to understand that this reminder also adheres to the poem: the poet has to interrupt and cut (*resecare*), snipping ropes that offer too much slack when hauling off the unwarranted hope for the future. This is why Nancy can repeat that poetry operates almost medically by cutting, interrupting, severing itself from itself.

I have mentioned the term *Witz*, a loaded German word meaning "witticism," "wit," "joke," and "pun," with which this collection begins. In "*Menstruum universale*," Nancy discusses the term in the context of his earlier explorations of German romanticism. The essay dates from 1977 and provides a blueprint for a section of the 1978 book that Nancy wrote jointly with Philippe Lacoue-Labarthe, his closest friend and collaborator, present in almost all the pages of *Expectation*, above all in the moving homage rendered to him in New York in 2008, as we see in "After Tragedy." *The Literary Absolute: The Theory of Literature in German Romanticism*[5] has a section entitled "The Fragmentary Exigency" showing why the concept of *Witz* has to be placed at the core of German romanticism. In the *Athenaeum*, Friedrich Schlegel developed a theory of the reduction of the philosophical system à la Kant or Hegel into a series of dense, independent fragments. Such fragments could be further condensed as *Witze*. As Lacoue-Labarthe and Nancy write:

> *Witz* is concerned with the fragment, first of all, in that both of these "genres" (insofar as they can be given such a name) imply the "sudden idea" (*Einfall*, the idea that suddenly "falls" upon you, so that the find is less found than received). The "motley heap of sudden ideas" implies something of *Witz*, just as, because "many witty sudden ideas" [*witzige Einfälle*] are like the sudden meeting of two friendly thoughts after a long separation, *Witz* seems to imply within itself the entire fragmentary, dialogical, and dialectical structure that we have outlined.
> The essence of the "sudden idea" consists in its being a synthesis of thoughts. As a result of a tradition that goes back to the seventeenth century, *Witz* is basically qualified as a unification of heterogeneous elements . . . (*LA*, 52)

In their groundbreaking treatise on the poetics of German Romanticism, Lacoue-Labarthe and Nancy remind us that *Witz* derives from *Wissen*, meaning knowledge. It is related to French *esprit* and to English *wit*, terms that refer to knowledge, but a different knowledge, a knowledge that is in some way always "other." It is a witty knowledge that eschews the stale and systematic discursivity of Reason. Romantic *Witz* thus brings to a climax the metaphysics of the *Idea*, the Idea's self-knowledge emerging poetically in its auto-manifestation. Therefore, the most bizarre or baroque manifestations become compatible with the highest knowledge capable of reaching the infinite. I quote their text:

> *Witz* is also a quality attributable to every type of genre or work, a spiritual faculty, and a type of spirit. Or perhaps it is the spirit-type, which in a single glance and with lightning speed (the assonance *Blitz-Witz* was often used, although it does not appear in the *Fragments*), in the confusion of a heterogeneous chaos, can seize upon and bring to light new, unforeseen and, in short, creative relations. "Witz is creative, it produces resemblances," Novalis writes in *Grains of Pollen*. *Witz* is an immediate, absolute knowing-seeing [*savoir-voir*]; it is sight [*vue*] regained at the blindspot of schematism and, consequently, sight gaining direct access to the productive capacity of works. (*LA*, 52)

Witz generates a poetry capable of "losing itself in what it presents" because irony is its key component. Romantic irony supposes the identity of the creative self and of the nothingness of works in what the romantics saw as a "transcendental buffoonery," a phrase that captures well Nancy's effort in his poem. At the same time, *Witz* appears caught up in a dilemma, an impossible choice between dissolution and recombination:

> On the path toward the absolute, toward absolute fragmentary absolution, romanticism will now follow two distinct and continually crossing paths. The first, that of Novalis, redefines *Witz* as simultaneous combination and dissolution: "*Witz*, as a principle of affinity, is at the same time *menstruum universale*" (*Grains of Pollen*) [*Blüthenstaub* fragment 57]. The universal solvent undoes the systematic, undoes the identity of the poet and sweeps it toward the "dissolution in song" evoked by a posthumous fragment intended for *Heinrich von Ofterdingen*, a dissolution that includes the sacrifice, in all its ambiguity, of the poet ("he will be sacrificed by savage peoples"). The ambiguity of sacrifice (sanctification), however, corresponds to the ambiguity of the motif of dissolution, which leads the chemistry of the *Witz* back to the alchemy of the *menstruum*, and therefore to the Great Work, while at the same time leading back to *Auflösung* (dissolution) in the sense, found notably in Kant, of organic assimilation, of "intussusception."

The second, Schlegelian path might be indicated by *Athenaeum* fragment 375 as the path leading toward "energy" or toward "the energetic man," defined by the "infinitely flexible . . . universal power through which the whole man shapes himself," well beyond the "genius" who "shapes a work." Energy extends to the limit of the work and of the system; its "infinite flexibility," linked to "an incalculable number of projects," effects an infinite fragmentation of work and system. But what is this flexibility, if not an infinite capacity for form, for the absolute of form; and what is energy, *en-ergeia*, if not the putting-into-work itself, the completed *organon*, whose works (of genius) are mere potentialities? (*LA*, 56–57)

This double postulation, either dissolution or energy, can be combined—dissolution *and* energy—which brings *Witz* closer to Maurice Blanchot's concept of "unworking," or "undoing" (*désoeuvrement*), also a manifestation of latent irony and parody. If *Witz* creates resemblances, it is by folding itself upon itself endlessly, thereby generating a process of dissemination and dissolution so pervasive that one can never be sure of avoiding pure chaos:

> The properly romantic—poietic—task is not to dissipate or reabsorb chaos, but to construct it or to make a *Work* from disorganization. For "potential organic beings," organization and generation can and must occur in the midst of disorganization, both as a parody of themselves and in keeping with the true "method and symmetry" of the System. The fragment, in this case, is the genre of the parody of the putting-into-work, or of the parodic putting-into-work, which inevitably refers back to "chaos" *also* as an exemplary Work, particularly in Roman satire and, above all, in Shakespeare (. . .). By also affirming itself as a dramatization, fragmentation would thus refer, both parodically and seriously, to itself, to its own chaos as the genre of the Work. Of course, through the well-known duplicity of parody, another value of chaos has been present from the start. (*LA*, 51)

In this sense, Nancy is right when he asserts that even Valéry's "La Jeune Parque" was not exempt from parody ("The Young Carp"). He insists that parody should not be confused with stylistic pastiche: parody is *parodos*, a "para-ôdè," which means the song near the other song, or the "discrepant moment of song," the moment when the infinity of Spirit will have to be confronted with the finitude of untranslatable signifiers. These signifiers provide echoes that obey apparently random echolalias; for example, my pun on the links between "rope," "hope," and "pope" earlier, words that could not be aligned in French for instance, or the assonance of *Blitz-Witz*, only valid in German.

This is why Valéry's original poem is structured by the roll-call of French rhymes; they cannot be rendered in English without creating an impossibly artificial style. Nancy's practice follows Valéry literally on that point. Even when lines are not rhymed, the practice of "verse" as *versus*, that is to say the regular return to the next line, a structure abundantly glossed in Nancy's pages, is sufficient to distinguish poetry as such: blank spaces introduced in the continuity of a voice mark the origin of poetry while accounting for its loaded links with philosophy.

Derrida pointed out in his essay "Qual Quelle" that it was because he was both a poet and a philosopher that Valéry understood so well that philosophy had to be "written." The wish to assert truth on its own, independent from any natural language, a desire manifested by philosophy since its inception, cannot avoid being compromised in its very essence by the accidents of homophony, by the unmotivated superposition of echoes, by the arbitrariness of sound shapes: "Valéry reminds the philosopher that philosophy is written. And that the philosopher is a philosopher to the extent that he forgets this."[6] As Derrida explains, this awareness already reached by Nietzsche (a philosopher who had influenced the French poet) entails three main consequences: first, philosophy breaks with the illusion of transparency condensed in the wish to hear oneself speak; then philosophy has to reckon with form, which should lead to a study of the formal practices and programs offered to philosophers; finally, philosophy can never be fully regulated by the law of pure thinking, as Valéry's innumerable remarks on Descartes's *cogito* aver. At the same time, in a consistent paradox, Valéry understood just as clearly that any poem required a certain vocal staging, a theatralization of the utterance, which is why he had been so interested in the description of Rachel's voice techniques. He wrote in his *Cahiers*: "The poem has no sense (*sens*) without ITS voice."[7] Following Nancy's use, one should translate *sens* as "sense," for in recurrent phenomenological explorations that are not limited to poetry and include the substance of the world, Nancy insists upon the interaction between the body and meaning, between flesh and words.

This almost direct confrontation between the senses and thought is one of the most salient features of "The Young Fate," a poem that was read early as a philosophical manifesto by French philosopher Alain. In his 1934 essay, "What Is the Young Fate?," Alain begins by stating that the poem, the most obscure poem of the French language according to him, presented the exact "reverse of our thoughts." He evokes poetically the movements of our bodies, their gestures, hesitations, fluxes, and dreams as the material basis for thought. He concludes his piece with an evocation of the clash between the spontaneous upsurge of life in our limbs and hearts with an inevitable petrification, an entropic death, once the images suggested have taken a definite form: "Now, as long as these signs are as lithe as water, we turn them easily into successful thoughts, and these are happy thoughts. But the crust hardens; rocks are formed at the bottom of that sea; nature shows its angles, folds, pathways; thought follows suit; irritation is assuaged by motivation. No longer a whirlpool but a hardened planet. Nothing to guess, one has just to wait. Minerals embody reason. We cannot explain reason; we can only explain nature. Thus invention perishes as whims die out. Finally the Young Fate turns into an aged Pythia."[8]

Alain was keenly aware of the inner tension between death and life in the poem—Valéry's initial plan had been to have the young mythical being die; the dominant tone was gloomy if not desperate, these lines being written during World War I. He changed his mind at the last moment and showed the young Fate turning at the end toward the Sun, which provided an opportunity for a final paean to survival and the enjoyment of the senses. A similar tension between life and death is perceptible in Nancy's poem, but these binaries tend to get blurred because of the numerous echoes of Homer, Lucretius, Mallarmé, Barthes, Blanchot, Hölderlin, and Heidegger—and of course, all of Valéry's works. It seems that this young carp could be a stuffed carp, an exquisite morsel of *gefilte fish*! Valéry appears in a section of the French original of *Expectation* between de Saussure and Jean-Jacques Rousseau,[9] and the section entitled "Within my breast, Alas, two souls . . ." in *Expectation* rewrites Valéry's play *My Faust*, a provocative reworking of Goethe's *Faust*. All these texts point to the creative division of the speaker in literature and to the demotion of the domineering Author replaced with a newly enfranchised Reader, each of which corresponds to a dramatic role in *My Faust*.

What renders the willing dispossession of the Author possible is that poets (I have mentioned Hölderlin and Valéry, one could add Paul Celan and Yves Bonnefoy) tend to be aware of a constitutive dissolution. Valéry expressed this at the end of another poem, a prose poem this time, entitled "Agathe." A young woman called Agathe pursues a monologue similar to that of the Young Fate when she deliberates with herself: "I thus keep the variety of my restlessness: I maintain in myself a disorder so as to attract my own power or any dispersion that I would expect."[10] Here, the poet's disappearance behind a feminine speaking (and kissing) mouth ushers in a poetics of dissipation opening onto the disparate heterogeneity of the sensual world.

What unites Nancy and Valéry would be a concern for a science of poetics that would be attentive to the absolute singularity and the irreducible specificity of poetic idioms. This is what comes to the fore in *Tel Quel*, Valéry's collection of critical jottings and reflections on poetics published a few years before he died.[11] His formalist leanings underscored a consistent rejection of authorial intention, for he would often say that his poetry had the meaning provided by his readers, while foregrounding the intellectual or reflexive element in literature. As we know, Valéry occupied the newly founded chair of Poetics at the Collège de France from 1937 to his death in 1945. His inaugural speech presented poetics as a study of "the positive phenomenon of production and consumption in the realm of intellectual works."[12] As Derrida had seen, one key principle was that language held sway over thought: "Literature is, and cannot be anything but the extension and application of certain properties of language."[13] A new poetics should usher in investigations of "effects that can be called properly literary,"[14] so as to distinguish them from the process of philosophy and its reliance on extra-linguistic ideas.

Following Valéry's *Tel Quel*, a sequence of remarks all insisting upon the technical aspects of literary craft, Nancy is thorough in his exercises as a close reader, as testified by "The Poet's Calculation," a systematic study of Hölderlin's use of meter. Hölderlin asserts that the task of poetry is to calculate and launches an *ars poetica* intent upon examining the "Whole" without trusting Reason. Exactitude or accuracy will be defined as a thought of primal difference within thought itself, but it is a difference that can be touched, experienced in the life of the poet:

> What is touched is a body. Not a body as organic assumption and
> internal finality but that opposite of the organic that Hölderlin called
> the *aorgic*, a materiality, a divisibility, a body as extension and distinc-
> tion: an "objective coherence . . . but also a felt and tangible coherence
> and identity in the alternation of oppositions," the unity of divisibility
> itself, of the "actual separation" that responds to the *arbitrariness of
> Zeus*, that is to say, the law of tangible and individual distinction.

(See "The Poet's Calculation" in this collection.)

In their joint experience of the absolute distance of the absolute, what distinguished Hölderlin from Valéry was that the French poet continued thinking and writing poetry without becoming mad, as his predecessor had done. For Hölderlin, "the point of contact is thus itself a distance or

separation" (see "The Poet's Calculation" in the text), an expression providing a last gloss on "The Young Fate," a poem that could be called an
exploration of "imminence": "Not an immanence or a transcendence but
an imminence, an infinite proximity that passes as close as possible, close
enough to touch the beating heart. This is the touch of the 'living sense'
upon the 'null sense,' it is the point of unity of the whole, and the space-
time of that point" ("The Poet's Calculation"). Thus, both Hölderlin and
Valéry convey to us what "sense" means in this poetics: an atheistic vision
of the gods allied with a materialistic conception of thought embedded in
embodied language. Both reinitiate a dialogue with Aristotle's *Poetics* that
had been lost since the seventeenth century. Indeed, true to Aristotle's
conception of *poiesis*, poetics will encompass any creative activity, which
includes practical activities, scientific inventions, and, in the case of poetry,
successive revisions of various drafts. Valéry asserted that there were works
that were created by their audience, and, less often, works that create their
audience.[15]

It is now time to recognize that the work of Jean-Luc Nancy has created
its audience, and that it cannot be reduced to an offshoot, albeit a highly
creative one, of deconstruction, even if we know the complicity that links
him with Derrida. One of the best introductions to his work is Derrida's
On Touching: Jean-Luc Nancy.[16] Here, I would like to suggest a different
partnership. Nancy's numerous publications on the most varied topics cannot but evoke the way Valéry composed his famed *Cahiers*, whose total
volume is estimated at around 30,000 pages. The more than eighty books
published by Nancy today—this is a conservative estimate—testify to a
similar amplitude and capaciousness. Let us leave the last words to the
Young Carp:

> Who sings this song, so simple, who imitates it,
> Unconcerned with being lost within? . . . (. . .)
> Who, then, would pass us on the way to this eternity
> Of albums, ancient verses, submerged in your binding,
> White shroud with its sharp crease readied?
> Oh, the fingernail beneath the sheet of paper, the number absolute
> That follows, on every page resolved,
> By the wistful ceremony of a reader
> Sacrificing the immense absence of the author
> To the pure meter by which all thought thinks itself."

"The Young Carp"

Coda

Philosophy, literature: expectation.

Expectations by one of the other: desire, expectation, solicitation, appeal, desperate insistence.

Each expects the truth. Each also expects the truth of the other, in two ways: each of them interrogates the other about its truth, each holds the truth of the other. They reciprocally expect that truth as a service, as an aid, an example, an illustration or explanation, a revelation. Each one knows that it can expect nothing of the other but nonetheless persists in its expectation, for each also knows that its truth is outside itself.

And each of them also knows that this outside is not called science or religion. For each of them, it is called by the name of the other. (The name "art" hovers between them, a truth, for its part, manifest but silent. This silent outside is what each of them does not forgo saying.)

II

Truth: the thing itself, the being or the other, the existent, appearance, sense. Each of them expects all of this at once: an expectation that everything be presented as such.

But each of them understands this "as such" differently. Philosophy wants the thing as thing to be a thing that is indicated, designated, characterized in itself *and*, at the same time, withdraws its being-thing behind or beyond that of any signification. Here, the thing as such is no thing: thing of the thingness of all things, nothing. Likewise, sense as such is the sense that makes itself known as sense—for example, not as a luminous impression but an impression such that it illuminates itself as "luminous impression." And with that, it grows dark. We are no longer concerned with seeing but with seeing sight. Sense in general will be true sense when it can show that it is sense and thus no longer refer to the other, or others: which is its very being of sense. Here, truth is an interruption of sense.

III

Literature views this "as such" as a comparison, a figure, an image, a form of presentation. For example: here we have a man like "Leopold Bloom." He is very much like him, he is composed of his features. His name, primarily. Then his history, for there is no name without a history. So, Leopold Bloom reveals the man as such, that is to say, as Leopold Bloom, which is to say, as the man who has a name and a history, his history. In this sense, the operation cannot stop: the truth of the man is in Bloom, whose truth is in the man whose truth is in Bloom's name and history. Here, truth is the impossibility of interrupting sense.

Where Bloom's history ends—or any other history for that matter, Don Quixote's or Mrs. Dolloway's—there occurs no more than a momentary suspension that opens and links to other histories or other versions of the same.

As well, we continue to see the interruption repudiated exactly where it is produced in the most striking manner: philosophy cannot desist from pursuing, continuing, resuming, drawing consequences; can never stop (even and, especially, when it is "the end of philosophy"). Literature cuts the narrative at some point, always arbitrarily, at the beginning as well as at the end, and simultaneously exposes the finitude of the cut narrative and the infinitude of the flow from which it is cut.

IV

Philosophy ceaselessly expects that truth be realized (system, architectonic, certitude). Literature expects that it be pursued (recitative, recitation, recital). But each expects the other under the assumption that the realization of the first would be the complete narrative of the second, while the infinite pursuit of the second would be the realization of the first.

Should this occur, there is no further expectation. In which case we do not speak of literature or philosophy, we speak of wisdom and myth. This is another world, a world that is the reverse of the world of the expectation of truth. We no longer expect, we summon or command.

Wisdom realizes by saying—for example, by saying "do this, don't do that." And in doing so, it affirms and orders, it asks nothing. Not even to be recognized as wise, for it also says "do not believe that Wisdom is wise: it is up to you to be wise, no one can transmit or explain wisdom."

Myth supplies the entire narrative, from the very beginning all the way to me (Mr. Bloom, for example). There's nothing to add, not before, not after, but at the same time the narrative is interminable for it continues to be narrated *by heart*. There's nothing to expect here either.

Philosophy and Literature are Wisdom and Myth that have become a part of expectation. Thus, each of them, having lost themselves or, even, both of them lost to the other. A loss—or, rather, a deployment. Both of them, or one by the other and one in the other?

V

Wisdom deploys its truth to the extent that it can, for there is neither wisdom nor way. It inaugurates the way that leads nowhere but as way always expects itself again: "method" as well as "narrative text" (*récit*).

Myth deploys, as far it can, the interminable of its narrative and its truth by which, far from being terminated in interminable recitation, it interminates itself in the termination of each narrative. Once told, Ulysses's story is opened up once more by its ending. There will be other wanderings.

Wandering and method, method of wandering, methodical wandering, way that is not traced but is itself the trace of an advancing step, a step about to pass by, about to awaken for itself the possibility of a direction, a destination, a desire.

Just making known its desire, which invents itself with every step, although being merely the desire of the step itself—which is, all in all, only the essence of desiring. Just desire.

A passing request: I would like to go there, toward whatever is on the other side of the side where I stand. I would like to leave here so that there would become here for me, and from there I'd leave once more. I would like to cross the river, the mountain, the sea. I myself would like to pass. I would like to overlook myself; do without myself.

I ask politely, without violence, but make no mistake: "I would like" means "I want," it is the will itself. The will of will: expectation of eternity, eternal return of the same step whose fleeting trace attests to the fact that someone is passing there.

That's all we ask for. Let us forget "philosophy, literature, myth, wisdom," let us forget knowledge and belief. There is only one expectation: I want to pass. I do not want to be or know, I want to pass and feel myself passing. Or you—it amounts to the same thing.

To pass—the limit, of course. To pass the limit of the interrupted and the uninterrupted. Neither completion nor incompletion. Neither conclusion nor suspension. But the passage we expect.

Perhaps the expectation must be divided before it can be heard: from philosophy to literature and from literature to philosophy. No doubt it must expose itself in this way because it has no answer. Response would exhaust it, but expectation always expects itself anew. It reexpects itself, and its repetition, its doubling, held between the course of saying (discourse) and its eruption or suspension (the announcement, the call, "that morning . . ."), compose a prayer, a supplication that appears to expect sense but already knows, irresistibly, that it forms every bit of sense uttered in the world.

Not even a prayer but simply the interminable arrival of the sense that is confused with its own expectation.

*

The work gathered here is scattered, as circumstances would have it, over a period of thirty-five years. Each with its own age. The texts that have been included are those that relate to literature, with the exception of the studies devoted to the analysis, overdetermined in this context, of certain individual works, specifically, those of Jean-Christophe Bailly, Philippe Beck, Michel Deguy, Gérard Haller, Philippe Lacoue-Labarthe, Roger Laporte, Pascale Quignard, William Shakespeare, and Catherine Weinzaepflen.

*

P.S. I would like to express my deep gratitude to Ginette Michaud, who was kind enough to take the initiative for this collection and was responsible for preparing most of the texts that appear here. The final volume has been put together and arranged, no less amicably and attentively, by Cécile Bourguignon.

I would especially like to express my thanks to Elisabeth Rigal, who authorized the republication of "The Poet's Calculation," initially published in 1997 in *Des lieux divins* (Éditions T.E.R.).

A Kind of Prologue
Menstruum universale
Literary Dissolution

Tell me, oh tell! what kind of thing is *Wit*,
    Thou who *Master* art of it.
For the *First matter* loves *Variety* less;
Less *Women* lov't, either in *Love* or *Dress*.
    A thousand different shapes it bears,
    Comely in thousand shapes appears.
Yonder we saw it plain; and here 'tis now,
Like *Spirits* in *a Place*, we know not *How*.
            —Abraham Cowley, "Ode of Wit," 1656

Witz as a principle of affinities is, at the same time, the *menstruum universale*.
            —Novalis

I

I want here to approach the study of an object nearly lost from the history of literature and the history of philosophy, an object that, in truth, has never been a significant part of either of those histories, namely, *wit*, or in German, which is the language in which it is most at home (even though English literature, from Sterne to Joyce, has been its favorite playing field), *Witz*. Witz can hardly be considered a part of literature or, so to speak, only just and in the worst way possible or only indirectly; it is neither genre nor style, not even a rhetorical figure. Nor does it belong to philosophy for that matter, not being a concept or a judgment or an argument. Yet it is capable of playing all those roles, but mockingly.

It is also capable of assuming the most decisive positions with the greatest seriousness: throughout history *Witz* makes a handful of remarkable appearances in key positions. Sterne, in his preface to *Tristram Shandy*, argues against Locke and on behalf of wit, ascribing to wit the essential property of every philosophical genre. For the founders of German Romanticism—Schlegel, Novalis, Bernhardi, Jean-Paul, and, later, Solger—*Witz* is a key concept, if not the principle of a theory that claims to be simultaneously aesthetic, literary, metaphysical, even social and political. And Freud wrote about *Witz* in his first work devoted to aesthetics, in which he constructs the principle of what will, throughout his career, define aesthetic pleasure for him.

But the nature of these appearances is such that, what is remarkable about them is their disappearance. Sterne's debate with Locke is, by his own admission, so lacking in seriousness that neither philosophy nor the theory of the Jena romantics can "truly" account for it. For them, *Witz*, even more so than other figures, is consigned to an ephemeral existence that characterizes the theoretical moment, limited to a handful of fragmentary writings that failed to produce any literary works and were soon replaced by what we have come to refer to as "romanticism." As for Freud, in spite of the importance of a number of questions addressed in *Der Witz*, after 1905, he never returned (aside from a few offhand remarks) to the topic or the work itself—in contrast to the frequent reassessments of *The Interpretation of Dreams* and *Three Essays on Sexuality*.

Witz does not hold the positions that theory—whatever it may be— might wish to assign it. It occupies them, yes—and in romanticism it even suddenly assumes the position of a metaphysical Absolute ("The essence of truth is to be *Witz*; for all science is a *Witz* of the intellect, all art is a *Witz* of fantasy, and every witticism is *witzig* only insofar as it evokes the Witz of truth," August Ferdinand Bernhardi wrote in 1803 in his *Sprachlehre*)— but it doesn't settle there. It does not create, or hardly so, a system, does not create, or barely, a school—in a way, it withdraws from the work as from thought. *Witz's* structures are as unstable as they are dazzling.

Why then attempt to grab hold of an object that is more or less forgotten, fading, negligible? Why take an interest in this minimalist category—one that is barely a category for that matter, imprecise and labile—which is most often reduced to that of the *"bon mot"*? It is certainly not for the fashionable pleasure of salvaging yet another of history's Cinderellas and brilliantly demonstrating the great importance of what everyone believed to be insignificant.

The intent here follows less along these lines, however, given that, today, nearly everyone recognizes the decisive importance of *Witz*. This quasi-consensus, never articulated in itself, is marked by the respect—even sometimes, the veneration—shown to *Witz* as an essential element of psychoanalysis as well as a no less essential element of a resolutely modern literature (always at least partly inseparable from a Joycean "tradition," whether through the European "nouveau roman," Faulkner, Burroughs, even Borgès—to arbitrarily limit our references). Such recognition borders on the religious: it is tacitly understood that *Witz* has aesthetic and *theoretical* virtues that are without equal anywhere else.

The question that must be asked, therefore, is extremely simple: how can the insignificant assume such importance and what does this operation entail? With respect to this first aspect at least, it is not *Witz*'s insignificance but its "fullness of sense" that we must address through its literary and philosophical history.

At the same time, this raises a second question: if *Witz*'s "fullness of sense" never *sticks*, if it is always dematerializing or melting away, in what way are we involved or drawn along by *Witz*? It is by this avenue that we should approach—so to speak—*Witz*'s insignificance. But it will then no longer be possible simply to identify and acknowledge the question as has previously been done.

In other words, if *Witz*—for reasons and in a context yet to be established—could be called by Novalis the *menstruum universale*, the "universal solvent" in the lexicon of alchemy, it is finally (but what *finality* could this bring about?) the very dissolution in and of *Witz* itself that must be addressed. Yet with dissolution there is nothing to be done—and it's even possible that nothing can be said about "it."

But here, too, there is nothing to be done; for we are unable to determine, or anticipate, or will, or control the fact that our own discourse might dissolve. This is so in principle, and even though all discourse—this like any other—can assume no other form than that of the intent and determination of such control. I must, therefore, and as abruptly as possible, cut short this introduction: my argument, as such, what I *propose*, can be nothing but an attempt to control as completely as possible an object designated by the name of *Witz*.

II

What do we mean by a *Witz*? Several things, sometimes combined, sometimes separate, depending on the time period or context. Therefore, all at once and separately, *Witz* is:

    —the specific type of utterance referred to as "wordplay" or "witticism" in all the variety the category comprises (from puns to logical games)

    —an operation of this type extended to a literary or artistic process other than that of the utterance itself (for example, the black page that appears in *Tristram Shandy*)

    —the psychological faculty capable of such productions: this is what specifically characterizes English *wit* and French *esprit* ("*l'esprit de finesse*," "*l'esprit ingénieux*")

    —the most general concept encompassed by these productions: this always involves an unexpected or surprising association or combination, or one not authorized by ordinary rules. In its state closest to a true "concept"—that found among the romantics—*Witz* refers quite generally to the union, mixture (or dissolution) of heterogeneities.

It is not a matter of choosing among these meanings nor of organizing them so they can be studied individually. They are not distinct or successive meanings of a given term. Each of them is, up to a certain point, inseparable from the others: *Witz* is the "structure" of a production called *Witz*, which requires a capability also called *Witz*. Which means that "*Witz*" is in a way inseparable, even in its semantic determination, from the expression "make a *Witz*." That is to say, *Witz* in general (if such "generality" can be determined) or some particular *Witz* is inseparable from the form and nature of the utterance, and an utterance is in turn inseparable from the one who utters it (from the *Witz* of the speaker and, therefore, from the utterance as well and, by inevitable contiguity, from the context, occasion, or situation of the utterance). Witz is inextricably—this will be shown—a logical, semiotic, semantic, psychological, philosophical, sociological, and pragmatic (in the sense of pragmatics as understood by linguistics) concept. Cowley's "Ode of Wit," which appears at the beginning of this essay, bears witness to this situation. Here, I'd like to add a quote from the same period, one that has lost nothing of its relevance today, and that reveals a quite different but equally legitimate approach to *Witz*:

Few people of distinction trouble themselves about the name of Wit, fewer understand it, and hardly any have honored it with their example. In the next class of people it seems best known, most admired, and most frequently practiced but their stations in life are not eminent enough to dazzle us into imitation. (Anonymous essay on wit published in *The Weekly Register*, London, July 22, 1732.)

In order to find our bearings in the space or the play of this word, I'll start with what the basic history of the word suggests (its German history because I'm using the German term, but the history of English wit is similar in many respects).

Witz acquired its current meanings only fairly recently. In old and middle-high-German, *Witzi* referred to an intellectual capacity, if not intelligence itself, then intelligence as sagacity, the natural power of discernment. By tracing its etymology, we would come into contact with the entire primitive family of *knowing* conceived as *seeing*: the Sanskrit *veda*, Greek *eidos*, the Platonic *Idea*, the Cartesian Latin *evidentia*. But instead of revealing itself as the organic growth of a primal root, the history of this family, along with its *Witz*, obscured any sense associated with knowing (*savoir*). *Witzi* is a knowledge of skill, calculation, stratagem. It is in this sense that it is distinguished from *Wissen*, the knowledge we possess, which can be rationalized and from which a system can be constructed—and will remain closer to its other twin, *Wise*, a concept based in aristocratic and courtly culture, and a form of knowledge understood as refinement. *Weisheit*, which appeared later, refers to wisdom. As for *Witz*, it will always be associated with sagacity, with the perspicacity of a clever, informed, and nimble mind and, consequently, of an intelligence that nature is assumed to provide and cannot be taught: Latin *ingenium*, a talent of mind that is innate rather than acquired.

Thus, the first *Witz* would be a knowledge that cannot be acquired or demonstrated (*mathemata*) but a knowledge that sees, that immediately grasps the *idea*, and which is able to make distinctions with lucidity.

The word retained the sense of this ability until the seventeenth century. Up to that point, it had been a feminine noun. It would become masculine and shift its meaning—not transform it but invest it with a new position and function. This change of gender and shift in meaning did not simply occur from within the German language. Uniquely, it required the intervention of two foreign languages. English "wit"—as we'll see—already occupied a portion of *Witz*'s future scope. But on the continent, by an effect of cultural privilege assumed by the French language—and by a misunderstanding of the foreign that followed from this—it was *esprit* that assumed this role. *Esprit*, in the sense of the expression *"avoir de l'esprit"* ("to be witty"), is, in truth, rather far from encompassing the semantic field of "wit." And yet it is this word that the Germans were unable to translate. In German, we say *"esprit*, like the French say." And in France, one hears, and reads, that the Germans are lacking in *esprit*. In reply, a German poet (Christian Wernicke) discovered that *Witz* was part of the German language. However, the poet's mother was English.

Strictly speaking, *Witz*, in the language in which it would reveal all of its conceptual scope, is the result of a unique nationalist quarrel. Cultures and languages, portraying themselves as identities, attributing to themselves an *ingenium*, glorify themselves for having *Witz* or scorn themselves for their lack of it. Those who do not have it cannot simply import it—*Witz* is not transportable, is untranslatable—but it so happens, by chance or the kindness of Fate, that they do have it without knowing it. When the time came, Kant was able to write, in his *Anthropology from a Pragmatic Point of View*,[1] that the German language had the advantage of distinguishing two terms— *Witz* and *Geist*—while French, not as rich, had only the word "*esprit*." But where did *esprit* come from?

III

I'd like now to describe the provenance of *esprit*—of *Witz*, or more accurately, what should be referred to as the *generation* of *Witz*, in two senses of the word: the genesis or engendering of *Witz* and—somewhat akin to the "beat generation"—what might be called the "*Witz* generation." *Witz* arises and puts its stamp on an entire era, almost by surprise it would seem and, at the same time, corresponds to a process of continuous engenderment in the history of literature and philosophy. Neither pure genesis nor pure event, *Witz* is always born and reborn like its hero, Tristram Shandy, whose identity is the identity of a *Witz*: Tristram is indeed the result of the natural process of generation but, as the result of an accident—his mother upsetting his father at the decisive moment by reminding him to rewind the clock—that is, as Tristram explains, by an "unhappy association of ideas which have no connection in nature."[2] Which immediately leads him to mention—long before the "preface," and from the very beginning of the story—Locke: "which strange combination of ideas, the sagacious Locke, who certainly understood the nature of these things better than most men, affirms to have produced more wry actions than all other sources of prejudice whatsoever" (ibid.).

Tristram's birth is the uncontrollable birth of wit, of a wit—the parodic birth of the hero who taunts or parodies philosophy—the birth of literature in philosophy, of literature as a *Witz* of philosophy, or of a "literary and philosophical" *Witz*, or even the deliquescent union of these heterogeneities.

Such expressions can only be provisional and subject to question once the generation of *Witz* is established. Yet Tristram's birth immediately indicates the difficulty inherent in such a stance. For we would have to begin our inquiry *simultaneously* from a division between literature and philosophy that has *always already* existed in the history of the West, *and* from the emergence, within philosophy, of the generation of literature, that is, of Tristram's era, our era.

The first direction would require that we return to the first known forms of grotesque or fantastic literature, including the Latin *satura* and its mix of genres and prosodies, the fragmentary texts of the Cynics, with their "bon mots" and their parodies of philosophy, the wordplay scattered throughout Plato's dialogs, and the genre of dialog itself, a sophisticated genre and preferred site of "witticism"—and thus to the first mimes and the birth of comedy, and to the imperceptible birth of comedy *and* tragedy, and to the "*Witz*" of their "strange combination."

The lesson is clear: in such an undertaking, we will never reach an origin or will reach it as *Witz*, through a circular kind of genesis, a vicious circle; but at the same time, we would have lost the *Witz*, confusing its modern specificity with all forms of literature and philosophy.

In a sense, this is the lesson of Witz: the uncontrolled, and uncontrollable, birth of the mixing of genres or of what one might be tempted to call the "Western genre," literature and philosophy, neither literature nor philosophy, literature or philosophy. In short, literary dissolution, where "literary" refers solely to the domain of text, of writing in general, the scriptural West.

But such literary dissolution has also occurred before in history. *Witz* has *occurred*, dissolution has been *repeated* under the strictly modern name and form of *Witz* ("*Witz*" has no equivalent at all in ancient languages). It is this repetition and this occurring that must be identified. And this is found in philosophy, in the philosophical rebirth of literary dissolution.

To begin, we must ask: where does *esprit* come from, as understood in seventeenth-century French?

To summarize to the extent possible without distorting the situation, we can say that *esprit* is the specifically modern product of the philosophical crisis of *judgment*.

What I refer to as a "philosophical crisis of judgment" is the modern repetition of a "crisis" that is integral to philosophical discourse. Specifically, the crisis of Greek *krisis*. *Krisis, krinein*—judgment, appreciation, decision— in philosophy (beginning with the *Poem* of Parmenides) refers to the act of choice, of decision, and the execution of the decision, an act outside the *logos* and necessary for the (good) *logos* to be maintained. In addition to the *logos*, *krisis* implicates a *tomos* that cannot be reduced to it. In this way, *krisis* marks the element or structure of undecidability in the "logical" decision itself.

Krisis and related words like *judicium*, on which English *judgment* is based, are words of a practical or pragmatic provenance, found in the fields of medicine, law, and politics.

Stoic semiology tells us that *krisis* is the decision that relates the sign to the thing. If accurate, it presents the *idioma* of the thing, if false, it provides no more than a disturbing or dangerous *phantasma*. *Judgment*, then, is the characteristic act of *composition*, of the combination of signs with things and the combination of signs with other signs. When *conceptio* is lacking, there is reason to proceed with *compositio*—that is, when there is no instantaneous self-suitability (or simultaneous production) of the thing and its *concept*. *Compositio* is a conceptual fault, a redirected or postponed engendering, a birth uncertain of how it came into being.

Long before scholasticism formulated a special discipline of judgment under the name *critica, critica* had already been established as a specific study or discipline, neither science nor art, involving the examination, commentary, and judgment of texts. Early literary criticism is the exercise of judgment in the most "appropriate" domain: that of works that are not based on pure "logic," which do not give rise to a pure "conception." The theory of judgment and literary criticism go hand in hand: they share— and indefinitely exchange—the order of the sign, of combination, of the establishment of relations and the act that determines such relations. Thus they share—and intersect at—the indispensible *subject* of such an act. This subject should not be understood as a *sub-jectum*, a substrate (Aristotle's *hypokeimenon*) but, rather, as the author and agent of the decision, the author or agent of the idiom or fantasy.

A similar subject—let's call it the critical subject—is not the "impersonal" universality *of the* Subject. On the contrary, it exists only in the inequality of subjects: if reason is the same in everyone, judgment is not. We are more or less endowed (by nature, by God, or by chance) with good judgment.

And it is very specifically upon the, already scholastic, division between *ratio* and *judicium* that all of the modern metaphysics of subjectivity and "generation of Witz" is based.

Descartes's operation consists in ascribing being and truth to the subject of the decision itself. Not as judging subject but as subject that *conceives itself*, and conceives itself conceiving. In a way, the *cogito* formulates the (re) conquest of substantiality by the subject-agent of the decision. (But except for the sole certainty of *cogito*, all the rest is judgment, which must be guided, clarified, guaranteed, or rectified by certitude alone.)

However, *cogito* is doubled—by its own double, the *man of wit*. Rather than being unique and unitary like the *cogito*, this double proliferates from the outset into a multiplicity of figures. The courtier (Castiglione, Gracian, to evoke its best known examples), the man of taste, the man of the salon, as well as the woman, the woman of taste, the woman of wit, form the polymorphic character of the subject of judgment that finds its certitude in itself. Unlike his double, he does not find such certitude in the light of intuition but in the shadow of a natural gift; he does not discover it as truth but as the sureness of the glance and the stratagem; he does not turn it into a substance but cultivates it as the exercise of a talent; he does not associate it with the deductions of science but draws from it works of political calculation, amorous strategy, and knowing wisdom; and, lastly, he does not offer us *Meditations* but "miscellanies," in which, through dialog, fable, or aphorism, the *sentence* reigns supreme.

Discourse disappears (or wants to disappear) before the truth it presents; the sentence says "true" only by the mark of its style and the extent of its wit. Discourse leads to conception, the sentence plays with the *concetto*. Discourse exposes the methodical order of science, the sentence, using mixture and fragmentation, tends to erupt momentarily into the maxim, the "*maxima sententia*," the greatest thought. The man of the Discourse purports to be an intellect, the man of wit knows himself to be the play of representation.

That the first is bound by necessity to the representation of his substance and the second conceives his actions as the very being of the subject is what each whispers to himself but can only deny. The first reinvents philosophy, the second reinvents literature—the man of thought, and the man of wit. They are the same, but the history of judgment is the history that divides them *and* unites them to one another irrevocably.

IV

Esprit, wit, *Witz*, which—given the incessant modification of their figures, their sexes, their genders, their style—now influenced *belles-lettres* and the *beaux-arts* (and the art of their criticism), are the doubles of judgment in that judgment is itself already, within the logic of discourse, excluded from conception. They are the doubles of the first *fault* of thought and, consequently, doubly fault ridden with respect to thought.

From the seventeenth to the nineteenth century, as far as philosophy was concerned, nothing was too severe for *Witz*—it was uncertain, disturbing, too obscure or too brilliant, flabby, effeminate, deceitful, and offered literary fantasies as idioms. Hobbes and Locke, who were the first to do so, ruled in favor of its exclusion, without appeal: *Witz* was dangerous.

But it is precisely this exclusion that provided the opportunity for a *definition* of *Witz*. In 1689, Locke wrote: "For wit lying most in the assemblage of ideas, and putting those together with quickness and variety wherein can be found any resemblance of congruity, thereby to make up pleasant pictures and agreeable visions in the fancy: judgment, on the contrary, lies quite on the other side, in separating carefully one from another ideas where can be found the least difference."[3]

In this way, the concept of *Witz* is supplied by philosophy—the concept that unites all the motley diversity and dispersion of its manifestations. While witty analyses of wit always relate it to the ultimate "property" of having a certain *"je ne sais quoi,"* to use an expression common in the seventeenth century, its rational analysts attribute to it a specific function: none other than that of *compositio* (for Locke's wit merely brings together things that are dissimilar, but already in his practice, and soon in his theory, *Witz* consists in establishing the resemblance of dissimilar things—that is, *Witz* brings about a necessary synthesis where Locke's judgment is limited to identifying a disparity). *Therefore, at the moment of its exclusion,* Witz *receives the initial qualification of judgment.* And "judgment" will be tendentially defined as the organization of *concepts.*

Philosophy banished *Witz*—and it banished literature along with elegance, charm, invention, ingenuity, the composition of figures, and imagination. But this was its way of baptizing them.

Moreover, philosophy, unable to cut itself off from judgment without excluding itself from *discourse*, brought *Witz* back into its purview at the very moment of its exclusion. In fact, all eighteenth-century philosophy could be analyzed, wherever it is not dedicated to seeking a "well-made language" (Leibniz's "characteristic language" or Condillac's "language of calculation"), as an attempt to use the resources of *Witz* on behalf of knowledge and truth. Truth now had to be adorned or ornamented to make it accessible, it required the assistance of rhetoric and fiction on the one hand, and truth itself on the other, the truth of mankind, the truth of a subject whose *cogito* lasted no longer than the Cartesian moment, *must* also be found in those unstable and unattributable functions known as taste, *talent*, *inventiveness*, *combination*, and *creativity*. Aesthetics is born of philosophy as the project of a science of *Witz*, a science of art and litera-ture—a science of the Other whom we have excluded—and because this exclusion is impossible, *of the sameness of the Other and the Same who excludes him*: philosophy wants to be the scholarly *Witz* of itself and of *Witz*.

But literature demands no less. The preface to *Tristram Shandy*, which gathers together the essential elements of the "defense and illustration" of *Witz* that had been in progress for more than a century, has to be read as a parody of philosophy and as a debate with philosophy, and as a philosophi-cal debate. Sterne insists upon the place, dignity, brilliance, and necessity of wit alongside judgment. In other words, Sterne considers *Tristram Shandy* as a whole to be the indispensible supplement of a philosophical treaty—providing what it lacks and completing its presentation. Moreover, this preface, lodged within the novel as if in its heart or center, highlights the literary self-production of literary theory and, therefore, signifies *at least* that it is literary (or critical) theory that most aptly constitutes a supplement to philosophy, and *at most* that literature, together with its own theory, is capable of providing the knowledge or thought of the identity of philoso-phy and literature—and can, therefore, do without philosophy.

Thus, we have the specifically modern possibility that literature and literary (critical, poetic, and so on) theory consider themselves or are con-sidered the site of truth; and reciprocally, the possibility that philosophy now considered itself in terms of its own *mise en scène* of truth, its own ability to combine signs and figures for things or for reason, in short, its aptitude for literary composition and, therefore, for *Witz*—a twofold pos-sibility that has arisen from the schism and chiasmus that *Witz* simultane-ously enacts, from the crisis of *Witz*.

V

This does not mean, however, that we're dealing with a simple exchange of roles, nor with the doubling of an identity. Of course, *Witz* was given an identity by its definition as a combination of heterogeneous elements—and, in a sense, it is this identity that literature wants to produce, or itself wants to be, just as philosophy wants to be. And this identity is none other than identity *itself*, in that it can be presented, and conceived, only through the mediation of nonidentity: in this would be found the definition of the fundamental "dialectic" of all Western thought, as Heidegger character-ized it. In that sense, *Witz* would be none other than the dialectical thought of identity and, primarily, the thought of the *identity of "wit" itself*, within the dialectic of "je ne sais quoi" and reason, of fantasy and demonstration, of the "witticism" and speech, of *compositio* and *conceptio*. And, strictly speaking, we would even have to conclude that the complete separation and opposition of *Witz* and Reason has only ever served to better enable this dialectic to operate. Literature has never been opposed to philosophy except to better ensure control over their separation.

From one point of view, it is the thought of this identity that is represented by the German Romanticism of the Jena group. We could say that romanticism (if we can call it such, as a form of shorthand, *this* particular romanticism) considered itself the thought of the novel or the novel as thought: thought in and as the mixture of genres, a generalized *Satura*, and not only literary genres but intellectual genres in general. The thought, therefore, of a higher fusion of philosophy, art, science, literature, and society. I present, without further commentary, several fragments from Friedrich Schlegel:

"*Witz* is the principle and organ of universal philosophy . . . the science of all sciences perpetually mingling and separating, a logical chemistry."

"Language is poetical, writing philosophical. *Witz* links them together."

"The supreme *Witz* should be the true *lingua caracteristica universalis* and, *at the same time*, an *ars combinatoria*."

"*Witz*, perhaps the pure principle of philosophy, ethics, and poetry."

For such thought, *Witz* must also reconquer spiritual unity and *erase the difference between intellect and "wit"*: "What was *Witz* originally, then, if not the most intimate mixture and interpenetration of reason and fantasy?" (Schlegel).

In this way, *Witz* comes to occupy the supreme place in the intellect with respect to philosophy as well as literature: "*Witz* is the creator, it fabricates resemblances" (Novalis).

It would be too easy and too naïve to write off these expressions as examples of "unbridled idealism" or "unrestrained romanticism." I hope to have shown the extent to which they represent the logical culmination of a *crisis* that is characteristic of the entire modern era. In that sense, romanticism is the closure of the crisis: "*Witz* is the point of indifference, where everything is saturated," wrote Schlegel, transposing to *Witz* the first principle of Schelling's metaphysics.

However, we must also consider how this same romanticism constitutes the radicalization of that very crisis.

Very schematically, the crisis can be characterized by three features:

1. Considered from the point of view of *Witz*, the work of the Jena romantics is primarily characterized by its . . . absence of a work. As theory,

the theory of *Witz* can be summarized by the platitude of the absolute affirmation of *Witz* and by the circle that condemns *Witz* to being presented, explicated, and justified only by the *Witz* or by *Witz*: "Language and *Witz* belong to metaphysics; a metaphysics that is not *witzig* is useless" (F. Schlegel). When all is said and done, it all comes down to the magic of a word, just as "the most intimate essence of *Witz* can only be explained by the magic of ideas" (ibid.). As a theory of literature, *Witz* authorizes nothing more than *Witz*—which remains in the state of a wish: "A theory of the novel must itself be a novel." And, finally, as literature, romantic *Witz* is more or less limited to the two incomplete novels produced by Novalis and Schlegel.

2. Although, in principle, there is but one *Witz* ("*Witz* is the principle of the novel, of mythology, and the encyclopedia" [Schlegel]), nonetheless, there is an irreducible multiplicity and, especially, hierarchy of *Witzes*. In this, the romantics repeated a critical gesture that can be found throughout the history of *Witz* and which we've neglected until now, and that is the condemnation of the vulgar *Witz*, of the "low" *Witz*, of the simple pun (Bernhardi, in the text quoted previously, adds that what he says should not be taken for a verbal pirouette, a *witzeln*.). Since the sixteenth century, to celebrate *Witz* always involved sorting out the good *Witz* from the bad—and, in particular, of criticizing the aggressive, cynical, and obscene *Witz*. There is a kind of trivial *Witz* that we must protect ourselves against: "To consider *Witz* an instrument of revenge is as vulgar as treating art as a means of tickling the senses" (F. Schlegel). That is why the richest works of *Witz*, those by Sterne and Jean-Paul, are acknowledged by the romantics only with the precautions required by the critique of their *poor taste*, of their "unhealthy" reliance (Schlegel) on the grotesque. But we must also see in Sterne and Jean-Paul how they themselves insist, even to the extent of self-criticism and self-derision, on distinguishing a "great" *Witz* from one that is minor, inconsistent, or vulgar.

3. There is one final aspect that I have not yet discussed. Ever since Shakespeare's famous "maxim" in Hamlet (repeated endlessly until Freud)—"brevity is the soul of wit"—the sole "genre" or the sole "form" that is always recognized as typical of *Witz* and is recognized as typical of all *Witz*, is concision, the rapidity of the statement that carries the *point*. Concerning the German *Witz*, the romantics, using an expression that has been repeated many times since, said that: *Witz ist ein Blitz*, *Witz* is a bolt of lightning. Brilliance, dazzlement, explosion—they express the form of the double of the *cogito* when the latter is *instantaneous*. But as often as the rapidity of *Witz* is recognized as essential to its "being" and to the *pleasure*

from which it cannot be separated, that same speed just as often disturbs or
deflects the thought of *Witz*: "in Witz there is a petrification, fright and
sudden coagulation" (F. Schlegel). The bolt of lightning blinds, the explosion deafens, pleasure paralyzes us. *Witz* hypnotizes the thought of *Witz*—
and at the same time also causes that thought to slip out of the supreme
unity in which it was held: "*Witz* is the characteristic form of our consciousness in that we are potential organic beings, *chaotic.*"

This last feature helps us understand all three together: *Witz*, in accordance with the dissociation out of which it arises, never corresponds to the
necessary *organicness* of a synthesis or completed work, much less to the
higher organism of a synthesis of synthesis (philosophical) and the work
(literary). Rather, it causes such synthesis to be dazzling as if it were a form
of chaos. That is why Novalis referred to the *menstruum universale* as a
"principle of affinities." This fragment is, of course, itself the synthesis of
a *Witz*: total affinity is the same thing as total dissolution. But stubbornly
there remains, at the (petrified) heart of romanticism, the need for the
statement of this synthesis to dissolve into itself, being incapable of con-
trolling the synthesis it states other than by the *Witz* it enunciates.

But *Witz* cannot *control*; that is why philosophy began with its exclusion.
It enacts combinations without *knowledge*, it remains heterogeneous even
after combining the heterogeneities it produces, it seduces without trying,
couples without fecundating, and we remain fearful of it as long as our
expectations remain high—it can literally do anything. Literary elegance,
which always remains "elegance," even when it descends into vulgarity,
once a literary project or proposal comes into existence, becomes a protest
against this "anything," against chaos—and, likewise, philosophical reasoning, always remains "reasoning," even when it makes use of the resources
of a brilliant *Witz*.

The triviality, the verbal chatter, the femininity and lack of consistency
of the "bon mot" have always worried and threatened the works of *Witz*
from below, even though those works have *also* drawn their resources and
justifications from them. Of course, it is always possible to control *Witz*, to
yoke it to the production of knowledge and of works that have always had
the finality of *judgment*. But because they had reached the peak of such
control, the romantics watched as it suddenly disintegrated in their hands.
Their attempt to use *Witz* to engender everything saw the return of something that was most characteristic of *Witz* (or rather, of that which never
creates the *Witz* but a *Witz*) but cannot be appropriated, cannot be *introduced* into any work (not even and, especially, into *Tristram Shandy*)—its
uncontrolled birth.

The romantics' quest for *Witz* in its entirety, and its crisis, can be summarized in this fragment from Friedrich Schlegel: "One should have Witz, but not want to have it, otherwise we end up with a *Witzelei*, the precious and erudite version of *Witz*."

If all differences were eliminated between *cogito* and "esprit" in the speculative *Witz*, the following alone would remain—we cannot want *Witz*. But philosophy has never been able to tell us what we cannot *want* and what it means *not to want*, nor has literature ever put it into practice.

Outside of philosophy, outside of literature (outside of psychoanalysis as well), outside the mixture or union of both (or all three), *Witz* provides us with nothing, and awards us with nothing. In its insistence, and almost in spite of "itself," it points to the longstanding dissolution of our *will* to philosophy, to literature (psychoanalysis), and of our will to mix and take responsibility for all our "genres." It leaves behind only something that does not yet have a name, either in philosophy or in literature, which could not have a name *without laughing*, not even the derisive name of *Witz*, something that would have the unattributable form and nature of this posthumous fragment of Novalis, which is not an *intentional* fragment but a note sketched for the unfinished sequel to his novel, a note that is sufficient, even in its fragmentary state, for carrying out the part of the program that it notes—the program that should be that of the *menstruum universale*, if this could ever be or create a program, but which, incapable of doing so, can merely be resolved or dissolved in this remark, which must remain unfinished: "*Dissolution of a poet in his song*: he will be sacrificed among savages."

April–May 1977

PART I

Literature

"One day, the gods withdraw . . .":
(Literature/Philosophy: in-between)

One day, the gods withdraw. Of their own volition, they withdraw their divinity, which is to say, their presence. They won't simply leave, they won't go somewhere else, they'll withdraw from their own presence— they'll disappear within it.

What remains of their presence is what remains of all presence whenever it has vanished—there remains what can be said about it. What can be said about it is what remains when we can no longer address it: cannot speak to it or touch it or observe it, nor offer it a present.

(Besides, maybe the gods withdraw because no longer is any present offered to their presence: no sacrifice, no oblation, other than through custom or imitation. We have other things to do: write, for example, calculate, conduct business, legislate. Deprived of presents, presence withdraws.)

Of that absent presence, there are always only two possibilities: its truth or its history. Of course, this has to be its true history. But because presence has fled, it is no longer certain that any history of it would be absolutely veridical: for no presence can attest to it.

What remains immediately splits in two: history and truth. Both have the same origin and relate to the same thing: to the same presence that has withdrawn. Its withdrawal is, therefore, manifest as the line separating them—history and truth.

Muthos is the story of divine actions and passions, among which are always found those concerning the world and its operations, man and his fate. *Muthos* signifies the saying of something, by which we make known the thing, the affair; in Latin, this is its *narratio*, which is its knowledge. When the gods have withdrawn, their history can no longer be simply true, nor their truth simply narrated. The presence that would attest to the existence of what is narrated as well as the veracity of the speech that narrates is lacking.

What is lacking is the body of the gods: Osiris dismembered, the Great Pan dead. What is lacking is the true body that by itself would utter its truth: its statue splattered with the blood of victims, impregnated with the smoke of incense, or the sacred wood where we can listen to the murmur of the spring from which a subterranean presence streams forth.

What is lacking is this speaking body; what remains is what can be said about it—and the *said* has become incorporeal, like the void, like place and time. These are the four forms of the incorporeal, that is, the interval in which bodies may be found but which is never itself a body. A property of the interval is to open and divide itself.

The *said* is no longer given, compact, with the divine body, orison of its lips: it separates from itself, distorts itself, *logos*.

*

Truth and narration, therefore, separate from one another. Their separation is drawn with the same line that is drawn with the withdrawal of the gods. The body of the gods is what remains between them: remains there as its own absence. Remains there as painted body, figurative body, narrated body: but the sacred body-to-body is no more.

Between literature and philosophy this intertwining is lacking, this embrace, this sacred entanglement between man and god, which is to say, between man and animal, plant, thunder, rock. Their distinction is exactly the de-intertwining, the de-embracing. The tangle thus untangled is separated by the sharpest of blades, but the cut itself forever bears the marks of that entanglement. Between them is that which cannot be disentangled.

*

Truth and narration separate in such a way that it's their separation that establishes them both. Without that separation, there would be neither truth nor narration: there would be the divine body.

Not only is narration susceptible to or suspected of lacking truth, it is deprived of it in principle, being deprived of the body, present as mouth of its own pronouncement, as skin of its own exposition.

This privation is identically the privation of truth, and truth, out of principle, here goes by the wayside, withdrawn, unrepresentable, unnarratable. Truth becomes a vanishing point that is anamorphosed into a question mark. Truth becomes: "What is truth?" To get past the question, even to break away from it, remains the vanishing point, the infinite perspective of what is now named *logos*.

Narration exposes figures: it invents itself as representability in general, which is to say, the trace of contours by which a body makes its presence known and, most importantly, becomes body, but it is doubtful whether the body that this trace outlines is true. The narrative trace exposes a bodily manifestation although it is uncertain whether it is identically a manifest body.

Rather, it is certain that it is not: by representing it, narration declares it absent. It is the same trace that makes god himself—jackal-headed officiant or resinous teardrop on the side of a tree—and which at present makes his figure. But this trace divides itself: the divine body is missing.

Thus, the perspective of truth also targets this absence as the site of what it desires, but whose absence it strives to show. By showing this absence— the figure itself, the imitation, representation, allegory, mythology, literature—it speaks the truth: that it is a defect, a mistake (error, illusion, lie, deception). Yet in speaking this truth, it speaks only half the truth: the presence beyond the figure or in the figure itself is lacking. But the discourse of truth states that this presence is beyond being. This discourse itself pushes as far as that beyond, where it is dissolved in an excess of light, a brilliance within which all possible representability is abolished.

*

Between figure and brilliance there remains the absent divine body. There remains a singular body of absence on either side of which narration and the perspective of truth touch. One describes the forms of the body, the other inscribes its excavation. Between description and inscription, forever stretched between them, torn apart, writing alone, interminable graph chiseled in the lead of a seal affixed to the site of withdrawal. The scene takes place around an empty tomb, a hollow mummy, a portrait resembling no one: around a body now produced, voiced as "body," in other words, an absent outside.

But this is a scene, and it is played very effectively. It is simultaneously a scene of mourning and desire: philosophy, literature, each of them mourning for and desiring the other (precisely the other), but each of them also competing with the other in the fulfillment of mourning and desire.

If mourning carries the day and is enclosed in endless dereliction, one or the other will descend into melancholy, the throat gripped by the lost body. But the latter is also, and on every occasion, for one the image of the other: philosophy strangles itself with impossible literature—a literature that is *its own* impossible. Or, rather, the reverse.

Sometimes it is literature that *leads* the mourning that philosophy experiences or denies. Sometimes it is philosophy that *sustains* the absence that literature embellishes. But the gesture of the one can also be the fact of the other. And there may also exist a philosophical poem that exhausts itself in the desire of the other and the desire to *poetize*: Zarathustra cried out in the end:

> I have long ceased to be concerned with *happiness*; I am concerned with my *work*.[1]

And there may be a thought here, bound without religion, in Lucretius's lines to Venus, which end as follows, exscribed outside words, his song of *nature* bedecked in red:

> They placed their own kin on the funeral pyres
> Of others, and with frenzied cries set light to them,
> And often in the fighting that ensued
> They shed much blood rather than leave the bodies.[2]

*

Not to abandon the bodies, possibly in spite of the work, that is the task. Not to abandon the bodies of the gods without, however, wanting to recall their presence. Not to abandon truth's function nor that of the figure without, however, filling the distance between them with sense. Not to abandon the world that always becomes more world, always further marked by absence, by interval, incorporeal, yet without saturating it with signification, with revelation, announcement, or apocalypse. The absence of the gods is the condition of the two, literature and philosophy, the in-between that legitimates them both, irreversibly atheological. But for those two, they are responsible for nurturing the in-between: for keeping the body open, for allowing it the possibility of that opening.

* * *

Attachment

"Whatever you wish," I was told by *La Quinzaine littéraire*: immediately, I
was paralyzed.[3] How would I choose? Nothing's been forced upon me: no
"subject." What is my "wish"? According to the word's meaning, it is my
manner, my way, but it is not my free will. "Wish" is not "will." It is obvious
that the offer made to me—or the demand—to write "whatever I wish"
mixes the two ideas. Strictly speaking, it's a given subject that I should
address "as I wish." If it's not given to me, I won't find it. In my lifetime, I've
never known what it means to want—I think that's more or less the expression Nietzsche used. For years, I've kept on my desk a sheet of paper on
which I've written this sentence from Seneca: "*Neminem mini dabis qui sciat
quomodo, quod vult, coeperit velle: non consilio adductus illo, sed impetu impactus
est.*" ("You can show me no man who knows how he began to crave that
which he craves. He has not been led to that pass by forethought; he has
been driven to it by impulse."[4]) In another letter to Lucilius, Seneca qualifies the philosophy of *bonum consilium*: careful consideration, deliberation,
counsel. Philosophy is a good counselor but it won't provide me with any
impetus. And without impetuosity, I won't be able to decide on a subject. For
the moment, this is what drives me to follow through with my wish:

"Philosophy," today, is a popular term, a desirable commodity. It is said
that it's the effect of a lack of sense in our world and the resulting appetite
for *consilium*. It so happens, though, that what is primarily sought—and put
up for sale—is an advisory philosophy: a giver of lessons, even solace,
instructor of virtues, purveyor of representation, attentive to wisdom (ori-
ental or orienting), dialog always upon its lips (in ordinary language) and
ethics within its grasp, together with a substantial store of values and senses.

But to philosophize is not to dip in any way into a reservoir of sense. It
does not make up for a deficit, it stirs up truth from top to bottom. To
philosophize begins precisely where sense is interrupted. That's how it all
began some twenty-seven centuries ago: through a great interruption of
the significations available on the shores of the Mediterranean (those significations would receive the status of "myths"). That we today experience
another suspension of sense (for example, the signifiers "history," "man,"
"community," "art") is nothing new—except for the exposure to new
requirements and new possibilities for thought, speech, and the writing of
thought.

This, to begin or to begin again—which it does ceaselessly, always essentially *in statu nascendi*—has a need for *impetus*. To philosophize does not
proceed without some driving force, even one that is violent, which rushes

forward and which also tears off: which tears from deposited, sedimented, half-decomposed sense and hastens toward possible sense, especially one not given, not available, which must be caught unawares, surprised in its unforeseeable and never simple, never univocal arrival. For a prisoner to leave Plato's cave, a certain violence is needed: the light wounds him, he is forced to turn back. Thought is not only fulfilled in a blinding explosion, it also begins that way. Between them is found the lingering twilight, when fear raises its powerful Hegelian wings until the coming dawn.

Certainly, we must think. Once more, everything has become not only worthy of thought but suffers from a lack of being thought. *Capital*, for example, before which it is not enough to stir up exorcisms or offer compromises; *identity*, which seems to have become incapable of stepping away from itself to relate to itself; or even *sovereignty*, about which we no longer know anything, except that it derives from a political-theological order from which we have become unmoored. I could go on like this and, of course, add *philosophy* to the list, whose intemperate use will soon render it sense-less. (And literature as well? But poetry continues to resist.)

This demands a driving force—in other words, it is especially not a question of seeking assurances. This demands an uprising, an insurrection of thought. Risk, therefore, and upheaval. One cannot be too wise to philosophize, it even requires a touch of madness. Nothing is closer to madness than the act of "creating oneself" and *"producing one's own object for oneself and giving it to oneself,"* which is for Hegel the "free act of thinking."[5]

To create concepts, to manhandle languages, to polish styles, to punch holes in thought—that's the work that must first be done. And it is also a festival, we mustn't forget that: not a matter of lanterns but a matter of impetuosity and a getting outside oneself. It's a fever contracted in the *open* to which thought exposes itself. If it doesn't expose itself, it deteriorates: this must be said without pathos, soberly, but with all the strength we can muster. In the end, we must not—as Artaud said—allow *the philosophical hum of being to fuck life all over again.*[6]

Reasons to Write

To Write, About the Book

In a certain manner—very certain, in fact—it is pretty much impossible today to write anything/nothing about the book. This particularity of the French language with respect to the word *nothing* [*rien*] forces us to simultaneously understand it as: it is no longer possible to write anything at all concerning the book, and it is no longer possible to dispense with writing about the book.

It is no longer possible to write anything at all concerning the book: if this entails the "question of the book," to use an expression found in one of the texts that serves as an outer limit of this impossibility ("Edmond Jabès and the Question of the Book" by Jacques Derrida[1]), we must immediately assume that this question has already been addressed (yet, it has not and cannot be the subject of any treatise). To attempt to present, to introduce anything at all about it, today, can only be a sign of ignorance or (true or feigned) naiveté. Regarding the question, something definitive has been provided by a body, a network, or however you wish to call it, of incomparable texts, which go by the names: Mallarmé, Proust, Joyce, Kafka, Bataille,

Borges, Blanchot, Laporte, Derrida. The list is, of course, incomplete and possibly unfair, but it is nonetheless certain that not only must we pass through these texts, we must *remain there*. There is nothing fetishistic, idolatrous, or conservative about this; on the contrary, we should realize this for ourselves. It is time to affirm that the question of the book is already *there*. Reactionary pietism consists, quite wrongly, in indefinitely soliciting these same texts, with zeal or voracity, in order to extract and reintroduce, in a thousand more or less openly stated ways, by gloss, imitation, or exploitation, questions about the book in terms of speculation, endless repetition, mise en scène, fragmentation, denunciation, or enunciation of the book for as long as there are books.

For myself, I would have been satisfied with patiently copying those texts here, even copying in this same volume, Blanchot's text, which opens, closes, and guides this book in which I write—this almost impossible book. Nothing can assure me that this shouldn't be done.

*

However—at the same time, by the same categorical imperative—it is no longer possible to dispense with writing about the book.

This question is not a question, it is not a subject we could consider as completely or incompletely explored, much less exhausted. Exhaustion—indefinite exhaustion—rather, forms the matter we must here confront, here as elsewhere.

As for the book (title, Mallarméan program), something has now been knotted into our history. The strength of the knot has nothing to do with the "genius" of these "authors" but signals the historical power and necessity, more than historical, with which the writing of the book had to wrap itself around itself. The West—what Heidegger caused us to think of as the West—having, as far as can be remembered, decided to consign to the book the science of a truth deciphered in a Book—the book of the World, of God, even the book of the Id—because neither reading nor writing was possible, the West tied itself up in writer's cramp. This is the primary, and quite well-known, reason for the fact that we must constantly reread these texts.

And re-write as well—providing that we do not allow, thereby forgetting the implacable lesson of Pierre Ménard, the concept of re-writing to tumble to the level of *rewriting*.[2]

Following a law that all these texts incorporate and articulate, following a law whose rigor need not be demonstrated, this history, grasped through the cramp of writing, concludes only through repetition. This is a question that has never been addressed; the question of the book marks the resurgence of repetition. Not its *own* repetition, for it is, to the extent that it is, a question of what remains without ownership (of literary ownership and communism, that is the question). Repetition is the form, the substance of that which does not have, once and for all (nor on several occasions) its identity printed in the untranscribable Book. For anyone who finds himself deprived of this identity—for any Westerner—it forms the question of the book, the question that must be written in order to be dissolved in its writing—to dissolve what?

To—but the gesture of writing never satisfies a teleology—dissolve—but a dissolution itself dissociated from the solutive values that metaphysics always confers on it—not only the ideal identity inscribed in the blinding whiteness of the Book

(I saw gathered there in the depths of it, Bound up by love into a single volume, All the leaves scattered through the universe—Dante[3])

but to dissolve to the point of deprivation, which is also the privatization, of this identity, to dissolve even the Book itself, even the deprivation, privatization of the Book. The Book is there—in every book are the virgin folds of the book (Mallarmé)—it must *be written on*, made palimpsest, overloaded, its pages muddied by added lines until the worst confusion of signs and writings prevails: its original illegibility must be achieved, aggravating the formless exhaustion of the cramp within.

Why? This risk must be taken: the book must be written in *for deliverance*. Which would have little to do with Freedom (I hear in this, in this subjective, subjected, subjugated, Freedom, that God or the Spirit of metaphysics is automatically bestowed). Writing must pass through the crack of the strange homonymy of *liber/liber*, through the contemporary ambiguity of *delivery*.

To write? to turn back one's nails, to hope, utterly in vain, for the moment of deliverance? (Bataille)

—and the sentence that follows in the same story, *A Story of Rats*: My reason for writing is to reach B.[4]

B. is the woman in this story, but her initial and the sentence itself mean that we read the woman, this woman, a woman, and a man, and B.; Bataille himself, and a place, and a book, and a thought, and deliverance "itself," in person, without any allegorism.

Such is repetition: resumption, rewriting the petition, the effort to reach and to join, the request, the demand, the desire, the claim, the supplication.

Rewriting the book is the renewed clamor or murmur of a demand, an urgent appeal. If the texts I have spoken of now *remain* part of our story, it is because they have addressed no question but have knotted that appeal in one or more throats of writing: a massive spasm of the glottis.

They have knotted the ethical, and more than ethical, appeal of a deliverance, to a deliverance. The imperative is not to respond (the neutral, Blanchot writes, de-nominating as neutral the literary act, which, bearing with it a *problem* without an *answer*, possesses the closure of an *aliquid* to which no question would correspond)—rather, it would be indispensible to distinguish, with as much care as possible, two incommensurable concepts: the answer to a question and the response to a call.

It's possible that we can only respond to the call by repeating the call—like guards charged with keeping watch. It's possible that the imperative is not that of the response but of the *obligation* to respond alone, which is called responsibility. How, in the case of the book, can it be a matter of responsibility? It is no longer possible to escape, any more than it is to avoid this: how, in writing where the Voice is absent (a voice without writing is both absolutely alive and absolutely dead—Derrida), can a call be heard, how can it be a question of vocation, invocation, or advocation? In general, how can the utterly different of the book be delivered?

All of these texts have exhausted the theme, the theory, the practice, the metamorphosis, the future, the fugue or cut of the book for no other reason than to repeat that call.

As for me, I wanted to write something else, something longer and for more than one person. That would take a long time to write. It would be as long as *The Arabian Nights* but entirely different (Proust).

Repetitions

Furthermore, it's no doubt preferable to dot the "i's" of repetition, even if it means repeating ourselves somewhat.

The reduplication of the book within itself, the self-representation of literature, the story of the work's own birth—its own deliverance—its self-analysis, or the involution of its message as an exhibition of its code, or the figuration of its prosecution within the process, narrative or demonstrative, of the formation of its figures, or the implementation of its rules by the very rules of its game, all of this, which in a word I would call autobibliography, all of this dates from the invention of the book. For this, our modernity has equipped itself with entire libraries—it had to, it was a necessity, by the very necessity of the book from which no writing escapes (this useless and prolix epistle I am writing already exists in one of the thirty volumes of the five bookcases in one of the countless hexagons—and its refutation as well—of *The Library of Babel*)—all of this forms the repetition of self, of which the book, from birth, can only be formed. My reason for writing is to reach B.: Babel, Bible, bibliology, bibliomancy, bibliomania, bibliophile, *bibliothèque*.

It is this that the book more specifically came to recite and brood over during the age of its material and technical invention: in the age of printing, age of the true book, age of the ripe subject and communication. Printing satisfied the need for some to be in relation with others in an ideal mode (Hegel). Since then, it's as if the ideal content of communication consisted in autobibliography. Every book exhibits the being or the law of the book: from the outset, there is no object other than self and this satisfaction. It gives me pleasure, my daughter, to write to you, although I have nothing to tell you (Madame de Sévigné).

Everything's been said, and we've arrived too late, for the more than seven thousand years that there have been men, and who think: the first chapter must begin this way, it must be about books, about a book called *The Characters*. The exhaustion of material imposes the infinity of possible ways of forming signs. It is the history of this world, the one we are now visiting, the goddess says to him: it is the book of its destinies. We move to another room and there is another world, another book—somewhere you'll also find the *Theodicy*, where this was written, and here you will read that Borges did no more than write down one of Leibniz's ideas, which Lichtenberg had already copied: the libraries will become cities. No place will be free of books, even when they are missing. You are quite right, Monsieur, an entire chapter is missing at that spot, leaving a hole in the book of at least ten pages, writes Tristram, the author who also narrates his own birth. Nor will any book be free of books, for not satisfied with inscribing our name on the anonymous thoughts of a single author, we appropriate those of thousands of individuals, eras, and entire libraries, and we steal, we even plagiarize, writes Jean Paul, plagiarizing himself once again. The textual anthology—a selection of flowers from books, the choice of a book so as to dispose the bouquet of its literarity in every book—continues unabated until it reaches us.

All this endless repetition of the book constitutes its native redundancy—and more naïve than we might imagine. Redundancy is overflow, the wave's excess: the Book has always been thought of as the infinitely resurgent foam of an inexhaustible ocean—a spurt of grandeur, a considerable thought or emotion, a sentence in bold type that continues for pages, one line per page in graduated placement—keep the reader breathless . . . for the length of the book (Mallarmé[5]). Respoken and fallen from the wave, this repetition may actually be writing: to write is to collect, to incorporate, to escort and to reduce. Every book escorts the redundancy of the Book to a space delimited by an inscription. In each of these temples, autobiography is venerated—providing that the other repetition, of which it is in fact merely the resumption or remuneration, is ignored. The age of printing is indeed the age of the subject—of the book there is only an *I*, and *I* repeats itself; that is how it recognizes itself.

*

I have no more made my book than my book has made me—a book consubstantial with its author.[6] The subject erects himself as a Book and only this erection has ever ensured the substance of a subject—whose frank dissimulation means that desire is read like an open book: thus, reader, I am myself the matter of my book: that is no reason for you to employ your leisure time in a subject so frivolous and so vain. I am not building here a statue to erect at the town crossroads, this is for a nook in a library, and to amuse a neighbor.[7] The others form the man; I recite and represent one in particular, quite poorly formed. I want my natural and ordinary pace to be seen, as irregular as it may be. My reason for writing is to reach B.—to reach myself, to reach in her my society, its solitude, to reach the one—man or woman—who says *I*, not natural, not ordinary.

*

I repeats its desire to itself—is any desire not in fact unsettled? That the *I* reveals itself does not necessarily make it see. Someone is irremediably lost in the material of his book—someone who will incessantly repeat: "the matter of my experience, which will be the matter of my book," and this time, it's Proust. Someone—he's the one who says *I* but he's not this one—repeats himself, lost in every book. Through the endless repetition of autobibliography and in spite of it, an autographer walks into the abyss. His wandering begins at the same crossroads as his erection.

The autographer is the one who takes a singular leave at the very beginning of his book. A-Dieu, then, Montaigne, this first of March, one thousand five hundred eighty. Signature of place, signature of name, signature of adieu, it enters his reading as it would a tomb. It is its sameness which, in altering its identity and its singularity, divides the seal (Derrida).[8]

Literal and literary repetition is the repetition of one who wanders within his own marks—within the discourse of his own funereal vigil, like

Finnegan, "riverrun, past Eve and Adam's, from swerve of shore to bend of bay, brings us by a commodius vicus of recirculation . . .," Joyce putting back into circulation and letting wander the signs of history and histories . . . an exodus, there, has begun again, and someone has entered the story of his diaspora. The repeated call always comes from him. It is the call of a solitude that predates any isolation, the invocation of a community that no society contains or heralds. How can the utterly different commonality of the book be released, someone asks, an ordinary writer, an *I* who is called?

> *bent over the book opened to the same page*
> *what he hears are the songs from*
> *the other side, where the others are found.*
>
> Jacqueline Risset

The History of the Book He Writes

is a history that conforms to his desire and his exodus. Writing, he says, marks the end of communism everywhere. That is, of what he has not known, for he is born with writing.

But he writes in his books—and he writes in all his books—that which communism was, the absence of the book. The book never claims anything other than to retrace that which exceeds it. The question concerning the origin of the book will never belong to a book (Derrida)[9]—and yet, O memory, which recorded what I saw, Here will be shown what there is noble in you (Dante).[10] He writes the world of the *aoidos*, the storyteller, the sacred reciter. The first poet, who took this step in order to free himself from the crowd through the imagination, knows how to return there in real life. For he will do all he can to relate to the crowd the exploits that his imagination attributes to the hero. This hero is, ultimately, himself. But the listeners, who understand the poet, know how to identify with the hero (Freud). This pure *poiesy* of the self in the pure community haunts but does not discontinue all of literature: and he is a man here, now, who is his own narrator, finally (Robbe-Grillet).[11]

It was, he says, the world of a mime who has no example to follow and will have no imitator, the world of the brilliant improviser, the dancer drunk with god, the beating heart, blows, the whistling of an unwritten music, the world of prayers, supplications, invocations. It is the tribe with its words and its chants, the cry sung by the primitive community around the hearth—silent writing of a fire so bright it tears itself apart without a trace (Laporte).

This occurs, in the story we tell ourselves, the society of writing that is not the book but the engraving of sacred characters, the inscription of Laws on tables of stone or metal, on columns, pilasters, pendiments, and fasciae, hard writing and the erection of stelae on which can be read Order and Disposition, Structure and Model—allowing them to be read by no one and, thus, by everyone: this is monumental communism, architectural writing, and hieroglyphic monarchy. All his words should seem hollowed out or in relief, chiseled or sculpted, as was said of sacred writing by the man (Joubert) who wrote in maxims.[12] And every book hopelessly tends toward this maxim: *maxima sententia*, the greatest thought . . .

At the end—from nowhere and from everywhere, from Egypt, from Ionia, from Canaan—comes the book; *ta biblia*, the irrevocably plural bible, the Law, the Prophets, the Writings as it is divided, arranged, specularly repeated and disseminated. It is and it is not the Book of one—author or people.

And finally, the very late, very ancient religion of books, which is where all exoduses begin. Egypt, Ionia, Canaan are set in motion for the crossing of deserts by villages that continue to be dispersed.

The history of books begins by losing itself in the book of history. No one has told us who wrote this very first pact that is called the Book of the Covenant (Exodus, 24, 7), not even if it was written. It is the history of the pact—pact of deliverance—broken, kept, betrayed, always offered—and the renewed call to sign it one more time. Broken though barely engraved, the Tables cannot be erected; they make their way in the Ark with the wandering tribes. The Rolls unfurl and the volume of history grows until it reaches us; the book is inseparable from the tale, the novel's story: romanticism is the era of the book. In our writings thought seems to move like a man who walks and does not waver from his path. But in the writings of the ancients, thought seems to move like a bird that glides and advances by turning round and round (Joubert).[13]

> Who does not see that I have taken a road along which I shall go,
> without stopping and without effort, as long as there is ink and paper
> in the world?[14]

Books begin with their repetition: two stories of genesis are blended, overlap, retell and contradict one another. Books, we copy them, reproduce them, *publish* them because they are not themselves public nor like a song or an obelisk; we transmit them, translate them—seventy-two Jews, six from each tribe, in seventy-two days, on the Isle of Pharos, turn the

Bible into Greek—they are betrayed, counterfeited, imitated, recopied, we recite them, we cite them. Whoever says *I* confuses books and signatures in his book: In the reasonings and inventions that I transplant into my soil and confound with my own, I have sometimes deliberately not indicated the author, in order to hold in check the temerity of those hasty condemnations that are tossed at all sorts of writings.[15] Here the so-called repetition is already starting again.

Books are corruptible. Books are made of wood: *biblos, liber, codex, Buch,* always bark or tree. It burns, rots, decomposes, disappears, succumbs to the gnawing criticism of mice. Bibliophily, as much as philosophy, is an impossible love of tanned, faded, worn, divided, lacunary objects. The book is miserable, detestable. Descartes hated the business of making books. There is nothing on the Subject—the other, the same, the one who says *I* (think)—in those "fat volumes," nothing but a waste of time, the pointless consumption of a life spent reading bits and pieces of a science that I can establish by myself. There should be some legal restraint aimed at inept and useless writers, as there is against vagabonds and idlers. Both I and a hundred others would be banished from the hands of our people. This is no jest. Scribbling seems to be a sort of symptom of an unruly age. When did we write so much as since our dissensions began?[16]—since we have been troubled with writing.

For, the one who says *I* must, however, write, the proof is inexorable: considering the problem of the *ego* and the *alter ego,* of originary coupling, and of human community, Husserl wrote: "All these matters are governed by essential necessities; they conform to an *essential style,* rooted first in the transcendental *ego* and in transcendental intersubjectivity which discloses itself in that *ego*—and then accordingly, in the essential forms of transcendental motivation and transcendental constitution. If we succeed in uncovering these forms, the aforesaid apriori style acquires a rational clarification that has the highest dignity, the dignity of an ultimate, a transcendental intelligibility."[17] Husserl writes what he does not want to—write. He writes that the originary alteration of the *ego,* the community of men, forms or deforms style, writing to the point of intelligibility, whose ultimate success it irrevocably deciphers.

Thus, supplication by the book began at the same time as the persecution of books. Writing is associated with the cruel simulacrum of suffering (Laporte). And now anyone can see through the glass the way the inscription is made on the body. Of course, the writing mustn't be too straightforward; it's not supposed to be fatal straight away, but only after an interval of twelve hours or so on average (Kafka, "The Penal Colony").[18]

At the end of the story, the officer who controls the machine is himself executed when the law he had violated is carved into his flesh: *Be just!* But only the machine remains for the savage application of the law—the communism and capitalism of writing machines. Yet, the appeal is the same: how can the utter otherness of the book be released?

The Apocalypse

What if books always heralded, always provoked the renewed beginning in this story of that which has no place? And what if we understood why, today, speaking and writing, we must always speak *several times at the same time*, speaking according to the logic of discourse and, therefore, under the sway of a nostalgia for the theological *logos*; speaking also to make possible a speaking communication that can only be achieved on the basis of a communism of the relations of exchange, thus of production—but also not speaking, writing, by way of a rupture with every language spoken and written (Blanchot)?[19]

With the end of books, there is the Apocalypse. It is the characteristically written genre of prophecy—which is to say, the call. It is the book of the end of the world, the book of renewal. The one who writes it speaks and I speak his name—John—and speaks his place of exile—the Isle of Patmos. This book is a letter to the scattered churches, to the community deprived of its communion. In this letter, a letter is addressed to each of the churches, each of the congregations. The letter is repeated, divided, transformed: To the angel of the Church of Ephesus, you write: These things saith he that holdeth the seven stars in his right hand (St. John).[20] To them in Ysat Loka. Hearing. The urb it orbs. Then's now with now's then in tense continuant. Heard. Who having has he shall have had. Hear! (Joyce).[21]

In this book, John writes the visions he is given to see: but he writes only because the visions command him to write. The Angel speaks to him while holding the Book, but John does not copy it, he writes what the Angel dictates to him. What is revealed is not the Angel, and it is not the Book: it is the writing of the man. The man who is announced through the revelation, the man who says in turn who he is is the one who speaks—the man, John writes, who says he is the *alpha* and the *omega*. He is the Book, of course, but also nothing other than the finite accounting of the characters of writing—this is all that is revealed in the seven broken seals of the book of the slaughtered Lamb. It is the end of religion.

John writes all his visions of scripture. But in the middle, he is forbidden from writing the words of the seven thunders. No book can release the unheard word, inaudible, deafening—the primitive tumult whose sound will accompany the exaltation of the mystical community. But the book knows the dispersion of communion—it is the inscription and it communicates the call: That the one who listens says "Come!" *Come!* declaims the Apocalypse—and our books about books. Come, and deliver unto us the justness of what is disappearing, a heart's movement (Blanchot, quoted by Derrida).[22] It is up to you to take a step toward non-sense. There is no possibility of determining, to determine, in any language whatsoever, what is coming in "Come" (Derrida).[23]

This is not an appeal to communication but the propagation of the repetition of the appeal, of the order and the demand that bear, produce, promote, teach nothing—come—that call for no response but only the obligation to respond, the responsibility of writing again with the twenty-six letters that harbor no revelation, merely their own exhaustion.

Here, the exhaustion is initial: My reason for writing is to reach B.—to get from the first to the second letter, to trace letters, connected to one another, which is called writing, which calls writing, which calls a woman, a man, a book, a story, and always like B. in the story, an impossible, unbearable nudity.

So far beyond and so far before what no word can reveal of truth—so far before and so far beyond any Book—the apocalypse remains to be discovered, the discovery that transforms every book: is that the book and communion are stripped bare, disclosed, in every book. The absence of the Book is the absence of Communion—our communion, or part of one in all and all in one (Mallarmé).[24] But also the presence—forever submerged in the moment—of the book. John had to eat a little book. I took the little book and ate it; in my mouth it had the sweetness of honey, but when I had eaten it, my belly was filled with bitterness.[25]

What communicates, what is communed, is nothing, is not nothing, nothing but bitterness, but a call; another communism yet to come without ending history, a communism of exodus and repetition, would like to say nothing (but, in Blanchot's words, *more* than what they want to say, what the words want: relations of exchange, therefore, of production?), but, it would write, this communism, the deliverance of books, in books. Vain insofar as it is bookish, or *livresque* (a word coined by Montaigne)— and how could it not be, starting right here?—this deliverance, assuredly, but certainly bookish as well insofar as it is vain, insofar as writing, again and once more, takes no risks openly.

*

I repeat: the reasons for writing a book can be compared to the desire to modify the relations that exist between a man and his fellow men. These relations are felt to be unacceptable and perceived as a form of terrible suffering (Bataille).

Far calls. Coming, far! End here. Us then (Joyce).[26]

April 1977

Narrative, Narration, Recitative

[. . .] the subject as subject of art, myth,
and story (is there any other?)
A story cannot have an end, never having had a beginning
—having (and this amounts to the same thing)
come to an end long ago.
—PHILIPPE LACOUE-LABARTHE[1]

I

Narrative implements and puts into play its narrator: there is no narrative without narration and no narration without a narrator.[2] The latter is never presented as distinct from the narrative, even when he is its subject, as he must be in an autobiography or a novel whose narrator is referred to in the first person, like those in *In Search of Lost Time* or *Tristram Shandy*, which are not by chance privileged *exempla* in the history of the modern narrative. The "I," of itself and by nature as much as by structure, is differentiated. Essentially, it is by distinction and by discretion: distinct, detached, separate, and discrete in the mathematical or semiological sense, discontinuous, isolated and impossible to break down for insertion into a continuity. Along these lines, the "I" of a first-person narrative is no more or less withdrawn than the absent, anonymous, and even voiceless narrator found in the most classical form of the narrative.

Distinction and discretion place the narrator some distance from the narration. Him or it—for it is unclear that we must limit ourselves to designating a "person," even though the *person* can be approached through the

43

historical biases of *personare*, "to sound through and through," as did the voices of ancient actors, narrators of Fable, through their masks. There is no person as interiority—unless we understand interiority to be nothing other than an infinite antecedence ever more withdrawn in the very emission of exteriority: the unsupposable supposition, unbearable, impossible to subjugate, of a subject of speech.

The narrator is the necessary and unlikely supposition of the narrative. He is the anteriority of the narrative to itself. The anteriority of the voice to itself.

II

Auto- or allographic, the narrative's advance is driven by a twofold necessity. On the one hand, it has to be narrated: it has to be enunciated, pronounced, must even be announced, must introduce itself as narrative. There is always a "once upon a time" that conceals or is concealed by, that reveals or is revealed by a particular time, be it imaginary (thus, Faulkner, when he begins "Old Man," in *If I Forget Thee, Jerusalem*, with "Once (it was in Mississippi, in May, in the flood year 1927) . . ."[3]). In this sense, it demands its subject, its narrator, its voice. In that "Once" there resonates—musically, I'll return to this—a vocal pronouncement or articulation. If there is a text, a discourse, or what have you, that is not narrative (which may be no more than a limiting assumption, that of an exclusively mathematical text, for example, if such a thing exists and if it is an example and not a unique case . . .) or not narrative in some sense—then, it is also a text without a voice and without an enunciator, which amounts to saying that it is not a text.

On the other hand, when the narrative is at least virtually present—and it can, in fact, it must be so against the background of the poem, the philosophical, legal, or scientific text, or anything that creates *diegesis* rather than *mimesis*, anything that is not a first-person statement, that is, anything that does not assume that the speaker speaks in our presence—once it implies its narrator, its subject or voice, as being absent but indicated or suggested in that absence: it detaches him as *sub-jectum* or *sup-positum*, it places that narrator along the edge, in the background, somewhat withdrawn from the narration itself.

Moreover, the narrative can seek out this subject in order to make him present, unmasking him in a sense, as Henry James does when he suddenly has his narrator speak in the first person after having kept the conventional narrator absent for three-hundred pages (in *What Maisie Knew*). In fact, such a process merely reveals how fragile is the separation between *diegesis* and *mimesis*, when presence in person shows itself to be the equivalent and the substitute for an absence. "Literature" may mean: uttered by no one— and "narrate" could be the name of the utterance that is not "mine" in the sense that it uses the speech of ordinary, non-literary life. At least it is supposed to be so, because it is not obvious that the simplest speech act does not imply that the speaking "me" should not, as "I," the subject of my speech, and at the same time as I come forth as speaker, withdraw into the interchangeability of all the "I's," which is nothing more, as far as literature is concerned, than a general condition of language as speech.

In this sense, the characterized *narrative*—history, narration, novel, short story—is nothing other than the specific treatment and intensifica- tion of a very general condition of speech—of actual language, of language untethered from linguistics, not from the language system [*langue*], for the latter impregnates and colors the act—and which is the condition of *oral- ity*. This latter—utterance, pronouncement, address—is far from being limited to the instrumentation of a phonatory apparatus. Orality is not phonation alone: it is the transmitting body, the body open to the outside as the transmitter of its "inside," which is only given in this transmission. Vocal production entails a resonance of the body through which inside and outside separate and respond to one another—and concerning which we should not doubt that the initial opening is of the order of the cry and the song together, of signal and invocation (here we could refer to those reli- gious, legal, and political values associated with the transmission of the voice and even with the vocabulary of the *vox*, as in Greek that of the *opa/ epos*). As can be seen, we would rediscover our literature at its birth and would find it adorned with the solemnity of a pronouncement that knows that it enacts nothing less than the possibility of producing on the outside, in the world, that thing or that one who inquires about the sense or the truth of the world, that is, its absolute outside (reversibility: the inside of the body is the outside of the world and vice versa). Here nothing occurs that does not imply a twofold dissociation: that of the given world and an "incorporeal" sense (as the Stoics said), and that of the narrator to the extent that he narrates *himself* or, rather—which amounts to the same thing—that he divides himself, while producing himself as narrator, between narrator and narrated.

What we refer to as *writing*, as the word is understood today, is merely the form in which is exemplified, while expanding—through the material inscription by which the movement, the path of pro-nouncement and pro- duction is retained and exposed—the facilitation of meaning as it strives to escape. With this infinite escape, the dissociation of the subject of speech is concretely inscribed in writing.

Narrative begins with this dissociation. It refers to it: not only does what it narrates precede its report of that narration, but even if it speaks in the present—this so-called "narrative" present or the present of a "mimetic" declaration—it cannot avoid exposing a gap through which it reveals itself to be preceding itself. A narrator will always have taken the initiative to narrate or will have received the directive to do so. In truth, speech has an absolute antecedent: in speech, "I" withdraws behind the "me" that speaks—but in this way it finds itself as well. No "I" becomes "I" other than by narrating itself as such or by being the narrator of some ordinary narrative.

III

Narrative alone establishes the tension—expectation and attention, notwithstanding any intention—in which the indisputable and irreducible privilege of the path, the way, the *method* that philosophy recognizes allows itself to be felt but, while recognizing it, cannot resist the tendency to reduce and absorb. If, as Hegel says, the True is the result arrived at by a path, this means ultimately that the path is integrated, absorbed in the result for which it will have been the means. It has been this way ever since the Platonic dialectic and the pathway leading to the heaven of Ideas and the *theos*. Nor is the True present on the path as something interminable or even as lacking a conclusion or direction—a path leading nowhere and losing itself in the woods that Descartes taught us always to cross by moving straight ahead: for, on such a path, it is the absence of direction and destination that, at every moment, with every step, is fulfilled as truth and surreptitiously confers the quality of a result to motion along the path.

For all philosophical and methodological paths, the result is presupposed. This presupposition may remain relatively indeterminate, similar to Cartesian intuition, Kantian liberty, or the Hegelian absolute; nonetheless, it remains a preexisting position, an already prepared reserve and viaticum. In spite of the considerable distances philosophers are able to cover and the distances they cross, their paths harbor a secret immobility. This immobility arises from their gaze being fixed—even though their eyes may be closed—on the idea of the result, of the fulfillment of the intention and the absorption of tension. Advancement along this path can and must comply with this idea: it must be such that its trajectory and speed can give rise to a result, a consequence that in turn illuminates the entire pathway and justifies its course. This will be adjusted to its end, its end will have served as rule, guide, and model: mimetic path of the goal, movement imitating position.

Every aspect of Philippe Lacoue-Labarthe's thought proceeds from an initial, deep-seated, and radical rejection of this mimetic conformation. Early on he recognized the subjection and immobility—the *typological* fixation—against which an essential rebelliousness drove him. Here, I want to postulate that this rebelliousness arose from a no less profound and no less innate sense of narrative in him—even if he never really engaged in such practice, although he may have approached it—and that this sense of narrative flowered through its attentiveness to music—by which it set itself apart, precisely, from the most ordinary activity of narrative. I don't wish to proceed by hewing too closely to the letter of his texts but by attempting to engage their fundamental movement based on a consideration of the narrative that I outline in my own way and at my own risk, in his memory.

Or rather: I outline it to pursue in my own way the narrative of his life and thought, the narrative that was his thought, the narration of the interminable and always too quickly concluded novel of his existence.

IV

I use the word "novel" to express what for us subsumes or indeed represents the narrative in exemplary fashion. That is, not the narration of picturesque adventures and highly colored episodes (not the novelistic), but the thought that is held under the major sign of arrival, of arising and disappearance. The thought that obeys what Philippe stated this way: "What we must think is the *"It happens that."*[4]

But with respect to this "It happens," the first condition for thought is understanding that the subject of this sentence, the "it" in "it happens," is indissolubly impersonal and personal. That this or that "happens," that a "that" happens, occurs effectively and fully—*arrives*, therefore—only when this "it" becomes someone. Therefore, no longer "it happens *that*" but simply "he arrives." "It happens that 'He' arrives." All of Philippe's thought has been turned to—and turned over, overturned by—this dread that "He" might arrive, He, himself, specifically, that he might finally arrive at himself, that he might finally arrive for himself.[5]

That someone arrives is as infrequently and as poorly determinable as the event of birth (in the same passage of Lacoue-Labarthe's text, he speaks of "we to whom birth has been 'given'"). We know that this event is an always postponed advent. Being born seems to be a one-time occurrence but begins before coming into the world and lasts—as Freud suggests—until we leave the world. We continue to be born in dying.

That is why he—Philippe—continues by writing: "But how is it thinkable without the [. . .] threat that the *He arrives* will cease to occur."[6] Yet this threat is inscribed in the nature and structure of the *arriving*. For that to arrive, it must also leave. It must first of all have gone—absent, not given, distant, lost even, nonexistent—for it to come or come back. Here, coming and coming back are the same, for coming always comes back from the same empty anteriority, coming comes back from nowhere, and returns there. (To come, coming, of course.)

This is exactly what philosophy ignores, rejects, or averts. Hegel objects to the fact that philosophy might have a beginning, as understood by the other sciences, that is, "the presupposition of a particular object."[7] Absolute knowledge is not total knowledge, integral and final: it is the knowledge about which nothing is presupposed as object but which subsumes into itself any object and dissolves its objectivity, that is to say, its exteriority. To know one is the subject of self, to return to the self, to the "concept of its concept" and, therefore, the absorption of any *arriving* and any *coming* (here Hegel speaks of "satisfaction," namely, that which profoundly contradicts *jouissance*. Coming surpasses the opposition between satisfaction and lack. This too belongs to narrative).

If the question of beginning is relevant to philosophy, it will only be so, writes Hegel, by considering it as a "relation to the subject to the extent that he is determined to philosophize, but not to science as such." The beginning is outside knowledge, it is empirical and contingent. It exists in some *Once upon a time there was a subject—for example, Georg Wilhelm Friedrich Hegel—who wanted to do philosophy*. Ultimately, you'll say to me, this subject will have been absorbed into the self-knowledge of knowledge. It's true, but this truth itself is infinitely projected outside any presentation that wouldn't strictly be the return-to-self of the concept of its own concept. Hegel himself knows this: this, this absolute return, strictly speaking, doesn't *happen*. On the contrary, it is that which, not happening, exposes the possibility of everything *happening*.[8]

This return-to-self is nothing, the insignificant, the lack of substance of an anteriority and posteriority to any *coming, coming-and-going*. In Hegel's work, this is called "being" as "empty copula." The emptiness of being—or the empty being, that is to say, philosophy itself—for Lacoue-Labarthe, shapes both what the narrative rejects and what it refutes.

It rejects it because it refuses to settle into the pretention of annexing, of reuniting the void to its satisfaction—either because it feels this dialectical accomplishment is impossible or fears the too unbearable truth within it. Or both of them together, as it should be. Rejection is also terror.

But it refutes it, for by opening up the narrative, by attempting to say that *it happens*, by struggling *to be able to say that it happens*, and to say *that it happens that* He *arrives*, it engages effectively, practically, and with exemplary tenacity—the tenacity of the narrator himself—the resistance to the mutual annihilation of the void and of satisfaction.

This is what Lacoue-Labarthe himself calls *mimesis without a model* or *originary mimesis*. The "he" of the narrative—"he" or "I," it matters little—or "we," or indeed no one, the anonymous voice, is the one who, "having decided to tell a story," begins to imitate an absolute narrator who never was because the absolute is unnarratable.

V

Under these conditions, not only does the self-referentiality of the concept (or the concept of the concept), in which the difference between void and plenitude is invalidated, turn out to be a form of self-strangulation—as well as of the self, or any "he" or any "someone" capable of arriving—but even the *path* so important to Hegel, to all philosophy, is invalidated. The path that matters to the result disappears within that result, indeed, just as the result does.

The narrative consists in separating itself from the metaphor of the path and of any concept of a means, whether associated with a goal or whether mediated as a goal itself. The narrative is not a path. It is pathclearing, which is quite different; in pathclearing, the path is not given, not even open.

Pathclearing exposes the possibility for the narrator to identify with the production and completion of the narrative itself. Without such identification, the narrator will remain lost outside the limits of the narrative. A narrator never dissolves into his narrative, any more than it is absorbed in him. The past of the ordinary narrative is merely a secondary effect of the being-already-past, that is, never-yet-arrived, of the narrator.

The narrative will have begun before its narrator, who, however, must have preceded it: this is the lesson of literature—a lesson that philosophy rejects in principle, satisfying itself with the decision to be contemporary with its beginning. The narrative, on the contrary, dissociates origin and beginning. When it begins it already has its origin behind it. The opening of any narrative can tell us this. When we read "For a long time, I used to go to bed early . . . ," we learn, before we learn anything else, that this *long time* took place long ago, over an insurmountable period of time, one that disappears behind these first words. And this stretch of time initially affects the "I" who claims to speak, who is written here. He distends it— here visibly, legibly, but every *incipit* distends it similarly: "once upon a time" dissociates the narrator from this unsituatable "time" that he nevertheless claims to be capable of situating.

In Lacoue-Labarthe's terms, we could say that this distension—the very dissociation of the narrator within his narration—is due to the failure to self-identify, the failure to become *oneself*.[9]

Dissociation *itself* represents that for which there cannot be any "sameness": here it represents the difference (or the *différance*) through which the subject establishes itself or, rather, is initialized or initiated, or, better yet, clears a path toward that which can only be concealed from the subject, given only as already withdrawn into a *long time* or a *once upon a time* that no story will ever recapture.

The narrative sets in motion something that is so withdrawn that nothing could disturb it or bring it to life: the absolute antecedence of the subject of speech. But "the subject of speech" is not independent of this antecedence: it is "*speech-itself*" and shapes it, this speech, helps it speak, at the cost of expiring in it—literally and in every sense. I quote Lacoue-Labarthe, who writes and describes

> [. . .] a precise trajectory that I would willingly identify, in one way or another, with the transition, between neck and larynx, from thought to utterance: to that elusive and most likely nonexistent moment, not subject to time, in which, at the back of the throat, *thought*, therefore (what other word can I use?), assumes a kind of intangible consistency—I'd say approximately: *draws breath*—and blends with the exhalation in which it seems that thought is not lost but is simply altered and, in being altered, is articulated or modulated as a vague atonal song [. . .].[10]

That—that or he—which expires not in speech but *with speech*—that or the one (he or she) who is called "thought" here, for lack of anything better, that is, for lack of a word for that which, being before words, rises to absolute antecedence, to the original separation, ever more withdrawn than any allocation, of a "one," of a "some" speaking subject, of some one speech-subject. Far from having to be thought of as separation *from* a broader unity or even from a unitotality (represented as maternal, oceanic, cosmic, take your pick), according to the known model ("castration," "loss," et cetera), this separation should be understood as the separation of the "one" in itself and from itself. This "one" who has always already been what it is but who only becomes so by expiring—death and speech together, speech and breath about to be lost in order to be found, formed in the hyphen between the immemorial and the unarriving.

VI

Recitation is the regime of this hyphen, of this line drawn from before to after and from the inside or the in-itself to the outside or the for-itself, which are the two poles of the infinite torsion through which "one" seeks, without ever finding, itself, but nevertheless extends and stretches, traces and withdraws, inspires and expires itself.

Recitation recites this ins-ex-piration, the rise and fall, the beat, the beating of this breath. *Citare* is to set in motion, to bring to the self (the Latin verb is related to the Greek *kinein*: there is cinema in every story). *Ex-citare*, is to awaken, *sus-citare*, to be raised (and *re-sus-citare* is not far), *in-citare*, to throw forward. All these motions and emotions are found in recitation, which excites, brings about, and incites a "saying," which is not just any saying but the saying that says an arrival and a departure, which says the tension of the fact that something is happening and that this something is, necessarily, some "one" or becomes or calls someone. That this someone is identified as "author" or "hero," that he is taken from a "personal" or imaginary history, matters little or only to take into account the extraordinary richness of narrative possibilities, the indefinite multiplicity of narrative stratagems. This profusion responds to the absence of a unique Narrative and this absence is inscribed in the very fact of the narrative, in its universal presence among speakers. For the narrative brings about the following: nothing happens without narrative.

Indeed, recitation is not satisfied with "saying" in the sense of uttering, expressing, or recounting events that have taken place. It makes them happen, it makes them *come to pass*. Nothing has occurred other than the sequencing of facts for as long as (but this time is never all that long) those facts are not seized, borne, pushed toward their manifestation. This thrust is the work of speech. Speech is not a tool, it is itself—in its phonation as in its phrasing, its syntax, its prosody—the thrust or drive of "meaning." Meaning is not added to or assumed by the facts, it is their *arrival*, it is their *coming*. In short, it is the fact of the fact, the thrust and pulsation that *bring into the world* and that thereby *make* a "world," which is to say, a space for the circulation of meaning.

The world is a world of narratives, of recitations of narratives. To begin with all those narratives of the world that every culture has always narrated, of which our "literature" is itself, in turn, the narrative: it endeavors to recount where we are and how, not only with this fact of the world and of our being-in-the-world but how we relate to our own narratives of the world, to their antiquity and their loss, to what seem to us to be naïve illusions or broken promises. How we have interrupted the myths and which voices are clamoring to speak through that interruption. Myth—a world narrating itself, a *tautegory* as Schelling remarked—has been interrupted by the injunction of the *logos*: truth made its appearance as the object of an *allegory*, a way of saying an other object, unpresentable, only representable.

But in truth, every narrative creates a new *muthos*: not that it fabricates more or less powerful, seductive, and credible figures, but that it opens speech itself to its own drive and pulsation. Speech, the voice, the perceptible narrative of meaning.

VII

That is why the narrative comes after. It comes after nothing and after everything: after no meaning that would have gone before it and after everything, for everything always settles outside meaning, in erratic blocks. The narrative returns. *Recitare:* to repeat the roll call of names before the court. The names that the narrator calls to appear before the court are his own names—his proper names, never entirely appropriate, in their non-significance, to this remarkable, unnamable property that forms the truth of what is happening, the truth of its arrival, the truth of the story told, recited, a truth called, invoked, evoked, unverifiable, itself erratic and spread throughout the narrative, weaving the narrative itself without ever revealing itself other than through the art of the narrator. What is called "art" is here, as elsewhere, a knowledge of unverifiable truths that have been modeled, figured, disfigured, and transfigured in keeping with the rhythm and pace of narration. ("The figure is never *one* . . . There is no unity or stability of the figural; the *imago* has no fixity or proper being. There is no 'proper image' with which to identify totally, no essence of the imaginary ."[11])

For *narration* is knowledge (*gnarus, co-gnosco, i-gnoro*): it is knowledge that reports, that relates what has taken place, the fact that it has happened, and how it has happened, how, therefore, the order and succession of things have found themselves and find themselves modified, modulated, altered thereby. This is not a knowledge of things learned (*mathemata*), it is the knowledge of things as they are grasped and released based on their incalculable provenance and destination.

*

The story or narration assumes the course of things, and that it has always already begun. Where philosophy wants to assume—and impose—the beginning itself, the point of origin and the point of ending, the narrative knows that these points are infinitely far and, in keeping with the infinite, meet and cancel one another in an identical absence of dimension. With the narrative, we fuse with dimension itself: the distention of the always-already and the never-yet, the suspense of the event. "But how to establish the exact moment in which a story begins? Everything has already begun before," Italo Calvino writes.[12]

I read the first sentence of a Faulkner story that Philippe liked, *As I Lay Dying*: "Jewel and I come up from the field."[13] Everything is already given, everything has already been given, begun and continued until the moment I read. Jewel and I are known, like the field and like this moment of return, at an unknown hour. Far from Valery's ironies about the outings of the Comtesse or the Marquise, this sentence brings with it a rhythm, a pace, a proximity already marked with the sonorous trait of a name—a jewel?—and with this other trait, which is the first person of the speaker. He's there, he speaks to us. We leave with him, at his own pace. We have *already* left.

About two hundred pages further in, the story closes with this sentence, "'Meet Mrs. Bundren,' he says."[14] The conclusion, comical or cynical—the replacement of the dead wife—that in truth completes the story, is joined to the already ironic but equally vague and indeterminate resonance of "he says," of this expression that in fact opens another possible story.

As implacable as the end of the story may be, it resonates beyond itself. It exposes its undoing [*désoeuvrement*] in Blanchot's sense. This is true as well of the end of *Under the Volcano*, to which Philippe was attached for literary reasons as well as by identification.

The Consul falls into the volcano's ravine and "it was as though this scream were being tossed from one tree to another, as its echoes returned, then, as though the trees themselves were crowding nearer, huddled together, closing over him, pitying . . ." The resonance of this last cry is followed, on the next line, by "Somebody threw a dead dog after him down the ravine."[15] This *coda*, which could be said to be expressly musical, picks up and amplifies the tonality of the cry with a precision that is foreign to the entire narrative. In the words of the text, and to stick with the French, the "*crevé*" ["dead"] repeats the "*cri*" ["scream"] at the same time as it stifles it. An extinguished but interminable sonority holds open the voice, the tone, and the song of the narrative.

That this has already begun and will continue beyond any narrative "end" is what music reveals. The common feature of music and narrative is based on an always open precedence and subsequence. What I hear when the music "begins" has already begun. What ceases to be heard when the music is silent continues to resonate. "In song," writes Lacoue-Labarthe, "we demand something of the voice other than what it produces spontaneously, we demand that it rediscover a little of the music that came *before* (birth) . . . ."[16]

Music doesn't only mobilize the actual resonance of the sounds it amplifies, intensifies, works, and modulates. It mobilizes their anterior and posterior resonance, the incompletion and unbeginning that belong essentially to resonance. The repetition—resumption, return, theme and variation, haunting melody, da capo, and so on—that haunts music, punctuates and accentuates it, governs the *re-* of *récit*, the iteration that picks up and replays what never took place and will not take place—but which defines the *musical moment*: the passage of time outside time, the composition of presents past and to come in a present that is not that of a given presence but of recollection and expectation, the present composed of a tension directed at the infinite return of a presence never given, always essentially— eternally—escaped.

A singing teacher said to his student, "You must never make it seem like you're beginning. One has already begun to sing."

This distension of the present, this expansion of presence beyond itself, until it becomes an absence replete with its own beating, filled with the repeated call of the absent burned by its "desire to reach itself,"[17] is what creates the true substance and challenge of the narrative.

Music is a narrative. Not a story. Not what we try to invent to transform music into narrative, as when we say that the clarinet is speaking to the orchestra or that the fast movement, with its energy, highlights and advances what the slow movement had set down and seemingly abandoned—or just the opposite, for nearly anything can be said when we make use of this register. Yet, we can and must make use of it, provided that we do not imagine any adventures or incidents between characters, landscapes, and images. Here, in particular, the image-less is determinant (the image-less or intimate destabilization of the image as it has been evoked): it is there, so to speak, to make room for the element I have been calling the "narrative," that is, the *coming-and-going* or *reciting itself and citing itself, calling itself and hearing itself*, but losing itself as well as finding itself in this echo of the self.

The Echo of the Subject—Lacoue-Labarthe's title . . . Title, we might say, of his entire body of work and of his life, his narrative. In an echo, I find and lose myself. I resonate in the space that must be opened if resonance is to occur. Rather than the encounter of the void and of satisfaction in absolute knowledge, it is the reverberation in the breach of an arrival that is about to depart. The breach is that which opens the subject and opens itself to the subject so that it might call itself there, might cite and recite itself.

VIII

For Lacoue-Labarthe, musical recitation is not or not essentially or primitively that of the melody. The melodic line can enclose a subjective representation (lyricism, expressiveness, effusion, as these have been understood since romanticism).[18] The rhythmic beat affects the structure of the Subject as such,[19] that is to say, the difference and *différance* between self and self, the Heraclitean "One differing from/in himself."[20]

The beat of this difference/différance does not arise in a given Subject: it exposes him to possibility, chance, and risk. It is born in the archaic pulsation around which—breathing, heart, listening, inside/outside—crystallizes, originarily, the enigma of "some one."

Rhythm engages time with a relation to self by exposing it, in its milieu, to the suspense of the beat, to the caesura or syncope that binds and unbinds measure during this time. Music, par excellence, has already begun and will pursue itself further into silence. No doubt there is no silence without rhythm.[21] There is no silence. We needn't focus on *pianissimo* introductions: when the first measure of Beethoven's Great Fugue (another of his major works) breaks the silence, cutting, tearing, demanding, imperious, the attack of sound alone and the thrust of its movement reveal an anteriority that could be called tonal and rhythmic (the melody only comes later). We have already been hearing something that was inaudible. Already a thrust, a drive and a pulsation behind the sound of the instruments, in an archi-sonority that is in some sense sonority itself: exposing the possibility of an echo. (We could say the same, to add one more example, about the attack of Albert Ayler's sax in Love Cry.)

Before music and before speech, like their obscure shared thrust, there is what we will call *recitative*. Not in the strictly musicological sense of the term (which, moreover, has varied and is today applied to a very broad musical spectrum[22]), but in the sense that it designates both that which, from speech, precedes song, approaches it without detaching itself in the form of a "melody," and that which, from music, enters into speech to distance time and relieve it of a cadence foreign to its meaning. Neither declamation—which is aligned with *pathos*—nor song—led by a *melos*—the recitative forms an *ethos*: a comportment, a behavior for language. Behavior that initially recognizes in it a "before" and an "after," which knows that it comes from further away and will go further than its linguistic constitution and phonetic utterance. The recitative awakens and maintains in language the *voice* that expresses it, while it summons and retains in music the *sense* that it alone can make vibrate.

In this way, a story is told all of whose intrigue or adventure cannot be bound together without undoing, from moment to moment, its progress in a cadence, nor without bearing away its signification in a pulsation that incessantly questions the birth of speech: the disturbance of the echo through which a subject knows and feels itself—here, it's the same thing—preceded and followed by itself in an infinite, eternal alterity. Consequently, much more lost than any narrative, but narrating, out of that loss, which it calls the loss of

> *[. . .] its own*
> *voice, which no more belongs to us than our*
> *way of moving or our gaze.*[23]

Therefore,

> *What we expected to see is not found, only a shadowless expanse with nothing to disturb it (just as the sea when, undisturbed by any breeze, remains at rest, not flickering but with motionless brilliance—to the point of invisibility), with a rustling just barely poignant . . .*[24]

May 2010

. . . would have to be a novel . . .

Literature is not part of written language: that is, at least, if writing is not the simple graphic record of speech.

Writing is prior to speech and perhaps even to language. For a language is possible only through implicit but constitutive reference to the impossibility of going beyond itself to establish itself in another language that would provide it with meaning. A language can only be established in itself, in the circular return to its own code. This law of language can be expressed by the formula: no metalanguage.

A metalanguage would not be a language, it would be the pure manifestation of the thing and, with it, its meaning. In truth, it wouldn't be a question of "meaning." There would be the thing and, at best, an index there to display it, or some method of presentation, and even that is uncertain because it's hard to understand why we would need to show that which shows itself (an axiom that defines truth for Spinoza and, ultimately, for everyone). Showing is necessary only when we are in the element of meaning: this relates to that, goes toward that, is based on, is lost inside, and so on. Meaning shows, it indicates a horizon, a destination. Truth shows itself: it is itself the horizon or destination, unless it is situated precisely beyond any horizon or destination (beyond or even before, as near us as possible).

Recently, "writing" has become the name in which the following expression is condensed: "there is no metalanguage." This signifies that writing has become the name of something that precedes meaning or succeeds it, rather than being the name of a way of assigning meaning. At the same time, this signifies that it is also, necessarily, the name of truth. Not truth as the correct correspondence with a given object but truth as that which manifests itself. Writing designates the novel of truth, the true novel, the true poem.

For this to occur, it was necessary that the operation of recording—or correspondence—itself be displaced or transformed. In fact, the recording model has gradually broken down to give way to what could be called the invention of an inscription, pathclearing, the engram of a trace. The expression of reality in a linguistic form has given way to the production of a fiction in which the real clears a path to meaning.

Of course, it's a question of representation: we imagine that we formerly believed in a language that translated the real; today, we imagine the real as the abyss of our creation. Each of these representations is a scaffold erected because of ideological urgency. Anyone who writes—from the tribal storyteller (for this orality, as we shall see, is also "writing" in the sense examined here) to the writer of narratives and poems—is hardly troubled by such representations. He can make use of them whenever questioned about his activity, but they do not guide the gesture of writing.

*

Here, we're in the situation of an informant. We are being asked how to think of literature. Maybe we should unravel the question. In fact, maybe we should . . . *write*?

Friedrich Schlegel wrote the following: "The theory of the novel would itself have to be a novel."[1] In other words, Schlegel posits that there is a literary metalanguage, which is itself literature and, consequently, immediately deprived of any claim to create metalanguage or metaliterature.

The recent use of the word "writing"—a slippage of meaning from "written form" to "style," then to that of textual creation—signifies no more than that we seek to identify how literature begins prior to any literature or language: it begins with a gesture that exposes a trace.

An ordinary trace follows a passage. The trace in question precedes and clears a passage. It is its provenance, its venue. It is an open path: but to open a path simultaneously assumes an anticipation, a choice of direction, and the precarity of the trace whose nature is such that it tends toward its effacement when it has only just made its appearance. In a way, it too, this effacement, is part of the anticipation of a destination: the destiny of a disappearance is inscribed in it with the tension of an appearance and an advance.

It is to designate this internal contradiction that Derrida spoke of the arche-trace (and *archi-écriture*).[2] The *arche* here is neither the oldest nor the most supreme: neither archeology nor architecture. It is not primitive, it is not first. It is immemorial—this time, the word is Blanchot's. The immemorial does not reside in a memory anterior to all memory but in an absence of memory. It concerns that which has gone before, but about which nothing can be connected to the present in terms of the past. It is a past so absolutely past that it hasn't even passed or didn't pass: it hasn't crossed a present to be deposited in a past present. It has never presented itself.

Rather, it is often said that it *will have gone before*. It's what we refer to as a "future perfect." But, in this case, the future perfect is, in a way, doubled: not only *will it have taken place* but that which will have taken place is referred to only as the fact of going before. In this doubling there appear two claims: one where nothing has taken place other than an indeterminate "taking place" (this is one of the possible meanings of Mallarmé's "*nothing will have taken place but the place*"); and another where the various values of the future perfect work together: the value of conjecture (it is not absolutely certain that it has taken place), the value of emphasis (a significant event must have taken place), the value of anticipation (which assumes a context such as "one day it will be revealed that such and such will have taken place").

The conjunction of these three values composes the meaning we've given to "writing" today. If "writing" does not consist in transcribing pre-existing givens—events, situations, objects, their significations—but in inscribing possibilities of meanings not given, not available, opened up by writing itself, then we must maintain:

—first of all, that no given has gone before other than the opening itself, which is not a given but the gift itself—because this shouldn't be understood as something like the opening of a tunnel, solid and stationary, but like the opening of a mouth that moves in harmony with the words by which it is affected, or like that of an opera that rushes forward to establish the musical key, initiate the movement, part the curtains before the stage;

—that nothing is certain concerning what may have gone before but without any precedence, any anteriority; "To write is to read where there

is nothing," wrote Philippe Grand;[3] but it may also be the case that everything has taken place, everything, the entire world, and that we've been
reading the great book of God or nature: it all comes down to the same
thing, that is, never recurs;

   —and finally, that what has taken place before anything might have
taken place—this empty or absent book, my absence between my two par-
ents, this origin without orifice (or the opposite)—constitutes an event of
great importance, in truth, so considerable that writing is devoted to its
consideration.

   Writing is devoted to considering the event that hasn't taken place or for
which the taking-place can only be conjectured because it has withdrawn
before any vestige, any trace one might discover. In fact, the event is itself
merely the initiation of the trace, the inception of language: the transmission of meaning. Haphazardly, or nested within one another, the creation of
the world, the appearance of mankind, the discovery of language.

   Essentially, this transmission precedes any possible meaning. But, here,
"precede" amounts to disappearing in the pure absence of any anteriority,
in the already-passed of any passage. This is what writing knows and this is
what writing enacts.

*

Literature knows that nothing has gone before. Every artifact of writing
exposes the trace. The same trace that signals the passage of nothing, of the
absent: that which has gone before me. We can call this "the dead one."
Not "death," which is neither a thing nor a person, but the dead one, the
one who has departed, who has passed, *the past* par excellence. We could
make it the principal character, the hero of the novel that would be the
novel of literature: *Passed, the Past, Monsieur Passé.*[4]

   But, yet, this hero is nowhere to be found—neither in the existence nor
in the imagination of the Ancients; he is simply himself, he *will have been* the
absolutely ancient Ancient. Blanchot speaks of the "terrifyingly ancient,"
terrifying because we can only be overcome with fright when considering
the empty darkness of the night that has gone before us. We leave that night
and we enter it, incessantly. *Passed—the Dead One*, no one, therefore, but no
one or the not-one, not-a-single-one, identified as *No One*, the one who,
like Ulysses before Polyphemus, is called *Outis, personne*, nobody, *niemand,
nessuno, nemo* (all are characters of stories, poems, or songs).

   Passed, the Dead One is the one who will always already have arrived
before I do, before anyone does. His arrival exposes the trace of what it
means *to arrive* in general: to come into the world, to come to light, the

arrival of the light itself. To be manifest, to be in the manifestation of things, to emit manifestation. Nothing comes before manifestation just as nothing follows it.

"Literature" has given a name to this, this knowledge of manifestation when it escapes the non-manifest, the hidden, nothingness. When did it assume this appellation, which is, after all, incomprehensible when we consider the earlier significations of the word: the domain of the written, then the literary thing, then "belles-lettres," then, in German, all the documents written on a given subject, as well as Verlaine's "rest," which is to say prosaic prose,[5] as well as Flaubert's intoxication[6] and, before Roland Barthes claimed, much later, that the writer "casts a spell on the intentional meaning, returns speech to a state before meaning"[7] (meanwhile, it's true, the rewriting of the epopee will be joyously referred to as an "allincluding most farraginous chronicle,"[8] which is to say, that literature will have attempted to unreservedly reenact its own meaning, within and without itself or, at least, the identity we might assume it possesses)—when, then, did it come to assume this meaning—today, distancing itself from a dominant representation that claims to be the witness, the report of the real, the lived experience we refer to as "autofictional," as if to signify that it is not at all fictional, for we are suffering from a loss of the real, we believe we are lost in the virtual, the fantasy, empty forms—since when, then, if not forever?

There is no storyteller, no fabulist or narrator of stories, myths, legends, tall tales, or channels of divine speech, no one who does not give his full faith to the story and yet knows that the entire substance of that story resides in his speech, in his utterance, which is also his invention.

Thus, the younger son, the mother's favorite, protected by her from the horde's dominant male, awakens one day to discover his own exploit and recounts how he killed the one who, thereby, becomes the father: this is the origin Freud gives to literature, the explicit myth of the invention of myth, of speech and the tribe together.

Literature is, precisely, speech that knows that its meaning runs from nothing to infinity, that it precedes literature and follows it, that it precedes itself and follows itself. This speech, which extends from the Dead One—the Father, the distinguished Figure fictionalized as immolated—and most importantly Death—the Mother, not a figure but the sharing of speech—to the possibility of some shared meaning.

Let us listen once again to the beginning of the songs for which we, Mediterraneans, have invented the invention under the name Homer, as name and birthplace of our literature:

Menin aeide théa Peleiadeo Achileos . . .
Andra moi ennepe mousa, polutropon . . .

Anger be now your song immortal one, . . .
Sing in me, Muse, and through me tell the story[9]

By asking the divine muse for her song, the singer declares it fiction, but fiction is also claimed to be sacred—inspired, insufflated from an outside that none would be tempted to situate elsewhere than in the deepest intimacy of the song itself.[10]

This outside is also referred to in song as that of events that will be told and celebrated: one man's anger, the activities and wanderings of another. This all takes place somewhere and at some time, and, yet, if we must question the story—almost in a prayer—whispered by a voice more than human, it is because we have everything to learn about these events even as we name them. What is being sung—the anger, the scheming—is already present but still yet to come. What is said in literature, as literature, is always already there and always yet to come.

This began long before narrative and will continue long after it. It is the most telling mark of story and song—in fact, prose and poem, words and music are wrapped together here—to have begun before the mouth begins to speak. The page, the screen, or the tablet upon which writing is traced are appropriate representations of this antecedence both virginal and initiatory—this opening.

A similar opening engages, structures, deploys, excites all of literature. It begins and is continued outside itself; in fact, it is it-"self" nothing more than this antecedence and this unrealizable succession. We cannot complete meaning. At every moment, we assume we are positing a signification: meaning displaces them all and deposits them somewhere else, near an earlier and later exterior. Patiently, hopelessly, this elsewhere inscribes, exscribes its traces.

March 2012

On the Work and Works

I

Seen from a no-doubt-questionable vantage point, but one we must occupy for the time being, we can say that the idea of the "work" annoys, irritates, and excites the entire history of our culture. It assumes pride of place in an uneasy way of thinking about reality, that is, a mode of thinking in which the real is no longer guaranteed, neither by its perceptible certainty nor by its drive toward an intellect that would, when all is said and done, be no more than that certainty itself. On the contrary, it is through the disjunction between perceptible presence and a breath held behind it that we are more or less forced to represent the constituent movement of our tradition.

From there we are faced with the question of the consistency of the real and its provenance or the question of its effectiveness and, therefore, its effectuation. The real, as effect and as effective, and thus the background of the "work" and with it the questions wrapped in the possibility of working it into shape, of implementing it, that is, in the realization of the real:

questions that are as much about the creation of the world as they are about human production.

In Greek, the *ergon* is the productive work and product of work that culminates in *energeia*, the enacted real in which an inherent power, a *dynamis*, is actualized. Latin translates *ergon* with *opus*, from which we derive "*oeuvre*" (however, German *Werk* and English "work," incorporate the root *erg-*). The work, or oeuvre, is an act in the sense that *actus*— accomplishment—is the past participle of Latin *ago* and, therefore, designates an action carried out or concluded: one that has come to its end, its finality, which Aristotle translates as *entelecheia*, which adds to *energeia* the idea of *telos*, a completed end.

The work brings with it the motif of production, which itself bears a threefold implication: that of productive action, that of the producing agent, and that of the act produced. As we know, the course of our culture, contemporary culture—that is, subsequent to the simultaneous growth of technology, democracy, and industrial capitalism—has come to view human existence and, tendentiously, that of the world itself, as the result of mankind's production of that existence. Agent, action, and act are conjoined in the self-production of a real whose essence is its very existence, which is thus given an absolute value—*value* itself, removed from any evaluation of use and exchange, consisting in nothing other than the capacity or, more appropriately, the dignity (that imposing word found in Kant and the rights of man) of self-productive *energy* or in a general operativity, ontological as much as axiological. To such self-production—which may also be understood as self-production in the work and as the work of its subject (author, actor, agent)—responds what we might refer to as autofinality: the work is realized as its own end, the effectiveness of the product is also the effectiveness of the production and the producer. It is this total sense to which the gist of the proverb *Finis coronat opus* (the end crowns the work) applies.

II

This is how, today, the most commonly held notion of the "work" has come to be identified. Within the very broad semantic field of the term— which ranges from specific lexicons, such as those associated with alchemy, justice, or architecture, to all the possible registers of operation, realization, or execution—there has emerged, beginning in the nineteenth century, a meaning we might consider privileged and which is found in the expression "work of art" ("oeuvre d'art"). This expression itself has come to resonate as tautological and "work" can refer, absolutely, either to a product or to all the products of an artist's activity. Zola's novel, *L'œuvre*,[1] is, in a sense, devoted to this usage, whereas, in 1831, Balzac was using the expression "chef-d'oeuvre" as a term derived from the world of artisanship. The two terms are not equivalent, of course, and the second remains even though the first has assumed a value that has come to resemble it.

Today, the emphatic, absolute value of the "work" subsists in current usage, whether it concerns literary criticism or art criticism or even an academic usage that assumes we are willingly showing our esteem for a young researcher when we say "that's a solid body of work [*oeuvre*]" or "you'll soon have a solid body of work [oeuvre]"—by which we highlight a significant difference with what the term "work" ["*les travaux*"] represents, no matter its richness.[2] Yet, and somewhat paradoxically, usage of the word has almost been entirely erased from the language employed in artistic milieu, where we now prefer to speak of the "work" ["*le travail*"] of an artist whenever we don't have a specific term at hand, like "book" in literature ("*ouvrage*" is outdated or too erudite and has never achieved the dignity of "oeuvre") or "film" in cinema (yet, whenever we need to characterize the unity and completeness of an entire body of work, we speak of the "body of work" of Ozu or of Ford).

Thus, there is a silent tension that works the usage and meaning of "oeuvre." In one sense, we know quite clearly what is involved. On the one hand, the word has gathered to itself all the force of the effective realization of this type of production for which we have, almost at the same time as history, reserved the very particular concentration of the word "art" taken in its absolute sense, that is, detached from the distinct values of the various kinds of know-how that constituted the mechanical and liberal arts, the skilled crafts, and the fine arts. The work [oeuvre] is filled with this type of fulfillment, which overflows any form of artisanship or technique that an "art" dissociated from any purpose of transmission, representation, or celebration of a content of historical, religious, political, or moral thought was intended to realize. The work sidestepped the effectuation of a reality that, in one way or another, surpasses every other real of nature or production. It produces itself far more than mankind; rather, it is in the work and as work that mankind produces itself beyond the "human, all too human." The work adds an effectiveness or excessive *energy* to the world.

In this way, the word is charged with what Proust states when he writes "I explained to Albertine that the great men of letters have never created more than a single work, or rather have never done more than refract through various media an identical beauty which they bring into the world."[3]

On the other hand, this same hyperbolic charge in the work has propelled it beyond itself, at least as representation of a fulfilled effectuation and the assured *entelechy* of its final end. We can date this excess, which this time is the excess of the work with regard to itself, from the moment—1923— when Joyce adopted the expression "work in progress" to characterize, indeed to title *Finnegans Wake*. The expression would characterize the book not only as a text always in progress but also as a work whose reading can indefinitely return to the beginning from the end. In one way or another, the work does not end, and this incompletion belies the assurance of completion and an achieved end.

III

Since Joyce, we have known how many forms the affirmation of the non-fulfillment of the work has been able to take, indeed the affirmation of the essence of the work in its non-fulfillment, in its "opening" or in its "undoing" [*désoeuvrement*], even though the work had been confronted with that other modality of incompleteness or destabilization represented by its technical reproducibility. At the same time, it is the author who finds himself destabilized as the figure of the agent or producer of the work. Moreover, his operative power as genius as well as its expression, if not its hierophany, in the work's various forms have lost their brilliance and their magic.

In all these ways, the work is damaged in both senses of the term: it is degraded in its monumental insistence on realization and it has renounced the edification of an architectonic real in place of or above the ordinary imperceptible real. On the contrary, it is this latter that has taken its place in a *mimesis* and *methexis* of the inconsistent, inconstant, and unconscious trivial existence of the things and figures of a world tending toward insignificance. The work has been replaced with the maneuver of a self-engendering of impressions, formal combinations, ways of saying that there is nothing to say or, at least, nothing that could be stated as the formula of an accomplished truth.

In that sense, the work and all the logics and symbolics of the production, self-production, or engendering of a world have not long occupied the place that in fact they had been encouraged to occupy but that was nothing other than the place of God, who himself, from the time of his metaphysical elaborations, had been represented as the image of productive energy. The death of God is the death of production and it is through sheer lack of inventiveness that we have not yet illuminated with a different light the shadow that grows before his tomb; on the contrary, we splash around in a productivity that can only further reproduce its lack of ends.

Nonetheless, we don't regret the work, assuming it was merely a substitute for God, no doubt, even more disappointing than God himself. We have learned something else, another reality of the work: not its fulfillment but its operation, not its end but its infinity, not its entelechy but its energy as act of a dynamic that can't be absorbed into a product—even if it were "mankind"—but which actualizes its tension, its vibration, and—why not say it?—its life.

IV

The life of the work may be something other than a cliché. If life consists of "the task of not ceasing to be," as Juan-Manuel Garrido has written, and if, to accomplish this, it continuously enacts the difference between life and death—a difference in which it manifests itself so that it is (so that it lives)—then the work lives to the extent that it continues to expose the difference within it of its pursuit and its cessation of being.[4] The completed work, *opus operatum*, by definition concludes its operation. This, however, continues in the *opus operans*. It is no longer the work in the sense of its completed execution and plenary manifestation, although this in no way excludes that plenitude.

It is no doubt necessary that a work be completed so it can manifest in its fulfillment that which exceeds it or, better still, so that it manifests its fulfillment as its own surpassing. At the time of death, a life surpasses itself, sometimes in other lives, which may be the lives of the living or even the lives of works, or even—since, as Proust says, "however far forward into future generations the works of men may shine, there must none the less be men"—neither living being nor work but the simple affirmation that that life has lived, has been lived, has struggled to be and to give rise to the event of that difference.[5]

Likewise the work, even in its fulfillment, may open on to other works and other authors of works, but it may also—exceeding the duration of human generations or even running out of them—surpass its own achievement in the affirmation of the existence of that tension for being and for giving rise to the enacting event. In a sense, there is nothing more to say about this history without historicity, which has brought us thirty thousand years of enacted works from the paintings in Paleolithic caves until today (bearing in mind that we have no documents, possibly older, on dance, music, and—why not?—even poetry). The life of men is indistinguishable from that of works and these live to the extent that we seek not only to make our life a work of art but also that we allow life to create through us—even out of us—its works of life and death.

This succession of works reveals its lack of an ending, of fulfillment, through the renewed end of each of them, of each of the ways and means in which they renew the same and always different energy that, once its fulfillment has been achieved—masterpiece or great work, twofold artisanal and alchemical model of every operation—separates to reveal that what it realizes, what it actualizes is always once again its *dynamis*, its power, which like every force is exercised only in the interplay of a difference of forces. The work is thus always the implementation of a difference between itself and itself by which it will always move beyond itself.

V

The work moves forward as often as it comes from behind: it doesn't project its realization as that of a blueprint might be projected, a determined anticipation of its completion. Just as this will not be the truth of the work, no longer will its production (assuming the word in this context isn't problematic) or realization, or its operation be associated with the prediction, not even strictly speaking, of the project. There is always an outpouring that exceeds expectation, just as there is always a groping about that escapes any calculation. Thus, the work overflows backward through the maneuver that haltingly approaches the work and that it ignores, and forward by the undoing that removes the work from completion, wherein it is nonetheless completed but also ruined. Blanchot writes: "The work, always already in ruins, is frozen: it is through reverence, through that which prolongs, maintains, consecrates it (through the idolatry inherent in a name), that it is stabilized, or is added to the catalogue of the good works of culture."[6]

Nonetheless, this does not prevent the manipulation of this ironical comment about "good works" from not being simple in every respect. For the expression leads us at the same time toward a lengthy semantic series that the overblown religiosity of all sorts of pious works has reduced to the figure of an *opus dei*. Yet, we must keep in mind that "works"—the *erga* of the *koine* subsequently transcribed into *opera*—have referred to effective action in opposition to the so-called spiritual disposition of faith (*pistis*). Saint Paul emphasized that works without faith remained without value;

James adamantly countered this with the primacy of works and, very specifically, so-called works of love (*agape, caritas*). We need not get into that debate here, except to point out that in the operation of the work, faith, that is, the confidence in that which must exceed all expectation, is inseparable from the action that works, manipulates, and undoes without respite. Additionally, from Augustine to Luther, we have always known that works are themselves love and faith, and moreover are not ours but the effects of grace.

What we refer to as good works is the sorry residue of a lengthy genealogy in which the effectiveness of acting has, from the beginning and for a very long time, prevailed before losing itself in the confusion of prescribed gestures, good works, and affectation. Mixed up in this we find the signification of practical, especially architectural, implementation: every cathedral was joined to an onsite office (a "*maison de l'oeuvre*"), which assumed responsibility for a set of social and financial problems associated with the construction site. This resulted in the "work" or the "assets," as understood by the management board of a religious edifice. At the same time, the "work" becomes the name of an entity for specific forms of support and assistance, such as the many forms of "missionary work," as well as, much later and now secularized, various kinds of "socialist work" like the "work for the construction of low-cost public baths in Paris" or the work of distributing books free of charge. An important newspaper, begun in 1904, was named *L'Oeuvre*, in an absolute condensation of the value of service to a cause (a newspaper, moreover, that focused on "signatures," the expression used at the time to refer to authored articles).

The work thus understood represents the energy devoted to a cause that calls upon but, at the same time, surpasses all possible realizations.

VI

It is in this sense that in the operation of the work there is no distinction between faith and works, no difference between an assured disposition and its realizations. As in the stronger spiritual tradition, works of faith or those of love—they are the same—are nothing other than the exercise and effectiveness of faith and love. Works of what we call "art" follow at least the same formal logic, even if they do not harbor true content. In truth, it is precisely a confidence that is realized; a fidelity that is confirmed in action, not as the apotheosis of a fulfillment—which would no longer have to be faithful to anything—but as the never resolved, never satisfied tension of a confidence whose object cannot be guaranteed.

What is this object? Something like an unusual, unforeseen meaning, possibly inaudible, whose premises and expectations come from deep within the work, its author, and all its circumstances, for it is a question of nothing less than the totality of a world or even—which amounts to the same thing—an entire language that seeks to make heard an uncommon voice, that of the newness of the world. What are Hamlet, the Great Fugue, or Madame Cézanne in the Conservatory? Each, a new expression and an expression of newness, of always the same energy renewed, relaunched, reopened.

What "newness" means is not something "never seen before" that the work suddenly brings to light. It is the possibility of seeing, of understanding, or—in the broadest sense—of saying, and this possibility is new in that it alone contains, "the language that makes it decipherable as speech." These words are taken from those used by Foucault to characterize the work as that for which madness supplies the "empty form" and "absence" to the extent that they both share the character of "speech that wraps around itself."[7] In madness, this envelopment is closed off and excluded from signification, in the work it displaces the significations received by way of unknown *signifiances*.

But the unknown, thus exposed, is not a forthcoming known that would be the end of the work, no more than *signifiance* is potential signification. It is here exactly that actuality comes into play, the enactment and putting-into-*energeia* of a *dynamis* that remains *dynamis*. The operation of the work consists in the revelation to itself, as well as to its author and "receivers" or "amateurs," of its own opening and its own exceedance. We reinvestigate Hamlet or the Great Fugue, continue to interpret them anew; looking at Madame Cézanne, we continue to wonder about the light that stains with white and almost slashes her dark blue dress in the midst of flowers whose brownish-pink is reflected on her cheeks.

Life itself lives upon those cheeks. It lives because of those cheeks, because of the movement of the bow across the strings. It couldn't live otherwise.

June 2011

To Open the Book

I

When the book is closed, there are three possibilities.

The first consists of not opening the book, literally or, at least, in the sense that opening and reading it involve repeating the text we already know, which we have learned and possessed since childhood, by heart, as they say, that is, with an intimacy that preserves it intact in its recitation. In that intimacy, we can say that the book remains open indefinitely, but contained in its dispersion.

The second possibility is to slip a pin into the thickness of the pages, at random, and cast Virgilian spells, finding an oracle in the first word or the first sentence we encounter. This was done with the *Aeneid*, which was considered a poem inspired by the gods. A generalized form of this exercise is called "bibliomancy" and, appropriately, *ta biblia* was its preferred terrain. A similar practice involves not opening the book: we merely cast a glance at it, take a quick snapshot.

The third involves simply opening the book and keeping it open while turning its pages. This openness is a movement. That movement is not only

the succession of pages raised and lowered one after the other—an anima-
tion that the new digital reading machines attempt to duplicate in the
suppleness of their images.

We use these three possibilities simultaneously, alternately, without
always realizing it. We read while softly chanting the text somewhere in the
back of the *camera oscura* that films the text; we are randomly gripped by a
word, by an expression in which we gather a kind of augury that doesn't
immediately relate to our life but to the sentiment of a possible and unexpected surfeit of meaning.

And we continue to turn the pages, keeping the book open, at least to
the extent that we wish to go on. For this is something we wish to do if
we have *entered* the book. And we express our feelings by saying things
like "I couldn't get into it" or "Once you start, you can't stop." So there
is a state, a relation in which the book is not only open before us but we
are in it, we proceed at its own pace, we recognize ourselves in it and
whenever we return to our reading after having had to interrupt it, an
entire world moves back into place. That world is around us, within us; it
is impossible to distinguish between them: we are there, in a place, which
is to say that events take place there, time rolls on or is shortened, spaces
open up before us or close in on themselves. We see persons, landscapes,
we share impressions, expectations, surprises. (Thus the almost inevitable
disappointment of any transposition of a novel to film: no matter how
well done, how careful or successful, what we cannot get over is the
imposition of images where we had created our own world of evanescent
visions.)

This is not just true of narratives and fiction. A reflective text—which
does not imply an informational document—is not without rhythm,
appeal, inflections, or the evocation of images or affects.

For example, Merleau-Ponty writes "only the central motive of philosophy, once understood, gives the philosopher's texts the value of adequate
signs. Through speech, then, there is a taking up of the other person's
thought, a reflection in others, a power of thinking *according to others* which
enriches our own thoughts."[1]

We don't simply understand the meaning of this sentence; it is com-
municated to us perceptively, in words like "taking up" or "reflection in,"
by the italics of "*according to*," and so on. We could say that the sentence
does what it says . . . that all speech is performative. This is something we
find in Derrida, for one, but also in experience and, uniquely, in the experience of literature.

II

For literature isn't so called for nothing: it enacts the letter. The letter is articulation, the heart of speech and language. That is to say, not only the two articulations—semantic and phonetic—inherent to language but the pronunciation, emission, modulation, tone, style and what we have ended up calling writing.

Merleau-Ponty continues: "Here , then, the sense of words must ultimately be induced by the words themselves, or more precisely their conceptual signification must be formed by drawing from a *gestural signification*, which itself is immanent in speech."[2]

Literature is gestural to the extent that it is speech. But it is essentially oral, as Lacoue-Labarthe liked to remind us.[3] This means addressed, sent, and discovering or providing its meaning only when sent (I don't dare say its flight, and yet . . .). To open the book is to raise the curtain on the scene of such gestures of sending. We find all the possibilities, postures, styles, and inventions of something that finds its initial energy expressed in Didier Cahen's words: "*I* speak *for the other*."[4] With respect to him, to him, in his place, in his name.

And of course the other—yes, the one whose address we've heard—is also "myself," who has nothing or very little to do with this *I* who speaks. And it is in myself, as it is in the other self, an opening to a *for the other*: for an elsewhere, an exterior about which it is fundamentally necessary that it has neither form nor function as goal or destination, nor completed trajectory or concluded operation. On the contrary, it is expected that we leave all these registers behind, that we forget them and allow them to be replaced with a kind of *dérive* concerned with itself: one to which the reader consents whenever he delves further into the book.

It is then that the book is open. Open to what it contains and delivers: a meaning unfolding (being produced, tracing its path) for itself and for no other purpose. There is nothing shocking in the fact that we might see this as relaxation or amusement: it's a matter of allowing oneself to be diverted, deflected from the needs of intention and production and letting a gesture materialize that makes a sign to the radiance in which we understand, for a moment, that the world appears whenever we make it appear. And "we" should always be understood as "I," a single *for everyone*, at least, for many.

"We understand": that's saying a lot, saying it badly. Rather, we are understood, captured, seized by the opening of the book into which we have been drawn (or not: there are books that remain closed to me, others that close themselves; we never sufficiently explore the delicate question of taste, penchants, singular impulses—here as in all perceptible or aesthetic matters . . .). And yet we understand, we are captured by a thought. Which thought is always simultaneously that of a story, a figure, a tone, a language, and thought of this, whether it is told to us, recounted there before us, in the book, at a distance, in fiction or in speech—in an element that is detached from the world and floats before it.

III

Which floats uncertain, labile, inconsistent, unreal: literature—all that remains! The remainder of the serious, the constructed, the important, the certain, the known. But this remainder is also that which precedes every serious occupation of the life-death, pain-pleasure, labor-repose genre. It precedes because speech is older than all of this and because in speech that is older still, we find this pronouncement: bear it before oneself, present it, declare it.

Declare—the way we declare a commodity, a love, an association, the opening of a meeting. This signifies (*calo, clamo*) that something is made to resonate. The real is not if it does not resonate in the unreal. It is there that what precedes us is found, without which we would not be these speaking animals, without which the animals themselves would not be, who in their mooing, hissing, and barking already cause the world to resonate.

That is why literature is oral: it opens up in a resonance that has no beginning and no end, in a glossolalia of presence without which everything would simply be absent.

But that is why it is written: the resonance has to return, has to be repeated, become an echo so that it might be heard and repeated. Literature is written in its very orality: it is recited, learned by heart, it is form and cadence. When writing comes, it is only the antecedence of this resonance that is exposed as such.

And that is why, among all the occupations, one alone ignores hierarchy: the scribe is his own master affirms the Egyptian Khety (whose clever remark contains its own very serious converse: it is indeed in the hands of the scribe that all other activities are consigned, counted, declared).

Literature: the declaration that owes nothing more than its own inscription, its articulation, its circulation, its recitation, its reading. Writing isn't really a part of the world of things: proven by the fact that the book has value only when it is opened and through its resonance when it is closed, always temporarily. The book is a remarkable and bibliophilic object only to the extent that it is an appreciably impalpable material. It is *liber*, thin film taken from between the *cortex* and the *materia*; it has the negligible consistency of a form.

The sheet—skin, papyrus, paper, screen—is the site of what Duchamp calls the *infrathin*, some examples of which are given by "*The emptiness in the paper between the front and back of a thin sheet* . . ." In turning to Hesychius we can estimate that literature owes its name to a transcription of the Greek word *diphtera*, which refers to the tanned hide, the thin piece of leather from which parchment was made. It is always made from skin, from a film, from that by which things are made known on the surface and to one another.

All the leaves of the open book resonate together and every book, in turn, opens itself up to all the others, in and for the others—eloquent remainder of this fortuitous world.

2013

Exergues

Dichtung und Wahrheit: Whence does this come to us? What is the origin of this phrase that is not a sentence and makes no sense?

It does not come to us from the too-famous titles of the great Counselor Aulique's Memoirs. He himself had already borrowed it: from an *old uneasiness of truth, from an old obsession of poetry.*

Am I true? Truth wonders. Is there anything truer than I who am truth itself? She answers: there is something truer than truth, something that tells the truth about truth and reduces the skeptic's strongest arguments to silence. She calls it "poetry," truer than truth, exact without measure, powerful without proof. This truth is manifest in and of itself.

Am I true? Poetry wonders. Is there anything truer than my splendor, my profundity, my chant? There is something truer: there is what neither chants nor enchants, what need not shine and thus could never become obscure, measure itself, proof, fidelity, and faith. This truth is manifest in and of itself.

So it was a waste of time, great Counselor Aulique . . . But it's true that you had, by a completely different path, found the secret of the distinction:

"I devoted the first hours of the morning to poetry. The middle of the day belonged to business."[1]

*

The Hatred of Poetry: He who risked this hostile and complicitous title overstepped his own dare. It betrays his resentment, his feverish desire for the power of poetry. Not a will to power, but a will to chance, he wrote. Thus, not will, but a receptiveness. This receptiveness is what makes poetry: the infinite welcoming of finite chance offered in the instant of utterance.

He hated the codes and beliefs of poetry. The codes: abundance of restraint, images or their effacement, and all the rules of narcissistic tongues, complacent to the splendor of words — and the beliefs: to name the unnameable, to seize the instant, to convoke the gods.

But he did not, could not, hate letting his mouth receive a declaration. For poetry is speaking without will.

Remembrance of Things Past: He had never gone to bed without a kiss from his mother, and this made up one phrase, interminable and endlessly resumed, the sinuous, uncertain, and yet invariable line of his mother's trajectory to his room, to his bed, a slow and obstinate declaration that opened the child's lips without unclenching them, while other, equally silent, lips — proffering what blessing, fervent or distracted? — came to touch his forehead or his cheek, with the *infinitesimal* movement of a kiss, not enough to form a word, yet too much for the lips to be simply mute, moved, on the contrary, by the same imperceptible articulation, by the same parting, not even murmuring, the long, desperate discourse of which, unknown to him, came to part his own lips before abandoning him to the night, to the absence of signs, to the insistence of linked phrases.[2]

Finnegans Wake: You find the book again without willing it. He had wanted . . . Now you can open it, anywhere, and close it — above all, close it . . . Having opened it, you've closed it: it won't say anything, won't let anything out. It is not unreadable — on the contrary — but it is not to be read. In closing it, you open it: this agitation of jaws, of lips, of tongues, it is poetry, a strange strangling. Shut its trap. (It laughs, surrenders itself at last.)

A Season in Hell: There is no more hell, there is no more poetry. The poet will go off no more, will be feverish no more. We move away from the annals of the poem. No longer will we turn our pain into elegies. We will no longer capitalize on our losses. And yet we will make the journey, right here. We will know the anguish of departure and the worry of return, of repetition.

Why this distress when there are poets?

Meditations on First Philosophy: Having thought it through . . . it could have turned out that I didn't exist, but I say that I am, so this must necessarily be true. Because I say it. I declare: "I am," thus this very thing is true, that I am the one who says that he is. I couldn't, if I weren't, say that I was without, at the heart of my non-being, being in that instant. I am nothing, no thing, if not something which says that it is. What thing? An existence, a poem, a surprise, a declaration. Having thought it through, without thinking, I don't think, I am. "I" is all thought and thoughtful of this being.—You, you are the existence that I am not, the truth.

XXX: To write, she wrote, is to blind oneself to everything else, to everything that is not the present object of the writing. Poetry should be writing without blindness. It wouldn't forget anything, wouldn't suspend anything. Not that it would say everything. Poetry would be fragmentary, multiple—but it wouldn't blind itself to everything else. It wouldn't be clairvoyant. But the light would not be limited.—She added: I wouldn't be forsaken anymore.

Being and Time: The existent, whose being is put into play in its very being, has a proper name. His being is to be gambled, risked, in his very being, and to be wagered on nothing but his future. He *is* to have yet to arrive or disappear. That is why he has a proper name, he is the only one to have it, he has nothing else. Or rather, he is nothing but this name.

It is not said, for it cannot be discussed. It's a secret lesson. It can only be a call. This existence must be called, each time the one who is no other, each time singular and singularly named. "Martin," "Georges," "Marie": each time the proper name is without propriety. It only calls him, calls her to come forward.

The Psalms of David: From the depths I cry out to you . . . Listen to my prayer . . . I cry out to you . . . Listen . . . How long?—But with you is grace, the abundance of few words, an obscure reserve. (He psalmodizes, he touches the chords one by one, pulling them and letting them go according to order and measure.)

The Tropic of Cancer: Naked and cracked, off limits, it defies intimacy. It will always be more intimate than the closest closeness, farther away than extreme enmity. It will always overflow, within as without. It is a mouth, which the lips open and close, proffering intimacy, offering and exposing the indescribable: a mouth kissed, a cadence, a gripping of the heart, a discharge.

Here words are no longer signs, nor appellations. They only touch the page and pierce the writing. Here it is forced, turned away, tempered, unoccupied. Literature is fucked. There is nothing more to describe, and nothing to name. Obscenities have no meaning. Poetry must not deliver obscenity; neither must it deliver us from it.

The Iliad: . . . the hideous and mortal, glorious and warlike anger that you were asked to sing, goddess, this anger still burns in us. It is an impatience for the Greeks' cause: their memory punctuates ours. But it is an infinite piety for the ramparts of the other side. For it is Ilion, and not the Greeks, that we have lost.

The Executioner's Song: How he recorded everything, how he investigated and had people investigate, searched for people, consulted archives, files, a whole arsenal of tape recorders, telephones, notes, typewriters, trips in airplanes and cars, a whole administration of memoirs, testimonies, fidelities, private documents, a whole machinery for consignment, detection, decipherment, confrontation, verification, gap filling. How this was recorded—mixed-up voices, mutilated discourses, fragments strewn along highways, in motels, television stations, and a long, continuous, indisputable declaration of distress and endless love, of space without direction, blinking neons, sweating bodies, little houses of wood, men of the law. How the policemen talked into their radios, and how he called her "Baby." The end of fiction, the beginning of poetry.

The Phenomenology of Mind: Past the phrase, past the discourse, there is not silence.

The pure element of thought is not thought, is not cognition. It is simply receiving immediate knowledge of what is immediately. This knowledge is not knowledge—nor science, nor theory, nor intelligence—it is itself the reception of what is, of what is offered. We must be receptive to it, and change nothing of it as it is offered.—We hold out our hands, our lips, in a desperate grammar.

XXX: He told her the truth, told her that it was the truth, and that he couldn't take telling it anymore, not being able to tell it, not being able to make it come, to let it come, to make of it the truth that would impose itself by itself. He told her that it was the truth, that he couldn't let it do what it would, let it undo itself.

Translated by Emily McVarish
1984

PART II

Poetry

The Poet's Calculation

1. Two hypotheses—partial and limited—will serve as axioms for a brief incursion into Hölderlin's poetics.

The first: for Hölderlin, the poet is more important than the poetry.

The second: above all else, the task of the poet is to calculate.

These two hypotheses are connected: calculation relates to the poet's activity and decision-making before it relates to the disposition of the poem, in which only its result is inscribed. This makes Hölderlin's poetics something other than a "poetic art," other than a literary and aesthetic theory. And yet, at the same time, it gives pride of place, in Hölderlin, to the *ars poetica*, the technique of composition, and to what its technician must be, the one who "knows himself." Poetry is something other than poetry and also something other than thought. In this way it is, very specifically, the double limit of itself: the poet himself and his calculation.[1]

*

2. This twofold hypothesis would, in its own way, already reveal the material distribution of a body of work in which the essays, together with *Hyperion* and the translations, occupy a significant place, even if they do not

equal the poems in quantity. It would also be characteristic, at least insofar as my feelings as a reader are concerned, of the poorly defined but tenacious impression of a relative disinterest on Hölderlin's part in the poem itself. Of course this might be overstating the case, and the exact nuance is difficult to grasp. It is as if the poet were inclined, ultimately, to a kind of abandonment of his poems—left, after all, to themselves, and to a sense of monotony in their development, without being too concerned with completion (of the piece worked on)—whereas in his "theoretical" research (as in the use of variants, often left unfinished), he grows concerned, reaches out, corrects himself, tries again, and often grows exhausted in making his way toward a precision that dissipates to the extent that it is imperiously required.

In this sense, we might be tempted to think that Hölderlin, in terms of his thought—and in the sense that such thought involves the *ars poetica* or even strictly philosophical themes—frequently exhausts himself in seeking a dialectic and speculative construction for which he can identify, strictly speaking, neither the figure nor the exact approach, unlike his two close philosopher friends, Schelling and Hegel, with whom he shared the post-Kantian ideal of a "system." And we wouldn't be wrong in seeing a form of clumsiness, an impasse along the philosophical path as such. Hölderlin doesn't really know how to approach the *ars philosophica*.

It is a question of temperament but it is also—and primarily, because it doesn't simply or solely introduce—a philosophical question. It specifically introduces the question of a different way of addressing "questions" in general, the question of another *ars* or *techne*. That is why it is not enough to say that Hölderlin is a thinker: we must also add that he doesn't think like a thinker but in terms of the *ars* of thinking. Hölderlin's first thought might in fact be this: that philosophers should develop a system, in the strongest, the most organic sense of the word, but the poet has to touch something other than a synthetic unity, even one that is alive and articulatory. The poet has to touch an absolute point of exactitude, which is the challenge of a calculation more than it is of a construction, production, or generation. He must touch that point or locate it on himself, or keep it in sight: it is quite unlike assembling the elements of an articulated totality. The point escapes the assembly. The philosopher's goal is synthesis—the poet's project is synopsis. The first signifies an operation, the second apprehension. The first requires time for its elaboration and unfolding, the second requires the space of time needed to identify and take aim, the moment—and with it, perhaps, the loss of consciousness.

*

3. What characterizes the poet for Hölderlin is described as the "constant precision of consciousness with which the poet examines a *whole*" ("*durchgängiger Bestimmtheit des Bewußtseins wird, womit der Dichter auf ein* Ganzes *blickt*").[2] *Bestimmtheit* can be rendered as "determination" or "precision": the poet has an absolute and constantly determined, complete, and unified consciousness, without repose, which keeps nothing for itself and gives itself entirely to its gaze. This might not be exactly what the philosopher understands by "consciousness." It comprises less the moment of relation to the self, of re-presentation as such, than the unique moment of looking— not so much the intention but the opening, the gaze directed at or cast upon (*Blick auf*), before, outside the self.

The thrust of this gaze achieves a *whole*: the totality of this whole is thus touched beyond—or above—any composition or synthesis, at the center, the heart, the joint that does not totalize but is the whole. This is the whole-being of the whole that is sighted and seen, directly, impeccably. And because it is the *whole*—Hölderlin doesn't emphasize the word arbitrarily—this center is no more inside than it is outside. It is identically and immediately contour and periphery. It is not the concept but the figure and existence of the whole: the whole revealing itself as whole. The whole letting itself be seen for a gaze and by a gaze directed precisely upon it—for a gaze and by a gaze that is, all things considered, the letting-oneself-be-seen of every self.

The poet: the whole clearly present. The indisputable and indisputably punctual presence of the whole. The act that exactly calculates the moment— the instant, the weight, the passage—of the presence of the whole. The act that leaves nothing outside itself: not the background of an "intention," not the background of a "thing in itself." But the thing itself in presence of the gaze itself, in the very clarity—and the distance, the wide-eyedness of this "itselfness," its exact calculation.

Nothing else—under these conditions it would be appropriate to write "no one else." The poet is not the "subject" of the representation of the whole but the place of the vision of the whole *in persona*. Hölderlin also calls this "the pure" or the "pure [poetic] individuality" (*Œuvres*, 622).

*

4. Hölderlin's purity is not something that would fail to contain either mixture or alterity. On the contrary, it is the pure coincidence of the same and the other, of the intrinsic and the foreign, of the human and the "divine": this coincidence in which the gaze is directed toward the thing—

rather than toward itself—only to the extent that it becomes, and is made, the very appearance of the thing. The unit of measurement here is accuracy itself, *pure* coincidence.

"Concision," "sobriety," Hölderlin's other keywords, do not refer to anything else. With them it is much less a question of an economy of means than of an extreme precision of the end—of that extremity where precision itself dissipates to the benefit of a rigorous exactitude: the whole, always the whole (of the world, of mankind, of the community, of an era, a form, a country, a river, a god . . .). The economy of means follows from this, that is, the brevity of what would elsewhere be referred to as "image" and which becomes "gaze" whenever we write, for example, "since we are become a dialogue."[3]

This is not an image, it's a strict predicative proposition, which states that we are, in fact, a dialogue (a discussion, a speaking-together or one-with-the-other, a *Gespräch*, a speaking ensemble). Not that we are in dialogue but that we are our dialogue. "We": all of us, those who speak, defined in their being by speaking-among-themselves. Thus, the indeterminate whole of "us" is absolutely determined: we are the between-us that is language and, reciprocally, language is the between-us.

Calculation consists in presenting or intending exactly this being and nothing else, without approximation, comparison, or metaphor. The philosopher is free to gloss this "between" or this "ge" of *Gespräch*, but here it is important that it be stated directly, straight to the point, that is, straight to the source as well: the poet who says "us" and who thus speaks already *for* us, that is, to us and in our place, but also in the place of the "between," precisely in the "between" itself. The linguist would say that the verse performs what it utters. It already speaks between *us*, it has grabbed us, calculated us, placed us at the source of the singular plural expression of the discussion.

The same holds true for "*since* we are." "Since" is the exact calculation of an indeterminacy. The poet doesn't say since when, because it's not measurable (any more than the "we"). The moment "since" when "we are a discussion" is as old as the discussion itself, which is, in turn, as old as any possible oldness—as the "morning" named by the previous verse—*and* as recent as its utterance, in the moment. It is absolutely immemorial and contemporary.

"Since" calculates the entire interval of the immemorial in the actual present: a null interval, infinite as well. "Since" measures a cadence of eternity.

But we need to understand the measurement as it is calculated in German. "*Seit ein Gespräch wir sind*": the conventional grammatical order is not respected. This should be translated: "Ever since a dialogue we are," and we could even interpret this as: "Since a dialogue we are." Rather than being woven together with syntax (*seit wir ein Gespräch sind*), "a dialogue" and "we are" stand as two blocks side by side, exactly juxtaposed. "We," shifted from its customary spot, bears the emphasis: a *Gespräch*, is what *we* are. And though we might not read the entire verse, this being will further specify: "*Seit ein Gespräch wird sind und hören voneinander*" = "Ever since we are a dialogue and we have news of one another," but equally possible: "Ever since a dialogue we are and hear one another"; we are *that* we hear each other, we are that we hear from one another what we are, what we are we learn from one another, as our conversation itself.

*

5. Whenever it is calculated, therefore, what is calculated is inherently incalculable. But this "which cannot be calculated" (952) is "the living sense" (951). The calculation consists in comparing this incalculable sense to the "mode" or "status" of "equilibrium" (952), which is that of the work.

The work is not a given standard of measurement to which the poet would submit the incommensurable, as a yoke and a limitation. But the measurement standard that is the work can be used to calculate the relationship of the incalculable (of sense) to a short word gap. In a way, the calculation is always infinitesimal, the calculation of an exact vanishing point or tangent: the coincidence of incalculable sense and abbreviated speech.

It is not the unsayable that would be said, fugitively or analogically and, consequently, hedged in a way. With respect to the calculation, there is neither unsayable nor sayable, there is only what is exactly said. That is why, if the calculation is "calculation of the status of the work" (951), this does not mean that it is subordinate to the work as product (in the romantic sense, as finite production of the infinite, which is why, we find no theme of the fragment in Hölderlin). Rather, we could say that the work is, tendentiously, the place of an exact saying: no transition, intonation, flexion.

Accuracy is inherent to calculation. It is also the infinite extremity and reversal of approximation. Calculation does not take place in the approximate, either from excess or from scarcity. It admits no margin (because it has no practical end). Consequently, it turns out right or it doesn't turn out at all. No approximation, no halo of sense, just the coincidence, without excess or remainder, even at a single point, of the saying and the said.

This accuracy is first and foremost that of the poets themselves:

> It is most important that perfect beings do not diverge too much from what is inferior, that the best do not distance themselves too much from what is barbarous; but neither should they mingle with them too much, *they must learn to recognize, exactly and dispassionately, the distance separating them from others and that this understanding dictates what they have to do and undergo.* (608)

Exactly: *bestimmt*: in a determined manner, clearly defined, delineated, in the way in which a voice (*Stimme*) presents and authorizes it. What we refer to as "the right tone," which is also "just the tone," nothing more, nothing less. Just the tone of the one who discovers the tone and how that tone accords with the others while separating from them.

(Of course, here, commentary trembles. We can hear these sentences, it is impossible to reject them, with the terrible tone of the Third Reich. We can also hear them with the tone of simple proportion, that which allows just the distinctness of a tone from the indistinctness of a murmur. Here, it is a question of Germany and not of Hölderlin alone, but I have nothing to say about this. Other than to note that the measure of measure, the measure of "sobriety" and "courage," the measure of exact "calculation," the appropriate unity is not given and that we should never imagine that it will be, nor that it could be. For Hölderlin, nothing is given, not even what he refers to as "German." It is always as "a stranger" that "the shaping Voice of man" arrives [841]. When Hölderlin identifies "Germany," "Stuttgart," "Heidelberg," or "the Necker," it is a question of the exactitude and clarity of the gaze, of specific locations where he finds himself, rather than sanctuaries of a destiny. For that matter, he also names the "Charente," "Provence," and the "lands of Gascony," as well as "Genoa" and "Lisbon." The divine is always errant [462], and for the "soul, deprived of homeland," the only "domain" [463] and "friendly refuge" is found in "song" [462]. If the country were given, the entire poetic of the calculation would be pointless.)

*

6. Exactitude requires the exclusion of whatever is extended indeterminately. The unity of the whole must be grasped in passing, as passage, and not pursued throughout its movement. The saying and that which is said, and nothing more, must suspend discourse. In this way, the accuracy of the

sequence, of the "rhythmic consecution," depends on its interruption, on the "caesura," which also consists in "pure speech, antirhythmic suspension" (952).[4] Rhythm is made of antirhythm, like the figure its outline, and that is why "the consecution of the calculation, and the rhythm with it, is divided" (952).[5]

The course of sense must be interrupted so sense can occur, so that it might be seized in passing—so that what is seized is the unity of a whole that is more and different than the whole of its moments, being, on the contrary, their shared scansion and syncope. This is the poet's calculation in its entirety, and his offered, unappeasable gesture, the gesture of an "uprooting" (952).

Uproot—everything that would result in excess, growth, excrescence of significations, everything that would make whole and totalization of the whole, rather than allowing the whole its unique pattern—uprooting must take place "at the right time and the right place" (607). This requires "considerable rapidity of comprehension" (607) because it is the whole, the purity of the whole as such that must be seized and scanned. But no criterion is provided for this, no guarantee. The unity of the whole, the sense of sense, is not a part one could deduce from the entirety of the others. The calculation is not a deduction, it's an aiming. And to aim at the unity of the whole, there is no measure outside the aim itself. The right time and the right place, the χαιρος of the poet, must, therefore, be the whole itself, its coincidence in person. The whole, every whole, and even the whole of all wholes, is not defined by filling up but by coincidence.

To get straight to the point, the opportune moment is not an external circumstance. It is part of the whole. It is the unity that presents itself (and which, no doubt, is nothing other in itself than this coming to presence, this exposition, this offering and this scansion). That is why calculation doesn't evaluate means, means of access. It doesn't calculate in that sense. Rather, it is the essence of the calculation: count of unity, the *one* presented, given, thrown as one. For that reason, we must not "fearfully linger" (607). The one who lingers (would it be the philosopher?) is afraid, afraid of missing the unity or, rather, afraid of unity itself. He thinks of it as too thin or too thick and, therefore, always ungraspable—whereas it is grasping itself, but a grasping that ungrasps itself in unity.

In addition, "it is through joy that you struggle to comprehend the pure in general." Intelligence is "always biased" (607). Joy, love, is not a higher intelligence, or deeper. It is this understanding in which it is rapidity that comprehends, because rapidity grasps the elusive and is dispossessed of it. It alone circumscribes the whole, its unity, the sense in passing. Rapidity doesn't go "faster": it is velocity itself, straight to the point. Love, similarly, is not a more impassioned sentiment or stronger connection: neither sentiment nor connection, it is the exact calculation of the "one" of the other, its exact pattern.

This circumscription, this outline, isolates the difference of unity. Without difference, unity cannot be unity. That is why one cannot "differentiate . . . by the spirit alone," without running the risk of "returning . . . to pure Being" (609). Pure being is indifference and not yet "pure." The pure must be the different, the singular, the whole as different from every other whole and, simultaneously, the whole different from itself and offering itself as such, as *one*. "One" is the difference between the whole and the whole. It is this alone that is counted one, always one, not sequenceable and not additionable, one without summation, suspension of continuity, the truth of sense, its arrival, its event.

*

7. Therefore, there must be "harmonic *alternation* and . . . *tension*" (610).[6] If harmony is agreement, agreement assumes difference, change and distance. Exactitude is the accurate determination of distance—between tones and genres, between metrical quantities and sonorous accents, and between the saying and the said—whereas approximation, even with precision, is the flight of distance, in the distance. Exactitude, on the contrary, advances by accurately estimating the deviation needed for there to be suitability, coincidence, and two-way correspondence between the *one* of the said and the *one* of the saying. The poet's calculation is first and foremost a consideration, without concession or hesitation, of the clear distinction of the one: the clear conscience of that which isolates, of that which suspends, of that which holds it back *vis-à-vis* that consideration.

Distinction is necessary within the "community, unitary simultaneity," the "kinship of all the parts" that is, in fact, responsible for "spiritual content." Community and kinship (or "affinity") cannot prevail within the order of union or communion. For "spiritual content" would be reduced to an "inconsistent phantasmagoria" (610) if the "spiritual" did not differentiate itself from itself and, thus, "progress outside of itself."

"Affinity" concerns "content"—and it occurs in accordance with "immobility"—but the "form" demands "alternation" and, with it, movement, "progression" (610), going ahead (*Fortstreben*). The *one* as such must, therefore, leave itself in order to be presented/scanned in alternation, in the inflection of tones, the cadence of rhythm, and the break with sense. The movement of leaving, the ex-position of the "spiritual" in exteriority, requires this break and its scansion: poetry is the scansion of sense, the poet accurately adjusts the angles of sight.

The poetics of the calculation or of exactitude is, then, the thought of originary difference. And as it must, strictly speaking, it is first of all this thought as originary difference of thought-in-itself. Which means, needless to say: it is this thought *only* in the originary difference of thought-in-itself. Which also means: it is implicated as difference-in-itself of originary thinking—as "poetry."

If thought in general, which is to say, practically speaking, for us that which philosophy represents, is necessarily implicated as ultimate appropriation of the thing—absorption of its "object" in the "subject" that it is, the "subject" itself being the principal subject of the object's self-appropriation—or, if it is implicated as elevation of the thing, of that very thing said, to the status and visibility of the Idea (in this sense, there is no thought that wouldn't be "idealist" and for Hölderlin-the-thinker as much as anyone else), then poetics, the thought of poetry, but more specifically, the thought of thought *in poetry*, is implicated here as the other of thought: as non-idealism itself. Poetry, or the defeat of idealism.

It isn't that poetry has to respond, as is the case for Hegel, to the need for an external and perceptible presentation of the Idea. In spite of the resemblances, uncontestable and numerous, it is not a question of a logic of manifestation, or of presentation or representation (in this sense we could say that Hölderlin remains outside *mimesis*, at least, up to a certain point, or rather from a certain point). Coming to presence is not (re)presentation. The release of the spiritual from itself is not its manifestation: it is its opposition, its opposing ex-position.

No doubt, Hölderlin also manages to engage in a dialectical process of the resolution of opposition. However, no part of that resolution is proposed as a resolution in the strict and comprehensive sense of the word. For that matter, it is what leads to the extreme, even the infinite complication of the analysis that Hölderlin tries to elaborate (in particular, in "On the Operations of the Poetic Spirit"[7]), without ever succeeding in satisfactorily formalizing it. Whenever there is a resolution, the perceptible manifestation of the spiritual is correlative with a spiritualization of the perceptible, and, thus, for Hegel, poetry leads, by right, to the dissolution of art by the sublimating dissolution of the perceptible element and exteriority. Hegelian poetry is inherently auto-resolutive or auto-dissolvent, just as, for that matter, it is in its auto-poietic, auto-plastic, or auto-mimetic principle.

But in Hölderlin we are not dealing with the mutual conformation between two orders—"spiritual" and "perceptible"—we are not dealing with the mimetic self-manifestation of "content" or "spirit." The order of "alternation" and "tension" is not the exterior of the "spiritual" interior: it is the outside, the without, the *partes extra partes*. The "content" is not, to conclude, the true form of form. Form is the uncontainable of content, the irreconcilable of reconciliation: the one of the whole, as break and not as totality. "The signification of the poem . . . unites by way of opposing, through the meeting of the extremes."[8] Contact is not confusion, just the opposite. In the language of logic, we would speak of "contraries" and not "contradiction": the two terms cited in presence do not exclude one another, they can be false at the same time. One is not the negation of the other and the other is not the manifestation of the one. But they touch one another in their opposition and the point of contact is the point of the *one* as much as the point of its vision, the scansion of its "outside," the moment of its coming into presence, a presence infinitely and exactly opposed to itself.

The procession of the Idea in the visible is replaced by this contact in which both clash with, cut, and capture one another at the same time. Such is the signification of "always opposed to itself," break and passage of sense—a rhythm that should be understood literally. The spirit, Hölderlin says, equalizes all opposites, whereas poetic "signification" separates and places in contact. In other words, poetic "signification" cannot be satisfied with "signifying," it must also be distinguishable from itself, be placed and presented outside, in a perceptible individuality. From sense to this atom, to this impenetrable point outside, there is contact, coincidence, and break. That is why there can be, within the poetic cadence, instantaneous comprehension that is also outside intelligence: not "unintelligence" but "love" of this *outside* by which the seizure-release of the one in the χαιρος can be touched.

The point of contact, the touching-of-the-opposite, is the opportune exactitude of the calculation that delivers sense or that delivers up to sense, by suspending the uninterrupted course of sense.

*

8. In this way, the poem can be "an autonomous world with respect to form, as [a] world within the world, and thus as a voice of the eternal directed to the eternal."[9] This world in the world is not a microcosm. It is not a reduced image of the other and it does not respond to the logic of mimetics. Rather than the reproduction of an other, it is the same confronting the same, in its opposition to the same: the point confronting totality, the whole that has left itself as one. The point of the totality, or the

point of totality, outside itself, facing itself—*punctum proximum* of the poet's gaze. Not the totality gathered into a point, in the manner of a synthesis, or a subsumption (therefore, dialectic and suppressing exteriority, redirecting it to the whole as whole)—but totality touched at its point of totality, the point of its unity: *touched*, which is to say, neither penetrated, nor kissed, nor sublimated, but affected in terms of a *sustained* and, therefore, inherently *felt exteriority*. To touch is not to highlight the difference between touching and touched: on the contrary, it is to present that difference as such, in its alternation and its tension.

That is also why the poem, the work as such, is not privileged, and that is why Hölderlin rarely engages in a poetics of rules, genres, and examples. When he examines "the difference of poetic modes,"[10] it is to propose a series of variations on the unique given of the "alternation of tones" (639), based on the necessity of their distinctions and mutual interaction. *Tone* marks the separation and distinction of the tension inherent in touch as such.

To be sure, what is important is the "operation of the poetic spirit," its "approach" or "manner of doing" (*Verfahrungsweise*), in other words, its technique and, consequently, its art: the act of this touching of the spirit that touches "infinite unity" and that touches itself by touching that unity—a unity that forms the "point of separation of unity" as well as the "point of unification" (*Œuvres*, 619). The theme of contact and that of the one (*das Einige*, the one as reunited unity) go hand in hand, because the touch—the touching gaze—isolates the point of contact. And it does so in two ways: on the one hand, it touches a single point and, on the other hand, it does not alter the face-to-face relationship of the touching and the touched. Nothing disappears in the overindifference of indistinctness, nothing is drowned in oceanic feeling. Everything is distinct, the whole is distinct as such.

What is touched is a body. Not a body as organic assumption and internal finality but that opposite of the organic that Hölderlin called the *aorgic* (*Essays*, 85), a materiality, a divisibility (*Essays*, 85–86), a body as extension and distinction: an "objective coherence . . . but also a felt and tangible coherence and identity in the alternation of oppositions" (*Essays*, 71), the unity of divisibility itself, of the "actual separation" that responds to the "*arbitrariness of Zeus*" (*Essays*, 86), that is to say, the law of tangible and individual distinction.

It would not be wrong to assert that Hölderlin's poetry is physical and erotic: if it is not so in its themes, at least ostensibly, it is in its mode and its gesture, in its address to the thing itself, its presence, its tangible existence in a distinct punctuality.

Thus—like a desire to paint and a desire for contact with the painting (it would be difficult to exaggerate the importance of accurate painting in Hölderlin; it grew in importance over the years):

> With yellow pears hangs down
> and full of wild roses
> The land into the lake,
> You loving swans,
> And drunk with kisses
>
> . . . straight   from dun-colored stone
> The waters trickle silver
> And holy green appears
> On a sodden meadow of the Charente,[11]

And the touch of language itself, the timbre and rhythm of words, and what can only be said in its own tongue:

> *Kommt eine Fremdlingin sie*
> *Zu uns, die Erweckerin,*
> *Die menschenbildende Stimme.*

Translation:

> A stranger it comes
> To us, that quickening word,
> The voice that moulds and makes human.

—where we lose the assonances and essential elements of the rhythm. We might attempt:

> One comes to us
> From afar, the awakener
> The voice maker of men.[12]

I can't speak with great technical precision about Hölderlin's language or prosody, that is, all things considered, his *ars poetica*. But I cannot insist too strongly on the fact that in them—language, prosody, rhythm—it is directly upon the words and song that the tone and tact of his poetics are arranged—that is, his thought, the outside of his thought, his thought outside thought. We should also keep in mind what he wrote at the beginning of "Celebration of Peace": "But if, nonetheless, some should think such a language too unconventional, I must confess to them: I cannot help it. On a fine day—they should consider—almost every mode of song makes itself heard; and Nature, whence it originates, also receives it again."[13] Language is singular, it must be so: not only as some precious and private idiom—there is no mannerism in Hölderlin—but as a language of extremes, which touches the impossible of the real, its distance and the correlative separation of all languages from one another, all songs. Every language must be one, just as every point touched. The "song," the ordinary metaphor/metonymy of the poem, is a more precise characterization for Hölderlin of that which "envelops" God's "ray," the brilliance or burst of the "storm of God" that the poet, "bareheaded," "grasps with his own hand" (835). The song does not dissimulate the light: it transmits its contact.

*

9. Touch is part of the calculation because it requires measure. The without-measure distinguishes neither the places nor the surfaces that touching requires.

> For sparingly, at all times knowing the measure,
> A God for a moment only will touch the dwellings
> Of men, by none foreseen, and no one knows when.[14]

Measure is the word, the word and the motif, on which intersect, very precisely—are shared in every sense, *sich mitteilen*—Hölderlin's thought and poetry. Because it is essentially the thought of measure, his thought must be a poetics, to think it must touch the outside of poetry.

This measure is not limiting, nor is it balancing. It does not maintain a happy medium. Hölderlinian measure is exact in that it measures the variance by which the whole and unity are possible as whole and as unity. The calculation observes the following sequence: Whole = Whole, Whole = One, One = One, but "=" equals the separation necessary to assert and count the One in the presence of the self, in the presence of itself, in the clarity of its distinction. Thus, poetics considers less the equality of the Whole with itself than equality in itself, the equality of equality, in a way, "=" "=" "=", or its measure, which is to say, the separation, the spacing needed only to assert the equality, its meter, its interval and scansion.

The idealism of unitotality moves beyond any measure, it knows only the absolute's self-correspondence in itself. It doesn't think in terms of equality but of identity (and in truth it thinks of identity itself in terms of the recovery of self by self rather than the exposure of self to self). But the poetics of contact requires the distance that is the essence of touch. What is touching is distinct from the touched, the touch is *discrete* or it is not. Feeling is possible only through the distance of an *appropriateness*— agreement and modesty, measure of the one by the other.

Thus:

> Here with his sunny gaze he awakens no warmth in her bosom,
>
> > Never with rain or with dew whispered those words that seduce;
>
> And I marveled at that, and I foolishly said to her: Mother
>
> > Earth, will you always, then, waste, widowed, your time and your
> >
> > > life?
>
> [. . .]
>
> Or in the heavenly beam after all still one day you'll be basking,
>
> Out of the dearth of your sleep raised by his breath after all,
>
> And like the living seed-grain, burst out of the husk that constricts
>
> > you,
>
> So that the world, unbound, tears itself loose and greets light.[15]

—here too, it must be made clear how the point of this agreement, the springtime of the earth, is given, in the final verse quoted, in the calculation of a tightly structured cadence: "*Los sich reißt und das Licht grüßt die entbundene Welt.*" "Los" triggers and discharges this explosion, the release, simultaneously, in the meaning, the sound, and the rhythm; we could say that this verse is the onomatopoeia of spring, or love, together with the following lines:

> *All die gesammelte Kraft aufflammt in üppigem Frühling,*
> *Rosen glühen und Wein sprudelt im kärglichen Nord.*

> All the strength so long gathered flares up in a springtime luxuriance,
> Roses glow and rich wine gushes in northerly dearth.[16]

—but it's not an imitation, it's a touch of the tongue that distances it from itself and from meaning, and which creates meaning in the interval, like the beat of the interval. There is no onomatopoeia of "living sense," but the impress of a sonorous touch, the impress of an accord of this separation of meaning: poetry is not meaning, doesn't create or express meaning, but it harmonizes with its separation, or it tunes its separation, like the tuning of its "lyre." In this way it is required to "*rhyme with joy*" ("*Sei zur Freude gereimt*").[17] Here, "rhyme" is a metaphor for "harmonize" only to the extent that it is also a metonym of poetry, and "joy" is "thought" (789)—or "said"—as the harmony that it is (or for which it is, in turn, the "metaphor"), only in the sonorous interval of poetic harmony. (Rather, we should say that it is still an imitation, this rhythmic movement of accents and assonances—*glühen/sprudelt/kärglich*, etc.—but an imitation of what? Does the rose imitate the embers or the embers the rose? Do *glühen*, *sprudelt*, *kärglich* imitate one another or do they respond to one another? Everything can rotate in every direction, around the same point: how does meaning touch sound and sound meaning—which is the same as saying "singing.")

The point of contact is thus itself a distance or separation. This point is not a geometric point of zero dimensionality: it is dimension itself, the distention of the poetic relationship to unity and totality. In short, it is the absolute distance of the absolute. This absolute distance is also a proximity: it is not measured according to the extent of separation but according to the simple nature and the simple intensity of the interval as such.

> This much is certain: be it at midday or should it
> Reach into midnight a measure remains
> Common to all, but to each is due also his own.[18]

The separation, the spacing of time and place, separation as such makes presence and its touch possible. Measure measures—it establishes and it expresses the appropriateness of—"the true, real, *determined* infinite" (627). Here, determination is not the limitation of infinity. Not its finitization in the sense of a loss and a fall within a finite horizon: on the contrary, it is the finishing, the exact completion according to "the fixed point that determines the mode of the line of the drawing, as well as the character and intensity of local color and light" (628).[19]

It is in this way that measure provides the *tone*, understood absolutely, the tension and tenor of contact: within the unity of the whole, and before it, against it, in the very moment of its cadence and its attack. Measure is the "beautiful precision" (631), not the precision—determination or exactitude—that might be beautiful elsewhere but the precision that is beautiful in itself because it precisely touches (or, *even more precisely*, exactly) the other side of beauty, "the beautiful infinite reflection that, in its continuous limitation, is at the same time principle of relation and continuous unification" (631).

This beautiful precision sets the tone, the contour, the color of that which localizes the infinite, that which reveals it and that which touches it—the gesture is the same—at the instantaneous point of its presence, that is, of its passage, at the point of that which delimits and isolates it as a zone of enjoyment.

"Measure in the beautiful precision, unity and firmness of its infinite agreement, its infinite identity, individuality, and attitude I its poetic prose of an all-delimiting moment" (*Essays*, 82). The *allbegrenzende Moment* is also the moment (read: the suspension) that delimits the whole, as well as that which delimits everything. At the same time, measure embraces everything, the totality of everything, and rigorously circumscribes the narrow space-time of the point and the touch.

But this simultaneity and conjunction are in no way a surpassing of one by the other, nor of one in the other, no infusion of the whole in the one. Measured language—the meter—does not overstep the bounds of measure (τεχνη itself is given over to working within them), just as that which measures it, and against which it is measured, naked presence, simply and firmly grasped in its passage, remains outside it and speaks this outside, this before, this face-to-face-with-itself. There is only the conjunction—the rhyme—of that face-to-face: the one and the gaze directed toward it, the twofold inscription of the poem, which is to say, its twofold excription. It is the unspeakable itself—but for the poet and in him "the speechless gains speech" (*Essays*, 55). Such is the effect of the "completeness and continuous determination of consciousness by means of which the poet is able to view a *totality* (*Essays*, 56).

> Heavy meanwhile with fruit and dark has my cherry-tree grown now,
> And to the gathering hand branches now proffer themselves.
> [. . .]
> Yet already I guess it: to holy remoteness they also
> Now have passed on and to me never again will return.[20]

*

10. Strictly speaking, meter is the divine: it is incommensurate in its strictly determined precision, the exactitude of the impossible. Thus:

> [. . .] here also gods are, and they govern,
> Great is their measure, but men take as their measure the span.[21]

The poet does not limit himself to this impoverished human measure, that of his palm, the "span," the measure for which he himself is the unit. But he measures divinely, that is, according to a measure that nothing measures, according to absolute greatness. This consists in the conjunction of the incommensurate and proximity, of two extremities of the infinite, the most distant ("and looked out into the African desert, unbroken Plains"[22]) and the most intimate ("but silent some thanks do live on").[23]

Absolute greatness is the exactitude of the meeting of suitability and separation: the suitability of the separation by which a presence, being-itself, presents itself, stays still, obvious, and disappears from that same place, at that some moment, in the unique passage of sense.

Meter measures that very thing, the "trace of the gods now departed"[24] that is neither pure loss nor the sign echoing in the distance, but the trace of the passage as veritable presence, definitively effective in that present whose contact distances itself as it is touched. Thus, the speech of poets "is *true*" and is addressed, especially, "to the angels or him"[25] not through the sense of what it says or what it evokes but through meter, which is itself—which is materially itself—the tangible and exact vestige of the passage of the gods, that is, of that passage that the gods *are*.

This doesn't mean that the poet's truth consists of anything at all in conjunction with a metric . . . It means that what must be said—the true, the just, the sense—the poet must say it in his condition of unity and passage, touched by his passage.

The divine is passage and only that: for this reason, the divine is essentially vestige not image, and at the same time remains the material and fading trace of a presence that is not worthwhile as sustenance, as being-present-there, stable and manifest, but which is worthwhile as passing, coming and going, arriving, occurring and departing.

Day-long, night-long we're urged on by a fire that's divine.[26]

The divine is in immanence and in the eclipse, in the approach, passage and withdrawal: its withdrawal is not its loss, but the condition of its fugitiveness, which is itself the condition of its sense. For the divine is the passage in that it makes a sign to nothing other than this passage itself. The place that melds "Olympus" and "Parnassus," the place "From whence comes and to which the coming god makes a sign in return,"[27] is the very coming and passage, it's the touch that illuminates itself and only itself (like Diotima, "You, only you, your own light, O heroine, keeps in the light still"[28]), thereby illuminating the one. The "coming god" is not going "to come," and in that sense is not "god"; he is the coming, all the coming and nothing but the coming: he is fully in the strike, the beat and metrical, syntactic, and semantic attitude of this verse, which causes the "coming" to revolve around itself: "*Dorther kommt und zurük deutet der kommende Gott.*" "Thence has come and back there points the god who's to come": that he might come—*kommt*—it is this that provides the assonance or rhyme of the verse—*dort/kommt/komm/Gott*—and this coming revolves around this sign or meaning (*deutet*) returned (*zurück*) to the *dort*, returning the *Gott* to

the *dort*. *Zurück* causes the coming to revolve around itself, in the middle
of the verse and an unvoiced assonance (*und/deutet*), which is that of sense,
an assonance that is itself embedded in the strong assonance of the extremities, *Dort/Gott*. God is merely the place, the place is the place of departure
and return, of the coming that is withdrawn and which thus creates sense.
Thus: that is, according to the verse, materially according to the scansion
of the verse. Poetry: material calculation of the atheistic passage. (To read
Hölderlin today is also to tear him from the romantic imagery that, of
necessity, is his, and of which "the gods" are one piece.)

(We could also interpret the verse in this way: the god who comes from
there comes and makes the sign "return," he orders the reversal of the verse,
that is, the reading of its scansion.)

Thus, the measure required is always that of passage as such. The act of
the poet is to take the measure, which by that very act also consists in measuring oneself against the "divine." To measure oneself against the divine is
not to confront it in some improbable rivalry but to measure oneself against
the incommensurability of the passage, against the incommensurable separation of the *place* of passage, so as to grasp it incommensurably but exactly,
with the absolute precision of the incommensurable, at the very point of its
incommensurability. That is, by its very evidence, its exposed patency, at the
manifest point of the presence of passage:

> [. . .] As long as in his heart
> Kindliness endures, ever pure,
> Man can be measured with the Divine
> Not without happiness. Is God unknown?
> Is he obvious like the sky? I would prefer
> to believe this. Such is the measure of man.[29]

The measure of man—what measures him—is the incommensurable
evidence of the divine, which is in reality the divinely a-theistic "divine" of
incommensurable evidence. This evidence is obvious "like the sky" because
it is neither the tangible evidence of an object nor the intelligible evidence
of an Idea, nor is it the self-evidence of a subject. It is unlike these three
evidences; rather, it is like all three together. It is evidence or the hollow-
ing out of the "open" as such. The sky: place of evidence as evidence of
place. Divine place because the "divine" is very exactly this evidence of
place, of all places. (The place is the locality: the separation and discretion
of passage, the place where the coming to presence necessarily takes *place*
each time—whether this is the "floor of the valley" or "the shore of Lake
Bienne," or "the room" with "the tables," or "the desert.") There is no gen-

erality of presence, there are only places of passage, exactly delimited, and including the place of the "gravedigger":

> He should take
> Everything
> Except the long ones
> To a clearing,
> Where ashes are scattered,
> And burn it on logs with fire.[30]

Similarly, there is no generality of the incommensurable "living sense." There are only its places of passage, always a word, a sentence, always a meter, a scansion. Meaning is the separation of language, its truth is local every time.

If, under these conditions, there is no measure on earth (*Œuvres*, 940), it is because all measure is of the "sky." Which, in turn, must be understood in two ways: every act of measuring takes the measure, in a specific place, of the entire sky, incommensurably open, and every act of measuring comes from the sky or returns to the sky, *zurück*, with that very thing that makes the act possible, and the encounter, measure itself, meter.

The withdrawal of the gods, the passage of sense, is both what is to be measured, that with which one must measure oneself, and that which gives the measure, the unit of measure, as well as its instrument, the measuring instrument that is no longer an instrument: meter, which is its own end.

The very exact response to the "lack of sacred names" is the appositeness of meter, which is the concern of the poet:

> Often we must be silent. The sacred names are gone.
> > Hearts beat, and would speech be absent?
> But a lyre to each hour assigns the tone
> > And perhaps delights the celestial ones drawing near.
> This makes ready and already, this too is ready to appease
> > The care concealed in joy.
> Whether he like it or not, a singer must harbor
> > Such cares in his soul, and often, though not the others.[31]

*

11. Meter satisfies the absence of the divine. Its accuracy is the point of contact, the tangent of two approaches, two approximations: that of the celestial (*Himmlische, welche sich nahn*) and that of the song (*beinahe [. . .] befriediget*). *Beinahe* should be translated as "near the near." "*[S]ich nahn*

[. . .] beinahe": as close as possible to the approach. That is proximity *itself,* the separation, but this separation, which is necessary to touch the thing itself—and that thing itself is an approach, an imminence. Not an immanence or a transcendence but an imminence, an infinite proximity that passes as close as possible, close enough to touch the beating heart. This is the touch of the "living sense" upon the "null sense," it is the point of unity of the whole, and the space-time of that point.

Meter measures the extent of the evidence, it measures it in its own place, at the point of its arrival, in "the beauty of the moment" (*Œuvres,* 511)—in passage itself. Meter responds to the evidence: to the clarity of the void, no doubt, but identically to the opening of clarity. Meter measures the unmeasured, the plenitude of the open. The eye directly upon the visible at the point of its totality. Such is

> How to speak alone
> To God.[32]

The meter speaks solely to the divine meter. Calculation seeks this accuracy: to respond to the rise and instantaneous passage of the incommensurable. This cannot be named other than with "words like flowers leaping alive"[33]—but here, too, language must be heard and the tightened measure:

> *Nun, nun müssen dafür Worte, wie Blumen, entstehn.*

> Now, now for this, words like flowers in bloom must be found.[34]

The meter's measure responds to the measure-less: it rises up like its pause [*coupe*]. The uninterrupted continuity of the "living sense" can become tangible only when interrupted. Not because interruption would simply expose an anguished gap of sense, but because it distances sense, grabs hold of it in its passage and exposes it to even more sense. The pause demands sense again—and sense slakes its thirst at the pause [*coupe*].

Take the following two lines:

> *Drin in den Alpen ist's noch helle Nacht und die Wolke,*
> *Freudiges dichtend, si deckt drinnen das gähnende Tal.*

The French translation by Michel Deguy reads:

> Au coeur des Alpes, nuit claire encore, et la nuée,
> Source du poème de joie, elle couvre là-bas la vallée béante. (*Œuvres,* 815)

> There in the Alps a gleaming night still delays and, composing
> Portents of gladness, the cloud covers a valley agape.[35]

It is not my intention to propose a better translation but to expose that which is untranslatable because it does not even allow itself to be translated into German—if, "translate" is limited to "restoring a signification." These lines should, in fact, be understood as:

Au-dedans des Alpes c'est encore claire nuit et la nuée
Composant du joyeux, elle couvre là-dedans le val béant.

In the Alps it is still bright night and the cloud
Composing joyful things, covers the broad valley.[36]

Drin—*drinnen* call and reflect one another from one line to the next, reinforcing and losing its assonance in this insistence, while *die Wolke/ [. . .] sie* (double pause, that of the verse, that of the prolepsis) suspends the "cloud" above that which it covers, and above its *dichten* (poetic composition, fiction, formation of figures in the fog). Referral and line break, repetition and return in addition to the line break, and, thus, by the break itself. *Drinnen* will be repeated twice more in the same strophe, and the entire poem (concluding with the lines previously quoted—"singer must harbor cares") can be read as the poet's penetration into depth or as his rising above it. Thus, the meaning is organized around the initial *Drin*, a cutting word (itself a contraction of *darin*) and as if cut again at the beginning of the line: *Drin in* . . . , and as it is rhymed at the beginning of the third line: *Dahin, dorthin* . . . The entire strophe is accentuated by the "*in*" and resonates with it (the penultimate verse of the first strophe reads "echo sounds all around")—that is, by direction, élan, transmission, as well as by what is within, a concealed, yet yawning depth: sense in all its senses. Here, the sense is the initial attack and the rhyme, the measure as well as the intended end—

Denn bacchantischer zieht drinnen der Morgen herauf.
For more bacchantically now morning approaches within.[37]

—but it is, precisely, only the infinite end, which consists in revealing other ends, revealing itself as end, and also as its only sonorous end, its only prolonged echo "*[f]reudiges dichtend*" ["portents of gladness"].

At every step of the way, Hölderlin's poetry—perhaps, in this sense, one of the most monotonous there is (but we would have to reexamine our customary evaluation of "monotony")—repeats the same thing, that is, repeats itself: a sentence whose own meaning is advanced and suspended, which surprises its meaning both earlier and later, and whose meter measures this earlier or this later, always infinite.

Thus:

So rivers plunge—not movement but rest they seek—[38]
—or, without trying to translate:
[. . .] thus falls
The river down, it seeks rest, is drawn,
Against its will, from
Rock to rock, unguided,
By the powerful pull of the abyss.[39]

The poet seeks the repose of revealed meaning—the "interpretation of legends" of which the end of the same poem speaks—and falls *gradually* into the abyss of meaning.[40] But it is a question neither of precipitation into the unknown nor of an evocative magic of arcane signifiers. This poetry holds no secrets. If the poet leads us continuously toward an incompleteness of meaning, if he calculates it thus, it is without mystery and without effusiveness. On the contrary, it is by a withholding of meaning, in the heightened awareness of its excess and the fleetingness of its passage, and by the exact measure enabled by the clarity of that awareness.

To follow the movement of meaning with clarity, its truth, not as a path with a goal or sense of progression but as a cadence that is maintained without, however, progressing—

And as the source follows the river
Where it wants to go, I must go there too
To follow its sureness through wandering.[41]

—or even:

[. . .] and see! the sublime star
Knows the changing road and follows it
The soul serene until decline. (*Œuvres*, 788)

The "living sense" (living until death, that is: its measure is not lessened)—

The echo of the festival is silent, and tomorrow everything will go
Its path along the narrow earth. (*Œuvres*, 831)[42]

—the incalculable is always that which is beyond sense, until we can identify neither loss nor gain of sense but the truth of sense, which is both "joy" (789) and "mourning" at the same time. The conjunction of joy and mourning—no doubt the Hölderlinian motif par excellence—responds to the conjunction of meaning and its suspension:

[. . .] when the holy cloud is hovering round a man,
We are amazed and do not know the meaning.
But you with nectar spice our breath, and then.[43]

Othem (the breath, the religious, Lutheran, form of *Athem*) rhymes with *deuten* (signify, interpret). The rhythm of the breath responds to the interruption of sense. Meter is the inherent measure of this: it is neither the expression (or *mimesis*) nor the knowledge, it is the mode and the tone.

*

12. Thus, "*Ein Rätsel ist Reinentsprungenes*," that is, "An enigma is the purely emergent" or "An enigma is a pure being-emerged." The meaning twists around itself, not in its sequentiality but in the emergence and the leap forward.

An enigma is the pure emergence. Even
Song can hardly unveil it.[44]

Even here the break separates the song from its enigma and, at the same time, touches upon emergence *itself*. The act of the poet, the act of measure, is to align himself with this "sudden presence" or "occurrence" of the divine that makes the divine as such. If "man / Loves that which is present,"[45] he must learn to support the arrival and departure—the departure "that goes with," if it can be so expressed—the totality of presence as the point, the unique break of "the measure that is in each of us."[46]

Calculation measures the moment, the presence, the brief scansion of life and sense, of the life of sense—and that is why it also measures, more than the poem, the poet himself, and in the poet "above all, the individual": "The apriority of the individual / over the whole" (Fragment 81, *Œuvres*, 935). Here, the individual is not the enclosed site of an individualism. He is indivisible punctuality, the precision of a measure that is always one, as well as being that of everyone. Its apriority is not a prevalence, nor a primacy: it is, expressed with purely Kantian rigor, the condition of possibility of the very experience of the whole. The whole can be present for everyone if it emerges and vanishes at a point that is unique each time.

Everything is intimate
That separates
Thus preserves the poet (Fragment 22, *Œuvres*, 924)

The poet must "feel and appropriate the common soul, which is common to all and unique to each."[47] And:

> The poets, and those no less who
> Are spiritual, must be worldly.[48]

> [. . .] Many give help
> To Heaven. And them
> The poet sees. It is good to rely
> Upon others. For no one can bear this life on his own.[49]

> For lonely not one
> Can endure the wealth
> Of the heavenly; [. . .].[50]

In this way the poet is an "individual" or individuated individuality as such: not the separate in the sufficiency or misery of isolation but separation itself by which everything is shared with everyone, each time whole and each time one—very exactly one as measure of the whole *in the measure*, where the whole is shared in itself, where it is itself only sharing: point, break, and passage, clear vestige of the presence that thereby presents itself.

That is why the "original poetic individuality" must itself be "abolished" in "the boldest and ultimate attempt of the poetic spirit,"[51] which must, by its very "freedom," put forth, present its own individuality outside itself, before itself, as an external figure, as the objectivity of its presence. It is not "in itself" that this spirit "can recognize itself" but outside itself. This outside—itself of the spirit—its body, its measure, its exactitude placed before it—is the real, present, impenetrable, and punctual.

Hölderlin's poetics is not a poetics of the possible and it is not, consequently, a poetics of the poem as *œuvre*, or work, that is, as possible world or as world of possibles, other world that imitates and sublimates this world. On the contrary, it is a poetics of the real: not "realism" but a poetics of exteriority to any work, and the work's only purpose is to inscribe or, rather, to exscribe. The exteriority of presence, that exteriority in which and in accordance with whose measure alone presence can come, come and go.

The real is always outside, always opposite, exactly where "the open gaze" rests, the one for which "light is opened," "the evidence of the sky": "Come into the open, friend!" The real is what must be gone toward, infinitely, exactly, and poetic measure supplies its distance and proximity, its remoteness and imminence in the moment of passage.

If man "dwells as a poet"—"Full of merit, but poetically, man [dwells] on this earth"[52]—it is not at all in the sense in which the "poetic" would modify the "dwelling," much less embellish or sublimate it. Nor is it strictly speaking "poetry that makes the dwelling a dwelling" (as Heidegger would have it). Rather, it is "dwelling on earth"—being in the real, being of the real—that makes the poetics: the earth, the outside, irreducible, unappropriable presence measures the separation of that which is found there, which essentially is found there—and also essentially lost there. Man does not dwell in the sky, where all is without distance. But he has the sky before him, whose evidence measures him. And what he risks "poetically" is turning toward the sky with his "attentive pupils,"[53] an exact gaze, infinite, at the right moment, at the carefully calculated moment—at every moment, providing that it is the moment of a given calculation.

> And, if you are able, raise your eyes
> To this light, the light that sees all![54]

The exact gaze does not appropriate his vision. It looks at what sees it, sees that it is seen from afar, always more distant in the unity of all. It touches this brilliance, its imminence, its miniscule, ungraspable, never guaranteed and yet so clear and so real passage.

> I am feeling increasingly well disposed to mankind, for I recognize in the small as well as in the large aspects of their activity and their character, one and the same original character, one and the same destiny. Yes, it's this need to advance, to sacrifice an assured present for something uncertain, different, better, always better, that I consider to be the principal cause of the activities of everyone around me.[55]

1997

Reason Demands Poetry:
An Interview with Emmanuel Laugier

EMMANUEL LAUGIER: *Jean-Luc Nancy, the question that first comes to mind, very directly, is about origin: whether it is the origin of writing or the reading of works of philosophy, poetry, essays on art, and so on. I'm wondering how it is that we've come to approach it in itself and, more specifically, how did Jean-Luc Nancy come to poetry? Is it philosophy—which, as we know, has always had an impassioned and bitter relationship with poetry, from the exclusion reserved for it by Plato in The Republic (with the exception of Pindar) to its self-dissolution in the Hegelian system, up to Heidegger's, in a sense, highly complex reading of Hölderlin—that has determined its reading or, specifically, at a given moment, the pure encounter with several verses at random in an open book, a strophe, something like a stunned reading?*

JEAN-LUC NANCY: How did poetry come to me? Did it only come to me? I have no idea. It so happens that I've written several texts on poetry and touched on certain poetic styles in some short texts, but that came relatively late in my life and required two things of me: one, the need to respond to a feeling of necessity, that of having, in a way, to defend poetry to philosophers; and two, to be able to free myself of an element of discomfort, shame, or modesty, to let go of the restraint associated with the concept of poetry and risk what Bataille referred to as the "sticky temptation of poetry." Each of these reasons would require a lengthy development, so I'll try to be brief.

But, first, I want to identify an otherwise quite ordinary trajectory: like so many others, when I was young, I produced a great number of "poems." I spent quite a lot of time on it between the ages of thirteen and twenty-three, roughly. This is quite banal, but this banality is telling; it identifies a model, almost a burden, if not an injunction with respect to poetry in our culture. Today, a boy of thirteen might be less subject to this model but I feel that, for all that, it's still there. To write, is to write a poem. To read, however, would be to read a novel—at least if it involved a silent reading, absorbed in its "read," if I can put it that way. But to read a poem is already to read aloud, it involves "reciting," if not "declaiming," and that too is part of the model. The *aoidos*, the troubadour, "I say: 'flower' . . . ," "music before all else," it seems to me that the aesthetic canon of my youth (which was very uncultured, very crude in terms of these subjects, and art in general) revolved around these references. But I rarely showed my poems to anyone, I was aware of their mediocrity even as I persisted in writing them and, at the same time, it was the exercise of discourse and thought that enabled me to speak outside. In other words: logical passion was clear and communicable in me, poetic fever obscure and shameful. One day, I was severely rebuffed by an author and literary critic of the time to whom I had shown the manuscript of a collection. I had conceived of what I would call "the Kant complex": Kant felt himself incapable of writing well and, at one time, I did considerable research on this characteristic of his work, which could be shown to affect many other aspects of his thought. I said "complex" jokingly, because I feel that, quite simply, one is a philosopher or a poet and rarely, if ever, both, and this is true for fundamental reasons; maybe we'll get around to discussing them at some point.

This was followed by meeting Philippe Lacoue-Labarthe, which was so important for me, and our collaboration (which continues, by the way; we're thinking of doing something together . . . about literature, in fact). Philippe, on the contrary, divided himself between poetry and philosophy. When I met him, he had just published some poems; he published some again a few years ago. In his work as a philosopher, I'd say that the conceptual rigor is always on the verge of becoming severe for philosophy to the extent that it is appropriated (sense, truth) and, consequently, of pointing to poetry as the truth of a recognition of something that cannot be appropriated. That would be Hölderlin's truth in contrast to that of Hegel, the

topic of innumerable discussions between us. But it also contains a condemnation of poetry when it is itself judged to be appropriating: for
example, Char, to whom I had been introduced a little earlier by another
good friend, François Warin, who had also introduced me to Heidegger.
Shortly after, when I met Jacques Derrida, I encountered yet another configuration: let's say, that of a continuous brushing against combined with
the ongoing dehiscence between poetry and philosophy, and on two planes
simultaneously, that of thought and that of writing, which were themselves
juxtaposed as front and back.

This is the context, and I think it's not simply anecdotal. It's the context
of a philosophy in the grip of a very powerful interrogation, which comes
from within itself, concerning its own "form" or "writing," that is to say,
obviously, concerning the "background" of its focus, which is called sense,
truth, *logos*, even "thought" in the Heideggerian sense (for whom all of this
existed in a nascent form). And with respect to our situation, I find it again,
differently modulated, in Deleuze or Badiou or Rancière.

I feel it plays a great and interminable role in all of this, one that begins
with Plato, as you noted. This is not the place to discuss it in depth. Rather,
as I've tried to do, it would be better to attempt to unite the features of a
cultural imposition combined with a malaise, with an uneasiness of thought
combined with desire, and simply state the following: we have not finished
with "poetry," whether we hate it (Bataille, Artaud) or venerate it. I wrote
several short texts on this, this theme (not even an idea!), accurately reflected
in the book's title, *Résistance de la poésie*.[1]

During this period, I was all over the place: I did philosophy, I even
risked a few poems (*sit venia verbo*), I played and enjoyed composing a complete parody of "La Jeune Parque" ("La Jeune Carpe," in an anthology put
together by Philippe and Mathieu Bénézet with the title *Haine de la poésie*),
and, finally, I experienced the "resistance" in question.[2] But with respect
to "La Jeune Carpe," I would like to add this interesting aside: this parody
of Valéry, whose meter, length, and manner are based on his poem, was
judged by Roger Munier—it's appropriate to give his name here given that
L'Animal devoted an issue (11/12) to him—to be genuinely poetic: he told
me he didn't see it as a parody in the comic sense of the term. I was quite
pleased, of course, but he was the only one to tell me so and his comment
always left me wondering about the possibilities, necessities, and criteria
for reading the "poem." (I should also point out that Valéry's poem itself is,
unquestionably, a parody in *one* sense.) With respect to this, you see, the
shadow of Heidegger isn't very far. I would say, therefore, that we are not
done with poetry by any means—but nor are we done with the question:

what poetry? Even if we remain inside a small, formerly "maudit" circle: Mallarmé, Corbière, Verlaine.

Finally, within this complex interest in poetry (and art, for one isn't found without the other) a decisive role was played by the recent renewal of poetry in France. For thirty years there has been a considerable, polymorphic body of work, obviously disorderly and risky in certain respects— but how could it be otherwise?—that bears witness to the tenacious, even bitter, forced, and demanding desire for a poetry devoid of romanticism, surrealism, conceptualism—and, we might add, fashionably depoeticized . . . I don't want to name names, there'd be too many or not enough. But the phenomenon is remarkable, and generous.

E.L.: *If I ask the question, it's also because the relationship between philosophy and poetry has not escaped unharmed: yet, what's interesting here is not to approach the debt that philosophy should apply to poetry, although it would probably be a good idea to consider their relationship, but rather to determine, in terms of the problem that Beda Alleman raises in the very first pages of his essay* Hölderlin et Heidegger (PUF, 1959), *how the* dialogue *between philosophy and poetry unfolds, or even* "how thinking finds itself in poetry and what takes place when thinking is resonant with poetry."

J.-L. N.: It seems to me that if thinking "finds itself," as you say, in poetry, it is precisely to the extent that it finds itself there as *thinking* and not as philosophical discourse. Let's first assume, if I may, the necessary— but not sufficient—condition that discourse must be scrupulously and strictly maintained, continuously, without interruption, and interminably (along the incessant course it continues to follow, one that cannot be arrested at the risk of failing to satisfy its most elementary duty: never close off or enclose a truth). Once this condition is satisfied—which means being indefinitely self-satisfying—there is, in effect, a resonance, as you say. In discourse, there resonates something that comes from elsewhere, from outside discourse. We could say: the meaning of discourse is not in discourse, to appropriate Wittgenstein. This resonance is the echo of a certain sonority, perhaps a voice, perhaps an appeal, which I'm going to try to situate—at least, if I otherwise fail to characterize it—by adding a detail to the Platonic allegory of the cave.

In this allegory I've always been intrigued by the moment of detachment of one of the prisoners—who becomes a philosopher. Who detaches him? Nothing is said about this. It is most probably someone who is already a philosopher because he's going to say that what he saw was merely "non-sense" (*phluariai*). It had to be a philosopher who made this gesture of deliverance from the violence upon which Plato insists: the violence of having him crane his neck and lift his eyes to the one who was chained. But who will have freed the very first future philosopher? Someone else, a non-philosopher. But who? I'm not going to try to guess. I only wish to point out that he must not only harm the prisoner but speak to him. Plato writes: "the prisoner was told that what he saw was *phluariai*." The word refers primarily to "gossip," to "verbal froth" (there's an idea of bubbling over, of excess, even of retching). Of course, the word already implies philosophical discourse but, here as well, during the first episode, we must imagine either an infinite self-antecedence of philosophy (in fact, this is its most consistent logic) or, in spite of everything, another, foreign voice, not yet philosophical, which names and denounces the idle chatter, the logorrhea. The background of the scene is found in a voice, behind the spectacular images of the shadow play and the blinding of the detached prisoner. Isn't this other, this same voice that denounces *phluaria*, poetry? Or, if not, if it is too soon to speak of poetry, another, close and distinct manner of questioning in order to disrupt the flow? Yet, that is what counts: the appeal to a language that doesn't bubble over, that doesn't propagate auditory signals but *speaks* and informs, that reveals or enunciates what it means to speak.

Bear in mind that there may be an echo in the cave: this was said a bit earlier. That echo is like a shadow borne by the voices of passersby outside. But everything must begin with an echo of a voice from nowhere that interrupts the flow of language, the futility of language, in order to *speak*. Not an echo as a reflection but as a resonance, because it doesn't come from an "outside" that is more "real" but, in fact, from within the cave, from its depths (or, because it's the same thing, from the surface of the wall itself). That's how philosophical discourse resonates once it opens the mouth, at the very moment when it begins to philosophize, when it will harass the freed prisoner with the unsullied *ti esti*, "What is it? Speak! Say what it is! What it truly is!" The resonance leads us to understand: don't say what it is but make your saying be. This chiastic reversal is not a pirouette, it's the simplest outline, and the poorest, as well, of what creates resonance between poetry and philosophy, to say being or to be (to cause to be) the saying. Which doesn't provide anything more than a starting point.

E. L.: *Because what "remains," nonetheless, as the exact point of poetic tension (or of the poetic?) is a kind of deviation that it incorporates into its process (into its techne, its poiein, its doing)—a deviation that leads it to arrest thought in it, to release itself, as you wrote in the* "Poet's Calculation,"[3] *from the spirit of* *synthesis or the inherent operation of philosophy, in order to apprehend something that, between language and the world, causes a syncope.*

J.-L. N.: "Syncope," yes, thank you for reminding me of a word I've liked for a very long time. I used it for the title of a work planned in two parts, the first part on Kant the non-poet, in fact, and the second was never completed (it would have been about the third *Critique* and on analogy, symbol, and so on). A syncope occurred: parts of that other volume were scattered throughout other essays. Maybe I was less interested in working systematically, which my initial plan would have required.

A rest, a suspension, a fluttering, a strong beat over a silence. And a loss of consciousness. Syncope versus synthesis or, more specifically, syncope at the heart of synthesis, smack in the middle. We can, and should, always ask ourselves if there isn't a hidden syncope in the middle of every synthesis, just as we can, and should, ask if there isn't a strange and paradoxical relationship between Hegel's *Aufhebung* and Kierkegaard's *leap*.

Between language and the world: we could say, the space where the concept is not possible, where reference leaps (in both senses of the word),[4] where, naming fails or enacts something other than a "denomination." The space where something is silent. What is it to silence something? What is it to *remain silent about something*? It is to hold and maintain at a distance, keep in reserve, because this is neither the place nor the time to say it, this thing. Speak at the right moment. Make it so that speaking takes *place* and doesn't simply flow (much less bubble over, no matter how frothy this taking-place might be!). Not to speak the just (the correct sense, the truth) but to speak justly: at the appropriate time and place, in a suitable ear, with the requisite tone. In this sense, when Kant forged his concept of the *transcendental*, Husserl his concept of *intentionality*, and Derrida his concept of *différance*, they are in the *poiesis* of a similar "justness": here and now this word was necessary, its invention was necessary and with it a suspension of sense, a deviation that maintains the suspense. Speech then continues but it can resume only because this arrested moment occurred.

But what I'm alluding to takes place by surprise in philosophy. Poetry takes this surprise as its subject, as task or intention. Which means, obviously, that it assumes the responsibility of abandoning any "subject," "task," or "intention" to allow surprise to surprise. But I specifically said "to allow": the difficulty, the aporia, may arise from this "to." The poet mustn't want what poetry wants, for there is the risk of getting lost in effects (silence or polysemy, effusion, incantation—return to the *hatred of poetry*). But he must want to be surprised in his very wanting. Or he must want by surprise.

Bit of a digression: I'm going to copy a quote from Seneca transcribed on a piece of paper that has been sitting on my desk for I don't know how many years. *Neminem mihi dabis qui sciat quomodo, quod vult, coeperit velle: non consilio adductus illo, sed impetu impactus est.* ("You can show me no man who knows how he began to crave that which he craves. He has not been led to that pass by forethought; he has been driven to it by impulse."[5])—I like this passage because I'm highly sensitive to the impulse in question, without which I feel that I would remain forever indecisive. But it's exactly the same impulse, the same shock that I feel determines the pertinence of saying. To be specific, not the discovery or invention of the *mot juste*, which is something quite rare, but at least of the feeling, which is so powerful, so heightened, that at a given moment, at a given place in speech and in existence, the *mot juste* is required, would be required. Not the first word or the last word, but the right word at the time. A *kairos* of language.

The poet must be a technician of this *kairos*. A *kairic techne*, there, that's the poetic bone—a bone like that of the skulls of the *vanities*. Hard, menacing, creating an obstacle and making us reflect. A *techne* that knows how to handle the *kairos*, but mostly that which allows *techne* itself to be grasped.

E.L.: *In the same book, you write and, one might say, consequently:* "*The course of sense must be interrupted so sense can occur, so that it might be seized in passing—so that what is seized is the unity of a whole that is more and different than the whole of its moments, being, on the contrary, their shared scansion and syncope.*"[6] *The line breaks and enjambment, by which poetry is distinguished from prose, would then be, as measure of that which exceeds sense (and thus beyond a simple calculated metric), of that which is distinctly outside its outside, the necessary uprooting by which it replays its experience* "all and for once."[7]

J.-L. N.: The break, yes—the verse: *versus*, the reversal of the plow at the edge of the field and the verses as furrows that turn back when they reach the enclosure. Compare this with prose, which moves *prorsus, always straight ahead—pro-vorsus*, we preserve the root *ver-vor*, but the "turning" or "turning around" only occurs in the beginning and doesn't turn back on itself.

I never tire of exploiting this mine, which is the etymon and thought of the *verse*. It enchants me because it gives us everything we need to think: the suspension of movement, reversal, return (to what?), the passage to the limit (the end of the field), the back-and-forth rhythm, labor . . .

Take the limit of the field, the enclosure: what is it? Apparently, it's a contingency, an accident of the terrain or a property right, or the need to accommodate woodland or pasture, or some other crop. But all of those accidents are the attributes of an essential necessity: the field cannot be extended indefinitely and absolute monoculture makes no sense. There's a necessity for a limit, for sharing. There is no unique, uninterrupted sense. Which can also be expressed as: there is no sense at all. But to avoid having this understood as implying non-sense or the absurd, which are nothing but the detritus or grimaces of a sense too ardently desired, I prefer to retain this word "sense," which my philosopher friends are not very fond of, especially not my poet friends. *Spilled sense*, that's poetry. The verse breaks and turns where the appropriation of sense we might have thought to be infinite stops.

Let's put it this way: the point where the line break occurs is no stranger to death, that is, to the fact that a meaning cannot be appropriated. All poetry celebrates death in this way. All philosophy, on the other hand, dismisses it, dialecticizes it, or overcomes it, at least potentially or based on some possible interpretation, for it's no less true that death also punctuates thinking that often appears to absorb it, as you find in Hegel and Spinoza. *The verse thinks death*, that's the proposition that should begin any consideration of poetry. "To think death" is to abandon trying to appropriate it, to respect the enclosure and turn the plow around. In this way there will be a field and a crop. The verse allows death to be heard at the point of the break, the terminus of the line. (And I also hear myself in this phrase: "the verse / the *worm* allows death to be heard."[8]) The verse doesn't imply a failure or loss, nor a release or recovery. It implies . . . that which doesn't allow itself "to understand," except, precisely, in the break, the beat, the syncope of the verse—and sometimes in the "enjambment," whose concept is contrary to that of "release" (enjambment is separation, great separation, which approaches the rupture or immobility planted along the two edges). Death: the assumption of the interruption of sense, assumption that does not make sense but that also knows, based on an unknowing knowledge, that without such interruption sense would flow away, evasive, chatty, frothy.

Somewhere, Lacan characterized the "sense of life" as that of a "desire borne by death." This may be a reformulation in his own idiom of the *Sein zum Tode*. In any case, it could also be read as: not a desire for death, not a race toward the abyss, and no longer the desire for an object that is always lacking, but desire as *conatus*, a perpetual tension of being that continues to tend—toward nothing, toward its own power—and that death carries, that is, which interruption itself supports and extends, whereas uninterruption would relax it and deliver it to *phluariai*. And under these conditions, and this is what I would especially like to emphasize, "death" is in no way opposed to "life," rather, they should only be considered together, joined and disjoined, joined by their disjunction—syncope, always.

E. L.: *In* The Literary Absolute, *you have shown, together with Philippe Lacoue-Labarthe, how early romanticism, the romanticism of Jena, had thought of poetry as an* "organ of the infinite," *reminding us in* Résistance de la poésie, *that this organ* "should be that which sets in motion an absolute transcendence of all determination."[9] *Is this something that, for them, will (or would) lead poetry to pour itself into prose? Is it in the rhythmic pouring of poetry into prose that there remains, for us, this time, this* "calculation" [this "measure," this "cutting edge skill" *Char wrote in* Hypnos (*the context not being arbitrary*)], *this suspensive force of sense, this seizure of another unit of scansion of the world, even to the extent of its uprooting?*[10]

J.-L. N.: The pouring into prose, to use your wonderful expression, is one of extreme delicacy and ambivalence. Mallarmé said, quite aptly, that there is verse in all prose. But it's to the extent that there is a return of the *versus*, no matter how hidden it might be. This might be a question of reading. A reader can scan prose that does not reveal its verses. Once again, the point is to scan accurately.

In the romantic movement, which continues to reproduce itself in various ways, there's a twofold possibility: either new prose believes it is opening an infinite furrow or it avoids this trap of belief. This could also be expressed in the following way: either the "infinite" is conceived as an indefinite extension of the finite or it is, on the contrary, conceived as absolute suspension of the finite to itself. In a sense, this is the Hegelian opposition of the bad and the good infinite. The infinite of poetry, like that of the surprise alluded to earlier, is instantaneous. It is instantaneously enacted, and that is where the *versus* is found. The tipping of the horizontal axis of the sentence into a vertical axis—therefore, a silence.

There is a decisive element within this concerning the moment and the present, the instantaneousness of a seizure or a divestment. The present of poetry is the present divested of presence. It is not the perpetual present of discourse, always in retention and protension between its past and its future. But a present suspended over its presentation. A breath held or a resumption of breath. Between inspiration and expiration, between first cry and last word. This restraint, simultaneously taut and lax, was foreseen but misunderstood by the romantics. We have learned—at our expense, through the terrible effects of intentions to perpetuate a present of assumed sense in an infinite melody—a renewed melody of the break.

But once again, we need to remind ourselves: the *right* break.

E. L.: *Finally, what is this attention to calculation based on and where does it occur, does it have any relation, even paradoxical, with the faculty of reason?*

J.-L. N.: Certainly. Reason makes sense of, that's its job. How can we make sense of the arrest of sense, that is, the suspension of reason? Of course, we must and can: that is what makes poetry. And that is how I understand or, rather, imagine, the connection in Heidegger between analysis of the "principle of reason" and poetry. There's no doubt that Heidegger "poeticized" to excess, that he succumbed to a pious and even nationalist (Hölderlin's "German song") celebration of poetry. It remains that his analysis of the "principle of reason," of its "incubation" throughout the history of the West and the renewal through technology of its lack of foundation or background cannot simply be withdrawn or struck out with a stroke of the pen.

In fact, Kantian reason, currently being reinvestigated, reveals this: to demand that we always seek a rational or reasonable world, while stripping cognitive reason of the means to construct that world (it constructs objects of knowledge not a "world" as a space of sense), or simply to provide a model (ultimately, this is the challenge of the "typic" found in the second *Critique*: the idea of "nature" cannot provide an organizing "scheme," only a remote "type," to indicate the form of a "moral" world), is a problematic we continue to grapple with. This does not mean we have to return to Kant—quite the contrary! What would such a return imply? Which "Kant"?

But I want to get back to reason. Yes, absolutely, reason demands poetry. It demands its own excess, which is not its forgetting. Reason calculates its own excess; reason then exceeds its own calculation: forgive me, again, for this apparent simplicity. Reason is not ratiocination. Kant knew this very well. Hegel, after him, was equally aware of this, if not more so. Poetry was there, every time, as the uncertain double—uneasy and disturbing, dependent on the moment—of critical reason. This is no small matter when you consider what "reason" implies for our entire tradition. If "poetry" remains such a powerful word, even at the price of "sticky temptations," it is precisely because of the uneasy and contradictory powers harbored by this so-called "reason."

When all is said and done, what did Plato want? To control poetry through reason and produce a rational poetry—for he consolidates all the elements of poetry to regulate them according to specific requirements. Philosophy is "the most beautiful of poems," as *The Laws* states. For a long time, until romanticism at least, this possibility of mutual regulation, this possibility of a "poem of reason" and a "poetic reason," existed or, rather, appears to have existed. At the same time, the fault was always there, because it consists precisely in the distinction between reason and poetry, or between two reasons, one philosophical and the other poetic, or between two poetries, one of reason, the other without reason, and so on. All the aspects of this division/confusion have existed.

E. L.: *Today, several writers are working at "tightening" the ongoing thread of prose; they're inventing another prosody, another way of rhyming that is another way of seeing and hearing the background noise of the world. Aside from the interweaving of verse and prose, or of cut rhythms and continuous, extended rhythms, in verse as in prose, don't we (also) have to consider a difference, to refold, to consider a refolding, as Mallarmé said, of that which differentiates experience from that which "cuts" itself off from it when it is continued in a straight line?*

J.-L. N.: I can't reply using formal criteria or references from authors, which would require a detailed examination. I'm not familiar with them all to the same extent, and I may not always evaluate them as you do. I'm aware of temporal changes, or what I take to be such, but I don't claim to have a genuine vision of the state of things, far from it. I read at random, haphazardly. I'm also very sensitive to the fact that texts are one thing, their readers another. I'm mostly trying to find out where, today, the judgment of taste is found. It's a very intriguing question. On the one hand, we no longer have criteria (as Lyotard said), on the other, we have, each of us, very marked tastes. But what is taste in a world without rules? It's not nothing but what is it? To what "universal," as Kant remarked, can it claim? I'd like to be able to grasp this question.

All the same, to address your question: certainly, today, in prose, the movement you refer to exists. What's more, isn't it as old as the reintroduction of poetry into the afterlife of romanticism (which, for that matter, was already putting prose into its poetic program, so to speak)? Baudelaire, of course. But perhaps more important would have been the event of Proustian prose, followed by—I'm throwing out some names here—Gide, Aragon, Joyce, Kafka, Beckett . . . throughout these very heterogeneous forms, isn't there a movement or agitation of this "tension" you speak of? Even though things were different with writers like Mann and Musil. And Hermann Broch as maybe somewhere between them. Faulkner, too. Hemingway. However, all of this is already behind us and, today, my impression (but it is, I repeat, very limited) is that it resulted in some confusion because the novel as such has disappeared. (How can I put it? The epic brand, if you like, although the word is unsatisfactory.) We have either the short story, the tale, which is something quite different, which might be perfect but remains within representation—or efforts specifically designed to poeticize prose, and that generally doesn't seem to me to be convincing. (Here, I disagree with some of my friends—I'd have to cite examples but that would take too long.) That's why I now prefer to read what is presented as poetry—even if I'm disappointed in it once in a while, or even frequently. The novel, I don't know where it's disappeared (any more than the theater for that matter). Very fine and beautiful things have been written on prose by Lacoue-Labarthe and Agamben, among others. But we're speaking of prose and not "about prose." Having said that, that's where we are today: there is more "about" than there is "that-about-which . . ." That goes for me as well, I'm worried about talking too much "about." Or maybe it's the fear, also the fatigue, that every theoretician experiences. For example, yesterday evening I was at a concert (James Blood Ulmer and Rodolphe Burger, in fact) and was overcome by a tremendous feeling of regret that I didn't play music!

E. L.: *If the practice of the poem is the passage, in implementing the break, of all that is* "difficult that doesn't allow itself to be managed," *in order, precisely, to make it yield to it, how can we conceive—because here it's a question of the arrival of a singular voice in language—of the link between the poem and a community, which is also one of language? Naturally, I'm thinking of the challenge raised by Deleuze when he speaks of an* "absent people," *or what Klee understood (although somewhat differently) by a people who* "do not support," *do not carry us (trägt) . . . From there to what you refer to as the* "resistance of poetry," *it seems that what you read (feel) in poetry almost enjoins you from thinking about it by separating it absolutely from what we believe to be its fascination with the arbitrariness of speech (semanticism) and that of the sign (semiotism).*

J.-L. N.: Yes, but at the moment, I don't see what I can add . . . Other than that the question of "people" means something to me. It seems futile to sweep them away with a wave of the hand. How can I put it? The "people," in the grand and even imposing division of its sense—between the population, the populace, the multitude, and the community—continues, for me, to refer to the place of a necessary interrogation: we cannot brush it aside because of nationalism or ethnomania. There's something else. To be without a people, absolutely—without language, without history, without references . . . which is what was attempted with those deported from the camps. We should reread the chapter by Améry, "Combien a-t-on besoin de *Heimat*" (I'm quoting from memory).[11] I know that, in this case, there are those very close to me who say they reject the word. I agree, but what then? We can't only say "language." A language can have more than one people and a people more than one language. I'm in no sense a nationalist or regionalist, I have no land of origin, I spent my childhood in Germany, then in southern France; I've lived in Alsace for more than 30 years . . . Nonetheless, I insist that a space of symbolic reference is needed, not only the "familial" . . . moreover, the familial always risks lapsing into infantilism: literally, the *infantia* that doesn't speak; a space is needed in which and through which we speak, we feel, we find our bearings and set forth. Allow me to be slightly provocative: people and poetry—how do we address this today? Do we deny the question? Do we repeat "the German song" with Hölderlin? No, certainly not! Mandelstam wrote, "The people needs to be wrapped in a mysterious verse" (January 19, 1937). Should we say that his poems of the time are suspect? Even if there's some truth to that, it's very unsatisfactory. I could also say that it's a people—the Jewish people—who bear among us the figure of a non-people par excellence, whether we understand this expression to have a destructive value or, on the contrary, elevation on a global scale. Mandelstam is Jewish; Jewish and Russian. How does he understand "people" in his verse? Obviously, in both senses together, Russian and communist . . . (this is more clearly seen from the context of the poem). But to expound would require another chapter and this interview is getting long!

I would, however, like to add—and maybe this will conclude with the essential: the separation of semanticism and semiotism, as you put it, what then? But what about the voice and in the voice or beneath the voice, what? What of the resonance of that which arouses desire and fear, a resonance we refer to as "lyricism," a name that must at the very least remind us of the proximity of music—a difficult proximity, ambiguous and uncertain, like any proximity, but indelible. Poetry cannot not be exposed to an unstable, even inconsistent, limit between speech and music. This means "song." Here, we would have to speak . . . once again—of song ("German" or otherwise). But of this as well, since song is love or death, together or alternately: I mean, very specifically, not that love and death (their asso-nance in our language) are the content or lyric themes, but that they (the "sense" of those words and of all their combinations) only take place in poetry, as poetry. And poetry embodies nothing else but them, ever since the *Iliad* itself, that is, nothing else other than that which escapes from between the fingers of philosophy (between its fingers, not between its lips, because it doesn't have any).

E. L.: *Finally, how and what constitutes your relationship (I'm thinking of the afterword and preface to Philippe Beck's* Dernière mode familiale[12] *and Gérard Haller's* Météoriques,[13] *and to the article devoted to songs in "broken prose" in Jean-Christophe Bailly's* Basse continue[14]*) to contemporary poetry or to what is being written in the field of contemporary writing?*

J.-L. N.: I gave a partial answer previously. I'll summarize as follows: on the one hand, I have a need, a very pressing, if not vital, need to understand contemporary voices, timbres, rhythms (as I have a need of electronic music). On the other hand, I take what comes as I encounter it . . . and I allow my "taste," my basic sensations, to make those choices, which may be provisional.

I wanted to avoid mentioning names for fear of seeming to engage in some ridiculous competition or of exhibiting a no less ridiculous private anthology. But because you do so by citing the names of those about whom or concerning whom I've written, it would be fair to add, in no particular order, Christian Prigent, Jean-Paul Michel, Michel Deguy, Claude Royet-Journoud, Pierre Alferi, and Olivier Cadiot (whose ephemeral review was the initial reason for *Résistance de la poésie*), who continue, each in their own way, to engage in an effective exploration of our "poetic" questions.[15] I'm limiting myself to these names because my relation to them is public and, consequently, belongs to my preoccupation with the "poetry" thing, but there might be others I wouldn't even be able to list. So many voices heard inside a review, a book received or glanced at—women's voices, in particular (here, in this same collection, and because I'm on the subject, I'd mention Ryoko Sekiguchi, one of whose poems is included in one of my texts[16]). Here, there's a joyous abundance, even with the risks or disappointments. There are so many voices or *verses* that touch or interest me: "interest" should be constructed as a category not of taste but as a quasi-taste for times of doubt and exploration. But here there's no classification, and it's not a standard formula. There are so many works I'm unfamiliar with and, perhaps, far more considerable! But I very much like the contemporary situation as such: it's a form of direct and immediate encounter. An opportunity brings us together, no criterion has preceded us, and we try one another out. It's a kind of readymade, in the design of which, as you know, the "encounter" plays a determining role. I have no claim whatsoever to legislate, no matter how little, in such a domain—that would be ridiculous. It's a form of pleasure, somewhat, a curiosity, a sensibility or, maybe a better way of putting it would be, susceptibility, an excitability. I'm susceptible to impressions that excite, irritate, tickle, or annoy certain foreign cords in me, about which I know nothing and, at the same time, think I know very well why they are there, falsely drowsy, next to the keyboards and calculators of the work of concepts . . . The sense of *verse*, of *pouring*, of *shower*, and *reverse*. The reverse of philosophy—there's a topic. But aren't philosophy and poetry, from their shared birth, structured like a Mobius strip?

One final remark. This ribbon simultaneously contains the possibility of anxiety (we'll never get off) and one of playfulness (like a *fort-da*! that goes back and forth endlessly). The conjunction—even more, the sameness—of anxiety and play is what poetry has the temerity to assume or, rather, to . . . play. Today, it's become very difficult for us to play; I mean this in the Nietzschean mode of "the world's great game" and the "divine child playing." But at the same time, the fact that there is some "play" in sense, in the world, in the most tightly integrated systems, and in love/death, play in the sense of an assemblage that plays and, therefore, doesn't assemble quite correctly, that too is part of who we are today. Paradoxically, where there is resistance, there is play.

Summer 2003

Wozu Dichter

I

The Hölderlin question comes up repeatedly. Its repetition confirms the desperation of the question and, at the same time, promises an interminable profusion of answers. It is remarkable, however, that in isolating this question—to the point of reducing it to these two words of German (*Wozu Dichter*, why poets?)—we risk blindly distancing ourselves from Hölderlin's thought.

In fact, Hölderlin himself does so little to isolate the question that it can be read in his text as a simple subordinate of the preceding proposition.

I do not know why there are poets in a time of want.[1]

Here, all is a matter of syntax and punctuation. On the one hand, it's certain that "I do not know" has, as its complements, the propositions that precede it, for the text reads:

> Often it seems to me
> Better to sleep than to be without friends as we are,
> Standing around waiting, but what to do and what to say
> I do not know, and why poets in a time of want.[2]

The *presence* of a question mark at the end of the last line (which follows two others in strophe 7 of the poem) seems attested in the manuscript, which did not prevent the German editors—before the latest effort at manuscript transcription—from omitting it from time to time. The omission makes sense if we understand the role of the original proposition played by "*I do not know*" in relation to what follows it and what goes before. Yet the question marks we find from time to time—at least in the French translations—after "do" and "say" are, unquestionably, imported.

Of course, we're well within our rights to read a break after "*I do not know*" and the introduction of a question: I do not know, I, the poet, and, besides, why poets? (or "why poet?" . . . in German we are unable to distinguish quantity here, but the following lines imply the plural). We're also right to think that the question mark comes to Hölderlin through habit, leading him, almost involuntarily, to the break, whereas he initially wrote "and why . . . ," linking it to the previous lines.

The French translator may object that we should expect, assuming some form of subordination, a "*ni*" before "*pourquoi*": "*ni pourquoi des poètes.*" But what is correct in French does not hold, especially in poetry, for German, in which this "and" is aligned with what comes before: "what to do *and* what to say . . . and why . . ."—specifically: here, the German has only a single *was* (what) as complement of "do" and "say," which would prevent or strongly interfere with a "*ni*" in French (which could be marked in various ways, *weder . . . noch, auch nicht*, but not as economically as in French).

All this micrology soon becomes tiring. What we want to point out is that the pathetic accent of this desperate, anxious questioning is not as marked, in any event, as what we are accustomed to perceive through the effect of an unwarranted selection of only half a line of verse. The dramatization of the isolated question falsifies the movement of the text and shifts the emphasis.

The same is true of the word "*dürftig*," often translated as "in/of distress," whereas "indigence/want" seems more appropriate, including in its social connotation.[3]

II

To these remarks on the text itself, two others must be added concerning the context. On the one hand, strophe 7 of "Bread and Wine" doesn't end with this verse. It continues with a final couplet, which reads:

> But they are, you say, like those holy priests of the god of wine
> Who in holy night wander from land to land.[4]

On the other hand, this strophe wasn't included in the final version of the poem. On the contrary, it is the one that, throughout the various versions and transformations of the poem by Hölderlin (six successive versions), underwent the most significant changes—to the extent that it would be more accurate to say that a different strophe was substituted for the first. Nothing remains of it, no more than the verse that concerns us here. Moreover, it would not be irrelevant to note that in its prior versions, strophe 7 is distinguished by having one less couplet than the others, whereas the final version reestablishes the strophe with nine couplets.

It is hard to ignore this wholesale erasure by Hölderlin himself of *Wozu Dichter*, and difficult as well to forget that he had produced, in its initial version, a type of misdirection—about which specialists have multiplied the number of conjectures. I will not examine them here. However, because the sixth version has kept nothing of the *Wozu*, I won't look into it, even if we cannot overlook it entirely.[5]

Let's return to the context of the prior version (I'm using the singular to simplify matters). The last couplet contrasts to the ignorance of the one who says "I" the affirmation introduced by "you say." This "I" is a unique occurrence in the poem and this "you" as well (if we neglect the other "you" at the beginning of strophe 4, which is addressed to Greece and not to that other you, here unnamed, whom it is customary to consider to be the man to whom the poem is dedicated, Wilhelm Heinze).

Although there are excellent reasons to see this as an address to Heinze, for whom Dionysus is certainly not absent and a close reading of which would no doubt provide the elements of the couplet in considerable detail, nothing prevents us from deciphering the dialogue as one of self with self. This self would be the one who writes or speaks (here they are the same). Moreover, Hölderlin may very well consider himself to be "one" with Heinze, one in the "we" that the poem has already spoken six times and will speak three times more (in strophe 7, which begins by interpellating the "friend," there are two "we's"). Yet, the "we" of the poem is, first and foremost, that of the community of childhood and culture through which the friends later—"too late" reads the strophe—would know something of Greece, something "true" as strophe 4 states.

III

The truth of *Wozu* might be found in the dialogue between the "I" who "does not know" and the "you" who "says that." I don't know why there are poets in a time of want but you say that poets are priests of the god of wine.

I don't know why there are—or would be—poets because this time is a time when man is incapable of "supporting the full impact of the gods" as he writes a few lines earlier. We can only await the arrival of the heroes whose hearts "*have a strength like that of the Celestials.*" They will arrive, that much is certain, but in the meanwhile, we may find it preferable to sleep because we don't know what to do or say.

We don't know what to do or say just as we don't know *why poets* . . . But *you say* what they are: you know, then, what to say and I know how to say it to myself, hearing it from you. If you know it, it is not absent. It is not merely a memory of Greece. You say it in the present: *they are.*

Further, I say it myself in the present. The last couplet is careful to lead with the affirmation of their being: "*Aber sie sind, sagst du* . . ." (but they are, you say . . .). This affirmation remains suspended for a brief moment as a pure ontological statement, independent of any other clarification. First, they are—the poets. And that's why they are also in a time of want. That's why there are poets.

They are the priests of the god of wine and they travel the world by night. But night is, precisely, the time when we are; the entire poem is sung at night, described in the first strophe, and the word recurs nine times in the entire text.[6] The eighth verse of our strophe says that "*distress and night make us strong.*" Night is the time of sleep (evoked, or invoked, twice in the strophe), the time of dreaming, named as well, during which time the gods distance themselves from us and become unreal, the time when sleeping might be preferable to gnawing away at one's impotence. During the night, at the edge of sleep, I hear that my alter ego is telling me of poets and their holy priesthood in the holy night.[7]

IV

From here it would be possible, and profitable, to extend the interpretation to the entire poem, then to its revision and transformation through the final version when the same strophe concludes by naming the night as "a clarity" and affirming the possibility of revealing the divine in spite of the slowness of his coming.[8] That approach cannot be adopted here. It was merely a question of allowing *Wozu Dichter* to be heard in its immediate context, without it being isolated as a kind of interrogative aphorism, more or less exclamatory and entirely plaintive—for which, at the same time, we nourish the hope and ambition of providing answers of even greater audacity and magnificence.

The response can be read between the lines of the poem and should at least be indicated. However, it is worth emphasizing this point by returning to the line of verse itself:

Weiss ich nicht, und wozu Dichter in dürftiger Zeit

The second line of the couplet is a pentameter, in principle iambic (one long/two short). But in German usage, even more so than in Greek or Latin, the meters can accommodate any number of variations, exceptions, or dispensations that prevent my too feeble science from scanning this line. Nonetheless, it seems to quite easily accommodate hearing in the very clear scansion of its first hemistich (if it's indeed that):

Weiss icht nicht/und wozu

No matter how fragile this incursion into prosody might be, it is highly likely that the rhythm here tends rather to connect what comes before the comma with what follows, thereby accentuating the sense of "nor do I know why . . ." It's the only reason I've allowed myself this detour. I don't want to extend it any further because the theory and practice of what is called iambic pentameter and Asclepiadic and Alcaic verse are far beyond my capacities.

More modestly, we can add here that two major alliterations or assonances can be heard in this verse. One refers to the hexameter that comes before the couplet and is associated with the *zu* that appears three times in the first line of verse, returning in the second with *wozu* and finally resonating with *Zeit*. The second entails the play between *ich*, *nicht*, and *Dicht-*. To emphasize the role of these recurrences, we'll compare the contrasted sonority of two verses of the couplet, the first being as follows:

So zu harren, und zu tun indes und zu sagen

This abundance of open vowels—*o, a, u* (pronounced "ou")—and the soft sibilants—*s, z*—and the internal rhyme of the two infinitives in *-en* are interrupted as if by a call, an awakening, almost an exclamation, in the strong sibilants, the fricatives, the stridency and accelerated rhythm of

Weiss ich nicht und wozu Dichter in dürftiger Zeit

I'm not trying to interpret these processes, only to feel the extent to which the poet is here at work, at his most intimate work of rhythm and song, and how, as a result, he is also concerned to make us hear, before any signification, that if he doesn't know *why poets* he is nonetheless concerned, *in a time of want*, with poetically sounding their name. The divine is lacking but the poetic makes up for it—unless there has always been truth, during times that were never, for as long as there have been times, without want or without poets.

Unpublished

PART III

Sense

Noli me frangere

with Philippe Lacoue-Labarthe

Of the fragment, little should be written. It is not an object or a genre, it does not form a work. (Friedrich Schlegel's fragmentary *will* is the very will to the Work, and enough has been said about that. But what Blanchot calls the fragmentary *exigency* exceeds the work, because that exigency exceeds the will.)

Fragment: the text is fragile. It's nothing but. It breaks and yet it doesn't break, in the same place. Where? Someplace, always someplace, an unassignable, incalculable place.

It is a mistake, then, to write in fragments on the fragment (that goes for Blanchot, too). But what else is there to do? Write about something else entirely—or about nothing-and let oneself be fragmented.

"That goes for Blanchot, too": nevertheless, it was the publication of *The Writing of the Disaster*, in July 1980, that came along to interrupt the composition of a completely different text, which I could now call, having abandoned it, a supplementary dialectic of the fragment. Blanchot's exigency was its guide. Blanchot's text interrupted it. I quote that text:

> The fragment, as fragments, tends to dissolve the totality that it presupposes and that it carries off toward the dissolution from which (strictly speaking) it does not form itself, but to which it exposes itself in order, disappearing (all identity disappearing along with it), to maintain itself as the energy of disappearing.

A supplementary dialectic of the fragment was therefore at work in that text as well. Perhaps it would not be wrong to call it a negative dialectic and to search for secret correspondences between Blanchot and Adrono. But that still means the dialectic—discourse—is indestructible. *Noli me frangere*, it orders in every text, and in the fragmentary text as well, and in the discourse in fragments on the fragment. Don't shatter me, don't fragment me.

This is not merely the effect of a will to self-protection, no more than the *Noli me tangere* of the Scriptures is. Don't touch me, says Christ arisen, because you couldn't, because you wouldn't know what you were touching, and because you would think you knew. You can't know anything or will anything about what is called a glorious body.

Above all, we must not believe that we could know how to fragment, that we could know ourselves in fragments, that we actually could fragment. No one fragments, unless perhaps it is that *Noli me frangere* that all writing utters: don't fragment me, don't wish to fragment me—fragmentation goes on, and I'm fragmented enough; anyway, it's not up to you.

All this is written in Blanchot's fragmentary writing. There's nothing to add, nothing to take away. Nothing to dialecticize, nothing to fragment. Above all, one mustn't fall into the double trap of overdialecticization and overfragmentation. Blanchot upholds to the point of exhaustion—to the point of no longer being able to bear it—the hazardous exigency of writing *right* between these twin traps. Thus his writing too (not just his discourse) declares: *Noli me frangere*. Don't shatter my insistence, my murmuring. You wouldn't be getting any closer to the fragment: it has already preceded my gesture and yours, and it will follow them forever.

Don't speak, don't write about the fragment. Or ever so little.

Finally, it is the fragment (fragments, the fragmentary exigency) that says Noli me frangere—thereby preserving no pure atom, no indivisible work, but, very simply, remaining unrelated to any operation, in any sense. The fragment is indestructible which is to say that destruction is assured and that this assurance is not assurance—not, in any case, for any knowledge, any subject.

Someone writes, someone reads, people talk, something takes shape, makes sense, completes itself in a work or in fragments—in a work, that is, in fragments. And it's indestructible: a conversation every bit as much as a poem. What is indestructible is *fragility* itself, more attenuated, more tremulous, more untenable, unbearable, than any fragmentation, the fragility that dwells in speaking or in writing, in opening your mouth, in tracing a word. There and then it shatters—nowhere else, at no other time. The fragility of a glorious body (neither transcendent nor immanent, neither yours nor mine, neither body nor mind) shatters a throat or a hand. There arises a word, a discourse, a chant, a writing. The glorious body will never stop repeating this order as fragile as a plea: *Noli me frangere.*

. . . . . .

—Well?

—I'm torn, I'm hesitating . . . *Noli me frangere*—all right. But it's a bit . . . "Don't touch it, it's broken"—and then it has this speculative, Sully Prudhomme aspect . . .[1]

—Let's not exaggerate.

—No, of course not. Because, at the same time, it's the non-ironic pole—or, even more, the "ironic" pole—of my *Schweben*, so I certainly recognize something there. What strikes me, I guess, is how closely the fragment is tied to an emotion of thought.

—Meaning . . . ?

—It's difficult. Obviously, I'm thinking about the "sentimental," both in the trivial sense and in Schiller's sense, which also contains the trivial sense. Therefore, I'm also thinking about the "subjective," about the thought-subject, whose body (writing) trembles from and is moved by its fragility, who is like the child that childhood abandons at the moment when the child opens its mouth to speak, to lament this abandonment, It's your final "plea."

— Or the "*chant romantique*," as Barthes defined it: the subject abandoned. Maybe the fragment isn't so far removed from the *Lied*. But in the Romantics, of course (and already in Schiller) there's something else. The Sentimental is what we tried to analyze in The Literary Absolute as the process of infinitization: it's the matrix of the speculative dialectic, but it's also the movement of excess. The subjective never stops going beyond itself.

—Music, too, at least for me . . .

—And your *émoi*, which would be better here anyway than "emotion."

—No doubt. As long as you keep to the strict sense, the loss of means—or keep to Witz, *é-moi*, out of the ego. But it mustn't be *Et-moi!*—and me![2]

—Precisely, *Witz* . . .

—Yes, just a moment ago, that's what I was also thinking about: the fragment as a spasm of thought. Today, naturally, we would immediately speak of *jouissance*, pleasure, orgasm.

—And why not?

—Yes, after all, why not? In the loss that *jouissance* entails, there is certainly an irrepressible movement of pleading. But the plea is contradictory: both "touch me (undo me)" and "don't touch me (help me, protect me)."

— The fragment, then, would be a moment of *jouissance* in thought. But "moment," when you think of the dialectical use of the word—

—Exactly: if your *Noli me frangere* is right—and I think that it is—it's still what makes *jouissance* a "moment." In fact, from the outset, that's where I hesitated. I have the impression that these fragments consolidate, paradoxically, a speculation on the fragment.

—It's quite possible. I myself had a somewhat similar feeling. But vaguely. You'll have to explain.

— That can't be improvised.

— Then write it! We decided to sign this text together. Why not follow the fragments with a dialogue, in the style of the *Gespräch*, only shorter?

— That's it. We'll dance on the edge of the abyss!

—Well, where we stand now . . .

—Really, who knows? It may not be the worst way to spring the specular trap.

—Well, then, my dear Lothario! To your pen! Cover one or two of those tiny sheets you like so much with your divine scrawl. I'll give myself the pleasure—and duty—of answering you.

—We can always try.

* * *

LOTHARIO: I find it quite difficult, dear Ludovico, not to see in your series of fragments a veritable discourse in miniature—with its own composition, its introduction, its well-articulate demonstration, its ringing conclusion (as the genre demands). You cleverly conceal a powerful rhetoric—that is, in this case, a powerful dialectic. You conceal it by noticing it—and in such a way that, as you may agree, these fragments on (impossible) fragmentation are properly speaking, a discourse on discourse, on the "indestructible" dialectic.

Far be it from me to reproach you: I know as well as you do the extreme vigilance needed in these matters. (There are so many weak repetitions of Romantic writing in our day, so many weak mimetic speculations!) And besides, I'm grateful that you give Blanchot credit for having avoided (or *known how* to avoid?) the "twin traps" of "overdialecticization" and "over-fragmentation." But a dialectic, even supplementary, even negative, remains a dialectic—that is, an economy. Mainly, I don't understand Blanchot's phrase very well, the one you're basing your remarks on. If I follow you, this phrase seems to you the best translation of "fragmentary exigency" (as opposed to the "fragmentary will" of the Romantics). What I don't understand very well is the phrase "to maintain itself as the energy of disappearing"—that sort of negative sublation that would be senseless if it were not precisely an *energy* that was *maintained*, put to work. There is still a will there (can one be avoided, in any case?), and therefore probably calculation as well, the guile of an ultimate calculation: that of the incalculable. It's your indestructible dialectic that utters the *Noli me frangere* . . . For my part, I'd wonder (more baldly) whether it isn't the energy itself, the will to the work, that gives rise to fragmentation, the unrelenting passion toward the work. That would be, in an exemplary way, but *short* of his "fragmentary will," what happens in Schlegel and in all those who have simply *suffered* fragmentation—a fragmentation they did not will.

LUDOVICO: You have read me very well, Lothario, every bit as well as you may have misunderstood one of my intentions, and for the same reason. It is indeed true that my fragments are a discourse. I will add that the *mise en abîme* (so tempting, so insidious and urgent) of the fragment ought, in my opinion, to display the irresistible reconstitution of discourse, from which the fragmentary *will* does not escape—and, even more, to which it yields beforehand, without knowing. But it's also this respect that Blanchot surprised me and interrupted a first draft in which I was expressly trying to discourse. For I was finding, in passages like the one I've quoted, a singular dialectical resurgence, and—very precisely, as you say—the *maintenance* of an *aim* toward the *work*. Like the Hegelian Spirit, the energy of the work—if you'll forgive me that redundant expression—is what seems to maintain itself here in fragmentary death. That Blanchot, in that case, should write *right* alongside the dialectic also signifies precisely that he repeats, if he will, its external contours. And it means that, in this way, we all ask not to be shattered.

But at the same time, I was trying to read or to hear the same dialectic as the admission (and not the will) of a fragility of discourse, which discourse admits even as it begs to be spared. "Energy" is such a strange word in this context that it is no doubt necessary *also* to give it the meaning (if it is a "meaning") of a renunciation of energy. I wanted to speak of "negative dialectic" in the sense of which Adorno writes: "the dialectic is the rigorous consciousness of non-identity." Adorno's book too, in its way, is written in fragments—without a visible *will* to fragment, but through the effect, it seems to me, of an extreme, almost unbearable, attention to the acute opposition, in Hegel, between the dialectic and the "viewpoint of consciousness," which brings back to its identity everything that differs from itself. Adorno attempts (I don't say he succeeds; that would make no sense) not to *maintain* the contradiction but to *bear* its rupture. The *negative* in Adorno and the *fragment* in Blanchot attempt to convert themselves from mastery to ordeal. In spite of everything. As if there were a space beyond Hegel and the Romantic absolute, *our* beyond—(not) one step beyond [*pas* au-delà], as you well know—where nothing more is willed, but where it is a question of experiencing non-identity. Of bearing in this way the weight of thought and writing. And that space begins, paradoxically, at the heart of identity, where discourse and consciousness plead *Noli me frangere* and thus admit that there is already fragmentation, that an interruption or a suspension has occurred, which did not involve a totality, and which did not shatter a unity, since unity is never achieved. A fragment that fragments—nothing. But I don't know whether I understand this ordeal in the same way that you understand the fact of "suffering" fragmentation . . .

LOTHARIO: "To suffer," as I understand the term, gestures toward "passivity." But the word that you yourself use, "ordeal," suits me perfectly; and everything you suggest about such an ordeal, I believe I can make my own—not just subscribe to. I believe I know—with no "knowledge" whatsoever—what it is to bear non-identity, to be doomed to this suspension, to this rupture or caesura that has always already happened (as what has never happened). I recognize this as the "difficult," the "impracticable"—as pain. In my pathos, which is not always so far removed from your own, I will say: write, think—*nothing* happens.

That, it seems to me, is how the disconnection is produced (without *production*). Adorno again: I'm thinking of the extreme acuity of his analysis of *parataxis* in the late poetry of Hölderlin—who in no way sought the rupture, even though, in full consciousness, he refused dialectical (conceptual) synthesis. When I spoke of "suffering fragmentation," I was actually thinking of him.

But the strange thing in all of this is that you have often reproached me—or at least you have often been amazed, mischievously so, by what you call my tendency to mysticism. And you, my dear friend? What about this "admission," this "pleading," this "spare me"? When I myself no longer dared to tell you how upsetting I found Benjamin's way of appropriating Malebranche's proposition on attentiveness and inflicting it to describe writing or thought as "a form of prayer."

So there is certainly a misunderstanding between us. It is in the place you're pointing to, but it's not just there. And, to take the ball back on the rebound, I would prefer to speak, while we're at it, of malaise. You see, what really bothers me—and maybe it would have been better to say right from the start—is your reference to the "glorious body." I find the resurrection, in whatever register—mystical, speculative—completely impenetrable. I have never found anything in Christianity more scandalous. That's why my mysticism, if that's what it is (which I greatly and deeply doubt), has little to do with the type of "negative theology" that you seem to deploying there and whose absolute positivity I can't help suspecting. What bothers me, finally, is that, with an extra twist of logic or rhetoric, as if carried along by a movement of what would today be called "maximalization," you reinforce the mysticism of the fragment under the pretext of combating it. If we find no solution to fragmentation—and here I quite agree with you—this is not because of the silent (and terribly eloquent) injunction of writing's "glorious body." Indecision is a *poor* experience.

LUDOVICO: A poor experience . . . I really have to grant you that. Or rather, I have nothing to "grant" you here, as if it were a question of matching thesis against thesis. You're talking about something in which or through which all theses and all positions of discourse collapse, but silently—or with a persistent murmur—concealing even the event of this collapse. Blanchot, writing about writing and about thought, has never stopped haunting these regions. The collapse is felt, and can hardly be expressed, much less justified. This is what happens: there is an exhaustion of discourse—an exhaustion of language—that can never be known or recognized, although it must still be said that the failure to recognize it dooms discourse to futility. This is not a mysticism of the ineffable, for it contains no secret of a hidden sense, of a Word beyond words. Instead, it is a mysticism of the fragility through which alone is disclosed what you will pardon me for calling, in spite of everything, a truth in human speech.

(There is no other truth.) As you see, I don't reject the word "mysticism." On the contrary, I will place it—to echo your *prayer*—under the patronage of a mystical teaching, that of Meister Eckhart: "Let us pray God to be free and quit of God."

If that still reeks too strongly of negative theology (and since the articulation, and discourse, of negative theology's very real difference from mysticism would surely be an infinite task), then I must make a confession to you, Lothario, about my "glorious body." I did not deduce the discourse of these fragments from the thought of a glorious body. On the contrary, the phrase from the Gospels came first, alone, to my ear. *Noli me tangere,* in that Latin suffused with the ancient sonorities of the Church, in a tone of psalmody and holy recitation. I couldn't tell you why. (Could it be that *The Writing of the Disaster*, having interrupted my work, having *touched* me in the complex way that I've been telling you about, made me say, "don't touch me?" I don't know.) But this phrase imposed itself, along with the dim memory of a narrative, of which I will now remind you: Mary Magdalene goes to the tomb and, seeing Jesus, on his feet, does not recognize him. Jesus says to her, "Mary!" Turning around, she says to him, in Hebrew, "Rabboni!" which means "Teacher!" Jesus says to her, "Do not touch me, for I have not yet ascended to my Father; but go unto my brethren."

You can feel how much this story—which John is the only one to relate—is made up entirely of an extreme, chased fragility. It's an ordeal, a joy, and a disappearance all at once. And the glorious body that disturbs you shines here with a glory so poor that it is neither recognized nor named as such. I admit that I didn't reject what a fragile phrase, a fragment of sound and sense, thus brought me. But the glorious body, as I have written, offers nothing to know or touch. It's there, and it slips away. It's not so much that I wanted to create an allegory of writing as that I felt how this phrase and this story, their spiritual meaning and fleeting emotion, were suspended, fragmented, instantly. And the idea "glory," of an invisible brightness . . . I believe that one always writes not only for glory but also *in* this hidden glory. I spoke to you just now about the weight of thought: in the Hebrew word that expresses Biblical "glory" there is the idea of a weight, a heaviness . . .

LOTHARIO: This "corpus," if I dare say so, is not very familiar to me. You know that: I really have forgotten quite a lot. Except, however, this figure of Mary Magdalene, who, for all sorts of reasons (some less admissible than others), has always been—how shall I put this?—very *close* to me. It's strange, besides—I didn't know she was implicated in this business of *Noli me tangere*—strange and, from a certain angle, troubling, suggestive. Perhaps that strangeness comes from the fact that, for me, she is first of all a secret, enigmatic figure from paintings. Or, if you like, the image of woman associated—memory immemorial—with La Tour's light. In fact, she's my image of love, or of the beautiful itself.

But, as you suspect, that has nothing to do with "glory," with splendor, which for me is inseparable—you'll laugh—from the Counter-Reformation, the Baroque. Ever since Plato, the beautiful has been a burst of light. But there are two kinds of such bursts, and ostentation (which is one of the meanings of the Latin *gloria*) puts me off a bit.

LUDOVICO: Do I dare say that it doesn't put me off? I must say so, at my own risk. I don't defend it, and I don't raise it in opposition to the restrained, vanishing, wholly interior burst of light that you seem to mean. I'll say instead that, for me, fragmentation is linked to this: that there is no (or no more) interiority. And, consequently, it is indeed linked to something of the Baroque. The passivity that we are both talking about can be concentrated or dispersed. Perhaps I'm incapable of letting it be concentrated, and so I see it dispersing in the Baroque fragmentation that Benjamin knew how to talk about, the Benjamin of *The Origin of German Tragic Drama* (Romanticism no doubt having mixed, in variable proportion, the two kinds of fragmentation). The Baroque emerges from the loss of organic totality as interiority and gives itself up to the "incomplete, shattered character of sensible, beautiful physis." Of course, in rupture itself and in its intervals, in brusque immobilizations and in surprising simultaneities, in the play of mirrors and of shimmering surfaces, writing also finds itself "preoccupied, in all willingness, with developing its own energy." I'll claim for writing (not for "myself," but for "literature") nothing less than the risking of this willingness and the hazarding that writing may shatter, burst apart. There is certainly something of *Witz* here. *Witz* (play, chance discovery, encounters with the incongruous) is very close to the dialectic, as we have written. (You'll also remember that Heidegger, in his *Schelling*, speaks of a "Romantic transposition of the idealist dialectic.") But *Witz* isn't absent from writing. It's simply that it can't be ordered around—and on that, I believe, we agree. A conspicuous failure of the will, or of the project, *makes* fragmentation—or writing. It gives me up to a kind of devastation, indeed a brilliant one, from which play is not shut out, the play of ridicule or of rejoicing. You seem to me, at this point, to fall into contemplation, and I must admit that contemplation is what I have forgotten, or have never known. And this, no doubt, is only a sign of the times . . . I can't, finally, dissociate the fragment from the closure of the modern world.

—So, there it is. I have the feeling we'd best just leave it at that. And, curiously enough, I think that with this method I ended up saying exactly what I wanted to say.

—And the posthumous fragment from Schlegel that you mentioned—didn't you do with that?

—No, fitting it in right would have taken me too far afield, and this is already long enough as it is.

—What did that fragment say? We can still put it into the little dialogue at the end.

—Here it is.

—"The activity whereby consciousness best reveals itself as fragment . . ."

—It's *Bruchstück*, piece. He doesn't say "fragment" . . .

—". . . is *Witz*, whose essence consists precisely in its being torn. . . ." It's good, but . . .

—But?

—But the dialectic has struck again.

—Yes and no.

—Anyway, in your text, it works. But when I think that, right there at the end, you hit me with interiority, with contemplation! And what if I'd hit you back, with piety? I restrained myself from elaborating on an *Ad majorem scriptionis* (or *cogitationis*) *gloriam* . . . But let's be serious. I don't know if that's what you were really trying to say, but when you speak of the fragment as a sign of the "closure of the modern world," it seems to me that you're touching on something true.

—I meant to say that the fragment, even in Blanchot, is too much the mark of the modern. It's impossible to tear it free from modernity . . .

—From Nietzsche, for example, who plays a large role in the origins of Blanchot's "fragmentary writing." In short, if you mean there's nothing to be done with the fragment as such (that is, ultimately, with the fragment as *genre*) . . .

—Yes, but not with fragmentation . . .

—Then I understand perfectly. No, the fragment as genre is still the will to fragment, with everything that entails: literature, in its very delimitation; the letter of the subject. In Barthes, it's striking: Montaigne, the recurrence of self-portraiture. And as for Blanchot's anonymity and self-effacement . . .

—That's something else again. How could we reduce anonymity to self-portraiture, even to the self-portrait of the subject of literature?

—There's literature and there's literature, and someday we'll have to make up our minds to distinguish them a bit more rigorously.
—Absolutely!

We talked much more about this question—that day, and later on as well.

Translated by Brian Holmes
1982

[At the authors' request, I have translated the majority of the quotations directly from the French, so as not to disturb the flow of the text. Consult the following references for more information; they do not always correspond word-for-word with this text.

Theodor Adorno, *Negative Dialectics*, trans. E. B. Ashton (New York: Continuum, 1973), 5.
Roland Barthes, *L'obvie et l'obtus* (Paris: Seuil, 1982), 253–58.
Walter Benjamin, *Illuminations*, trans. Harry Zohn (New York: Schocken Books, 1969), 134; *The Origin of German Tragic Drama*, trans. John Osborne (London: New Left Books, 1977), 176.
Maurice Blanchot, *The Writing of the Disaster*, trans. Ann Smock (Lincoln: University of Nebraska Press, 1986), 60–61.
Meister Eckhart: A Modern Translation, trans. Raymond Bernard Blakney (New York: Harper & Brothers, 1941), 231.
Martin Heidegger, *Schelling's Treatise on the Essence of Human Freedom*, trans. Joan Stambaugh (Athens: Ohio University Press, 1985), 82.

For the authors' previous reflections on the fragment and fragmentation, see *The Literary Absolute: The Theory of Literature in German Romanticism*, trans. Philip Barnard and Cheryl Lester (Albany: SUNY Press, 1988).—Trans.]

Responding for Sense

Write to me. Write anything at all.[1]

—EMMANUEL LOI

The sentence—literature—is oral.[2]

—PHILIPPE LACOUE-LABARTHE

Who writes responds.

To whom or what he or she responds, has been given many names by tradition. The Muse, poetic Fury, Genius, with or without capitalization, inspiration, sometimes mission or vocation, sometimes a necessity of the soul or the nerves, heavenly grace, sacred injunction, a duty of memory or forgetfulness, self-creation of the text. But the oldest name is *thea*, found in the first verse of the *Iliad*: "Sing Goddess, the wrath of Achilles. . . ." In this *incipit* of Western literature, the poet utters merely the first line—or at most the lines that lead to the question: "What god has cast them into war?"—and the response ("The son of Leto and Zeus") engages the entire poem, it being understood that it is *thea* who sings.

It is not Homer himself who writes: he allows the divine voice to sing. He, the *aoidos*, sings to the extent that he interprets the divine song—the song that asks to be sung ("*menin aeide thea . . .*"): in this way he does what he expects her to do so that he himself might withdraw into this song— hers becoming his but always remaining this divine song. He allows the voice to sing or allows it to be heard, he recites it. Since then, the one who writes does so only by letting himself dictate in the several senses of the term. *Dicto* is to speak through repetition, insistence, it is to command, to prescribe. To write is to let oneself be enjoined to write: to respond to a command, or an entreaty, or an exhortation, excitation, or pressure. But also, he receives the dictation: writing, he lays down the text that another voice composes and recites for that purpose, a voice that does not write, a voice that writes primally. From the word *dictare*, German has drawn, alongside *diktieren* (dictate), the verb *dichten* (to compose a written piece, uniquely a poem). The one who writes responds in one way or another, by echo or execution, transcription or translation, to the *dictatorship* of a *dictatio*. What, in the *Iliad*, appears to be manifested as the response by *Thea*—of the *thea*, of an unnamed, unidentified *thea*—is in fact, the opposite, the response of the *aoidos* to the dictation of the divine voice: but, precisely, this response is given by its opposite figure because, in truth, it is the *aoidos* who responds—rather, even more truthfully, there is only response to some response, and none—neither *aoidos* nor goddess—has ever begun.

That responds to itself: this is the expression for what today we call writing. That responds to itself: responds *in itself*, responds *to itself*, and responds *for itself*. *Res responsoria*, the subject that succeeds the *res cogitans* (unless it has always preceded it and inhabits it)—if we recall that the *responsorius cantus* referred to the alternating song of lessons (*lectio*) and verses (*versus*) or *response*. In writing it is a question of song, and the alternation or internal resonance that forms the song.

The *aoidos* and the *thea*, therefore, do not respond in the sense that we respond to a question but in the sense that we meet, or satisfy, an expectation, or in the sense that voices reply to one another, correspond to one another. They respond or correspond to one another in the sense that *respondeo* is to be reciprocally engaged in a *sponsio*, in a religious or legal engagement: to satisfy a promise with a reciprocal promise (as in marital engagements, a form of *sponsio*, from which French derives "*épouser*" and Italian "*sposare*"). He who writes listens and is engaged in his listening, by his listening. Similarly, in German, *Antwort*, and in English, *answer*, the "response" is the word that comes to the encounter. To write is to agree to an encounter: it is to go toward the encounter and it is to accept the commitment of the encounter. To write is to arrange a meeting. (The encounter may be furtive, it may be no more than a simple crossing of paths, a brushing against, but it may also be a lengthy conversation—and it can also occur "counter to," through the shock, confrontation or repulsion. But it is always a question of some confrontation or other, and that never takes place in isolation.)

To listen is to resonate: to let vibrate within oneself sounds that have come from elsewhere, and reply to them with the reverberation of a body, made cavernous for that purpose. This cave is not that of Plato. It is not closed and only barely open to an exterior that projects shadows but is *openness in itself* in both senses that the expression can assume: the opening up to the interior of the self and the opening itself, absolutely. In fact, it is "me" as opening, me as sounding box against which the harmonies and accents of voices from outside, divine voices, strike, slide, and caress. But the resonance is not a shadow, it is not the remains of a subtraction but the intensification and reharmonization, the remodulation of a sonority. Who writes resonates and, by resonating, responds: he shares the engagement of a voice from the outside. He is engaged in turn, renders polyphonic the voice that was monodic upon arrival. For without that polyphony, the monody would not even be *heard*. That is, *no one* would hear it and the monody *itself* would remain deaf to itself.

*

The response, or reply, is the resumption and renewal of the voice—of what it says, its accent, its articulation and phrasing, its singingness. But without resumption, without response, therefore, the voice would remain in itself. A voice in itself is not a voice, it is a silence that doesn't even have the space of an address, a mutism sealed in its own buzzing, in its mooing or its murmur (the repetition of a silent *mmm—mutum*). A voice is always at least two polyphonous voices in some respect. One voice must always say to the other "Sing! *aoidos!*" *Aoidos*, from which is derived, *odè*, the song, the ode, is related to *audé*, which characterizes the human voice in contrast with *phoné*, which can also be used for the animal voice. *Audao* is to speak to, to address, to utter a reply or call out to. The human voice always reverberates toward another voice and from another voice or even in another voice. Its sonorous resonance is inseparable from the reverberation of saying and listening: even as I speak alone and silently "in my head" (as we assume we can say), that is, while I think, I hear another voice in my voice or I hear my voice resonate in another throat.

"Writing" is the name of that resonance of voice: the call, the encounter, and the engagement that the call assumes at the encounter. In this sense, all writing is "engaged" in a sense that precedes the notion of political or moral engagement, in the service of a cause. To write is to engage the voice in the resonance that makes it human; but "human" in this case signifies nothing other than "that which is held—or happens—in resonance."

Thus, writing is the very resonance of the voice or the voice as resonance, to the extent that it is self-reference, through the distance of a "self" to the "sameness" that enables it to identify itself: absolutely singular each time for an indefinite number of encounters that are singular on every occasion. Writing "fixes," as we say, the flow of speech (*verba volant, scripta manent*); this fixation is nothing other than the recording, storage, or residence of the capacity for resonance. In living speech, or even in speech that speaks only to inform the moment, with no delay or rendezvous, resonance is extinguished as soon as the information has reached its destination. In writing, the destination is first of all, initially and always, resonance as such: Homer did not write for fewer than his millions and millions of readers, each of them one by one and as peoples or groups of singular cultures for roughly 30 centuries. And that is why he begins his poem with an appeal to the divine voice whose resonance he, the *aoidos*, becomes. Writing fixed, engraved in wood, wax, stone, or paper, digitized on screen, as well as recorded in the speaking voice of an orator, a singer, an "addresser" in general, were we to forge the term—writing is stationary and invariable only because it thereby inscribes the space of an always renewed resonance.

When Hegel states that a written truth loses nothing when preserved outside the singular circumstance of its utterance—thus "it's dark" or "it's getting dark" spoken at noon—doesn't he mean that truth isn't part of the order of empirical verifiability but, rather, the order of the address and resonance? If I say, "It's dark" at noon, what is it I'm trying to say and what form of listening is implied when encountering my utterance?

To say "it's dark" at midnight states something but announces nothing; or, rather, the sentence announces a sense that exceeds the immediate referential meaning attested. Similarly, this same sentence spoken at noon— that is, this *written* sentence—announces a meaning that, from the outset, escapes reference and makes a sign to something else. This "something else" consists primarily of the address of the sentence and the resonance through which it is addressed; we could also say that it engages its meaning through its *phrasing* rather than its signification. The *phrasing* refers to the manner or art of articulating, in writing or in music, aggregates considered as units of meaning: the song of sense.

*

The song of sense is nothing other than sense itself. Sense is not signification or designation—referral by a signifier to a signified concept that is itself assumed to exist outside language; rather, it is the opening of the structure and dynamic of *referral* in general, through which something like a signifying referral can take place: referral of signifier to signified, itself accompanied by a referral of signifier to signifier through the interplay of differences in language and, finally, or to begin, the referral of a voice to a listening, without which neither of the two previous referrals could even have taken place, because one and the other and one through the other, in short, assume that *understanding* (*entente*) is possible (in both senses of the word in French; in German, we could say obedience to or belonging to— *gehören, gehorchen*—other modes of "response").³

What is meant to be *heard* is not primarily what the word *intends to say*, in the sense that this intention would have already produced the completed reality of its intention or desire. Before all else, it is this desire itself that must be heard: we must hear the "wanting-to-say" *try to be* itself in its *saying*. (In German we should hear the *deuten* of *bedeuten*: hear in the "signification," the declaration, the announcement addressed to all—to the people, that is, *deutsch* or *dutch*, as well, because, here, the name of the people, that of its language and that of the appeal or announcement, resonate within the same semantic space.) To hear saying desire itself as saying is to already hear it resonate while hearing it desire the other as its place of resonance and referral. Sense as song is in no way the setting to music of a statement or a text—it is the resonant primitive character of sense itself.

In all saying, the wanting-to-say [*vouloir-dire*], before it says something, is initially expressed as wanting, and this wanting, before wanting something, initially apprehends itself as able-to-say-itself, that is, able to call and respond to itself.

In other words, if writing is replying to a call with another call, or producing and giving shape to the *call* as such—as in Homer, to call upon the goddess who calls from the depths of language and legend, inextricably bound up in one another—we now learn that the call and the address are themselves nothing other than sense: sense as opening up of the possibility of referral.

Sense can absolutely never be the result of a single subject of sense because that subject itself would, at the very least, have to hear the sense it would produce or discover. It would have to *hear itself* and to hear itself would have to have *called itself* and to call itself it would have to be able to resonate—and, finally, to resonate it would have to, first of all, provide the space in itself, the interval or spacing, the *opening* that is the condition of possibility of a resonance, because this demands a relation of vibration to vibration, a "sympathy," as physicists say when they speak of "sympathetic vibrations," or the "harmony" musicians speak of. But resonance as it should be understood here is not only the relation between two distinct orders of sound; first and foremost, it forms sonority in itself. Sonority is defined, precisely, by the fact that "in itself" it is a distancing from itself. The sonorous is its own expansion or amplification and the establishment of its own resonance.

Song is the human sonority of sense: sense is itself formed and defined by the internal spacing of its referral and, above all, by the transmission through which it destines itself and desires itself as a reply to its own transmission. *In this sense*, we are never, each of us, one alongside the other, anything other than singular points along a general transmission that sense makes of itself toward itself, and that begins and is lost far before and far after us, in the indefinitely open totality of the world. But at the same time, these singular points that we are (or the several singular points that fragment within each individual or collective identity) are themselves the necessarily discrete or discontinuous structure of the general spacing within which sense can resonate, that is to say, *reply to itself*.

In communicating itself to all the singular points of listening or reading, of understanding or interpretation, of recitation or rewriting, sense does nothing other than divide itself among or into so many singular senses (here, the word "sense" can be understood both with its value of "wanting-to-say" and its value of "able to understand," as when we speak of "good sense" or "artistic sense"—and those two values, it should be understood, cannot be separated from one another: both are present in the very sense of the same sense). Sense taken absolutely or in itself is nothing other than the totality of singular senses. Infinite sense is identical to the infinity of singularities of sense. It is neither a general sense nor a sense by the summation of or as a result of singular senses: it is the succession *and* discontinuity of those singulars. The fact is *that-there-is* passage and sharing between them, passage and sharing of a "wanting-to-say" and an "ability to understand"—of an activity and a passivity—that together are one and the same thing, *the thing of sense*: but this thing is such that its reality is nothing other than its dissemination.

If *I want to say*, this means, above all, that I want to say *to myself* and, thus, immediately, that I want to say *to you*, that I want to *say "I" to you* and, thus, immediately, to *say "you" to you*, to you, who, in my wanting are, therefore, already the one who says "you" to me to call upon me to say "I" and to say "I" to you.

*

Writing—whose name recalls an incision (*scribo, skripat, scaripha*)—is quite precisely the name of the disjunctive spacing in which and through which sense can reply to itself: desire itself, send itself, and refer to itself indefinitely from singular point to singular point—which also means from singular sense to singular sense (from Homer—who no doubt was himself not just one—to his reader Plato, to his reader Virgil, to his reader Augustine, to his reader Joyce, and so on to his millions of millions of readers and rewriters, respondents, and correspondents). Writing incises the shapeless mass in which, without it, neither mouth nor ear would be opened. Every written work is a mouth/ear that exchanges with itself, calls to itself, hears itself, and replies to itself: *aoidos, thea*!

*

The one who writes responds to sense: he is, to the extent that he writes, the response to the call of sense or, rather, the "response-in-call" of sense. But this sense—*thea*—to which it responds, also responds to it. The *aoidos* is responding for *thea*: he is the only one who attests to her presence and her voice. His call to her song bears witness to her presence, which has no other attestation. The *aoidos* is the respondent for *thea*, he answers on her behalf and for her and, thus, he is responsible for her—and with her, for everything that we can hear from her.

If the responsible one is the one who responds not *to* but *for* or *on behalf of*, it is because he is the one who thereby agrees, indirectly or mediately and belatedly—belatedly, but promised, engaged—to respond *to* that which could be demanded concerning that for which or the one for whom the responsible assumes responsibility. The one responsible takes charge of and assumes responsibility for another's commitment—the commitment that another cannot himself assume—or the commitment that the present state of things makes it impossible to assume knowingly: for example, by stating that I'm responsible for a project, I assume the unforeseeable that it contains. Responsibility is the anticipated response to questions, demands, and interpellations not yet formulated, and not exactly foreseeable.

He who writes makes himself responsible for absolute sense. He commits himself to no less than the totality and the infinity of that sense. At the same time, he bears witness to the existence of *thea* and assumes her desire: the desire he assumes from *thea* and the desire that *thea* herself is.

As witness to *thea's* existence, he declares himself to be her *aoidos*, that is, her *hermeneut*. The hermeneut is not initially the one who deciphers and decodes significations, although he may sometimes be called upon to do so—and to redo them endlessly or up to the point where all signification frays to the point of exhaustion and escapes through the very incision of writing. The hermeneut is not initially the one who signifies *that which* is said: he is the one who carries the desire to say further. The hermeneut stands in for the subject of that desire: he presents *thea* and allows her to be heard in the very voice—his own voice—through which he convokes her. He allows that voice to be heard singularly each time.[4]

But in this way, he who writes does not only bear witness to the existence of *thea*, he also bears witness to her nature and that she is entirely made of this sharing of voices of which he is, he (or she) who writes, a part, a moment, an accent, and a sense alongside so many others.

By responding to the desire of sense and, thus, to sense as desire, by acceding to that desire and allowing himself to be possessed by it, the one who writes assumes responsibility for the totality and infinity of sense as sharing of itself. Sense is shared and does nothing other than that: it opens the continuous and discontinuous circulation, the exchange of the inexchangeable and always singular desire to say. This desire is inexchangeable, for what it desires is not the communication of a signification, it is the cut and the touch of a singular truth.

What happens to sense at each point or singular moment—in each writing—is not the fulfillment of a moment that one final instance could enhance and capitalize upon in some final satisfaction of sense (completed exegesis, closed interpretation, sense made current forever). It is neither a moment nor an end in the trial of sense—and in this sense, there is no trial of sense: there is only its desire and its sharing. What happens to the singular point is the singular itself as the scansion of truth in sense.

The one who writes cannot fail to adopt, while he writes, Rimbaud's words: "There's no doubt about it, an oracle, I tell you."[5] He utters these words without arrogance of any kind, but also without confining them to the derisive angle of a subjectivity. Here, certitude is the truth of engagement and responsibility in, and for, sense. The oracle is the one who speaks in the name of the gods. This oracle—the writing oracle—speaks in the name of the divinity, always the same, *thea*, the one without a name, the one who does not even have the unpronounceable name and who is "divine" in no sense other than the sense in which her truth is shared, here and now, in this singular speech that undertakes to open the mouth (*oraculum*) to let sense pass—or better: who undertakes to open the mouth to sense, in both senses of the word.[6]

No doubt, singular truth does not arise for any occurrence of speech or writing. An "oracle" is not the one who thinks he is an oracle, nor the one who decides to become one. (For they enclose themselves in the representation of a "me"—which is a generality with the appearance of particularity—rather than opening themselves up to the singular referral of an "I.")

Truth can come to sense only if it is given access to its cut and its touch. This touch that cuts, that incises with writing undifferentiated space and the closed mouth, can only come from outside. This outside is not that of an authority or a spirit that breathes. It is the outside in which and for which responsibility has engaged itself: this outside in which there is nothing and in whose silent breast no god, no muse, no genius keeps watch over—or observes. It is this silence of the outside that holds all authority and exhales all inspiration.

In one sense—in one quite initial sense—this outside is that of absolute sense itself to the extent that it is foreign to any signification and, therefore, primarily to language itself: to language, in any case, formed, composed, and articulated in the order of significations received and even possible.

Truth arises from language already lost or yet to come. It comes from the voice that desires itself and seeks itself behind the voice—at the bottom of the throat, where the incision exposes an initial separation, which rises to the lips but which the lips have not yet known. It arrives like a yet-to-come of language: an unheard-of language, a figure of language that will only occur this once, an inflection, an accent, or a *style*—the incision engraved by a stylus. This is not a carving, it is truly an incision made in conventional language by the blade of an outside that consists simultaneously of non-language and language-yet-to-come or a desire for language.

The "style" of truth or truth as style owes nothing to ornament nor to the solicitation and exploitation of available significations. It can only come from outside—the touch and cut of an outside that is properly the outside of all signification, which is, thus, sense outside itself, the truth of sense as its infinite excess or its bottomless fault.

*

To come from the outside, to respond to this outside and answer for it, the incision must owe something to chance, to surprise, to the *kairos*, the favorable moment whose favor consists only in offering itself to the one who is exposed to the outside, and who, as a result, has come to *no longer want his wanting-to-say*: to let this desire be touched by the favor of an excess for every possible "saying."

But in allowing oneself to be disposed to this favor, to its rarity, a withdrawal of language is required. One must have been led to a point before language, where language itself already knows—always already knows, there where it is formed, there where a being liable for sense is outlined, a being susceptible to sense—that there is, once and for all, nothing to say, nothing that doesn't envelop in some way a nothing of signification and that, through this nothing, touches the thing itself, the thing *in itself*, which is to say, the thing outside and *the thing from the outside*.

The one who writes responds to this thing and responds for this thing. The thing itself is *thea*: it is sense and the desire to say, it is the infinite sharing of saying. It is not the inert mass that would remain outside language as a "real" that language was unable to reach. No, it is the outside that language itself incises in itself and presents in every truth to which it gives rise or to which it sets fire.

Language is knowing—and, therefore, it is the knowledge itself of writing: not what writing knows how to do, nor what it might know in order to write (like an "art of writing"), but the knowledge that writing *is in the process of writing*. It is the knowledge of that for which it bears witness. It bears witness to this—that sense, because it is going and coming, because it is call and response, is given or arises in withdrawal or in excess: withdrawal or excess for every signification that arrests and appeases desire and its response, the response that can in turn be nothing but another desire and the desire of an other. *I* who desire *you* and who desires that *you* say *I* to him and that, in saying *I* to him, you say *you* to him in turn.

In this dizzying constriction, the knowledge of writing is hidden—which is to say, the knowledge that it is the instrument or is recognized as such. The one who writes knows the desire of the other and also knows that this knowledge must be divided from itself so it can be what it is: response, engagement in the truth of this not-knowing.

2000

Body—Theater

Every time I come into the world, every day, therefore, my pupils open upon what there can be no question of calling a spectacle, for I am immediately caught, mixed up in, drawn forward by all the forces in my body, which makes its way in this world, which incorporates its space, its directions, its resistances, its openings, and which moves in this perception for which it is only the point of view from which this perceiving, which is also acting, is organized. Like any point, the point of view has no dimension. And it is, as we know, a blind spot, a stain that enables perspectives, relationships, near and far, to arrange themselves around it. This dark vanishing point resides within me, but within in the sense of the back of the room, the background I could represent as a point, as a non-space lodged immediately behind the space that develops like my head, my skull, my back, and all that within-itself by which a perceiving and acting body knows it is carried forth and projected.

Concerning this point, therefore, there is no possible spectacle, only engagement, the free-for-all of the world, attraction and repulsion, crossing and stopping, holding and detachment, capture and release. To be in the world is the opposite of being in the spectacle. It is to be inside, not before. Moreover, what we have grown accustomed to calling, even outside philosophy, "being in the world," translated from the German *in der Welt sein*, by which Heidegger sought to signify an *in*, a "*dans*," which is not exactly one of inclusion—of a "subject" in a "world" that would preexist—but of the co-belonging of the two and, more specifically, in the manner of what he referred to as "being-thrown"—*Geworfensein*—in which can be heard the thrust, the projection into this fall that results in "finding oneself there" and its delineation—*Entwurf*—the projection of a gesture, of a possible aspect of existing—existence itself being nothing other than the incessant requestioning of its own outlines.

I've taken this short detour through Heidegger to indicate the extent to which, in this most powerful insistence on the primacy of "being-in," of being as given over to, launched, devoted to, mobilized in its being by the very fact of being, we also find as little concern as possible for the phenomena of representation—which demands a "subject" for whom it takes place, a subject that can only be, with respect to the existent, perfectly secondary, derivative and limited (for example, subject of knowledge, subject of a concept or vision). To the extent that it thereby concerns dissociating, as profoundly as possible, the order of existing from the orders of knowing, representing, picturing, and also measuring and evaluating, shifting them all, without denying them, but at the last moment, upon condition of existing, we must acknowledge that which has initiated, irreversibly, the era in which the "subject" found himself "pulled away from"—like Rimbaud's peninsulas—unmoored, detached from "ancient parapets" and cast, projected toward another moment of this quite singular destiny for which we are, we and the world, the infinite destination.

However, this sendoff, without hesitation, without return, doesn't prevent us from noting that something is lacking in this description of existing. Not only are we not prevented from but are even led, very precisely and also very insistently, to identify this lack. What it consists of can be stated very simply: existence also wants to be part of the show. This is part of its project, its projection, its being-thrown. It is part of its being in the world.

No doubt Heidegger wasn't unaware of this—it would be too easy to assume he was shortsighted in this regard. However, this need for staging was never addressed by him as such. Presumably, it was part and parcel of the attention he gave to art in general, to poetry in particular, but at no time did that attention involve theater. This was pointed out by Philippe Lacoue-Labarthe, for whom it became a decisive element in the distance he insisted on maintaining from the depth of his closeness to Heidegger.

In particular, he pointed out the extent to which, in Heidegger's consideration of Hölderlin, theater is never mentioned, while its importance for the translator of Sophocles and the author of the tragedy, *The Death of Empedocles*, cannot fail to be obvious.

I won't go any deeper into pursuing the questions that concerned Lacoue-Labarthe. They're his. But I do note the following: the existent wants to make an appearance, and this wish (desire, impulse, what have you) belongs to existing itself. We'll see shortly, if possible, how to justify this second proposition. But for now, let's examine the first.

I want to return to the scene of my arrival in the world. Each time it occurs, everyday, therefore, my eyelids open not only on the non-spectacle of the world perceived, experienced, acted. They also open, at the same time, on this darkness I initially referred to as a blind spot located within or behind me: thus, they open not for me, for my gaze, but for the possible gaze of an other, a multitude of others. A possible and, no doubt, certain gaze, for even in complete solitude, I am also part of this multitude of others. I am a part of it, at least as one who knows he is not allowed to see that on which this small double curtain has risen: my gaze. But in doing so, I am like a spectator unable to find a seat in the theater but who nonetheless knows what he's missing: within that closed circle and against a background presented against the darkness of the city, the curtain rises on a scene, that is, on the very space of a coming to presence. The number of characters, the intensity of the lighting, the construction of the set matter little: it is solely a question of a coming to presence and of *representation* in the sense, that is, of an intensification of presence.

When this other is not myself but an other self who, for his part, must face the same impenetrability about himself—who knows he is held to the same impossibility of seeing himself and knowing his "self," other than through the unique vanishing point of his blind spot—when the other, therefore, sees and hears me, he knows that he is at the theater. Not the spectacle we call "world," by which we most frequently designate a kind of panorama of perception arrayed before a subject and that, in the final analysis, is part of the being in the world of that subject, but rather a spectacle in the sense of the theater: he sees that a presence is staged and presented to him. He receives, more than he perceives, the intensification of this presence, its staging.

There is no need to have recourse to the weightier meanings of these words—"spectacle," "staging," "mise-en-scène"—and to consider all the ways roles are assumed, the showiness and swagger, the ways of exhibiting oneself and making oneself stand out, the ostentation and posing. It is sufficient to experience, as simply and discreetly as possible, the following: that what we call a "subject" comes into presence, that is, once again, into "representation," according to the intensive and, in fact, originary and proper value of the word. And in this sense, a subject is a body.

*

Need it be spelled out? The subject thrown into the world, engaged in the world, for all that, is not yet a presence. Though he is distinguishable from the subject of knowledge, nonetheless, he is something of an immaterial point, viewpoint or decision point, bifurcation, the branching of acts, behaviors, thoughts. In this sense, the "*da*" of Heideggerian *Dasein*, the "there" of existing, harbors an ambiguity: if there is opening and spatiality in the sense of the ex-position by which he ek-sists, he is at the same time, and this in spite of the desire of Heidegger himself, limited and, in some way, held within the subjectivity of his "ever-mineness" (*Jemeinigkeit*). Here, "subjectivity" does not signify relativity and interiority of viewpoint but only and primarily—and once again in spite of what Heidegger wants to attempt to say—the immateriality of this limited "my" position, the summit of the angle or articulation of the decision of existence. In a word, he is not body. He doesn't achieve his own body.

That is why this subject is no more theatrical than any of the subjects of representation in the ordinary sense (idea, image, signification) or the subjects of knowledge, action, judgment, even subjects of relationship and affect.

In truth, for as long as we've thought in terms of a "subject," we think, whether we want to or not, in terms of an incorporeal subject—even though this substance becomes subject strictly speaking, as Hegel intended, that is, the relation to self passing through a self-estrangement and self-alienation before its return. Nor with Hegel do we really touch upon the theater and, maybe, we never touch upon philosophy either (except in Aristotle, but that's another story and I don't want to go into it here). On the contrary, we're always more or less in the incorporeal configuration of a projection point (including the projection of self) connected with signi-fications that are themselves incorporeal by definition.

In this sense, there is always only one and that is also why the question of the other presents itself with such complexity when we ask how a subject is able to recognize another subject, how the *ego* relates to the *alter ego*. For, starting with the one we never reach the other. Heidegger himself was aware of this, which challenges every mode of introducing the other except that of the originary given of a *Mitdasein*, of a being-there-with and a being-with-the-other-there. But this "with"—to which I am far from denying that it should be assigned the greatest importance and which is even, in the form of the *common*, no doubt that which all modernity has the most difficulty conceptualizing—this "with" again always risks remaining a side-by-side of subjects. Nor am I challenging the importance of mingling, of copresence and compearance; or the importance of this other dimension, orthogonal in a way, which is that of the face-to-face and which refers us to the tradition of the "I and thou" (Buber) and the "face of the other" (Levinas).

What is important to state here is of another order, prior in a sense and outside any form of compearance, whether side-by-side or face-to-face. It concerns the condition by which presence can be. The presence of the world, of course, but what is the world if not a disposition of presences, it being understood that in the "disposition" there is an element of the topological—simple spacing—and dynamics—coming and going, arrival and departure, presence never consisting of pure position, of the situation with its coordinates, but of exposition, presentation, arrival, approach, and distancing? The word "presence" is constructed from a "pre" of proximity and not anteriority. That is why it is temporal as well as spatial: neither before nor after, but nearby, arriving nearby, and the spatiality of "nearby" is itself a temporal spatiality, an arrival, an approach.

*

We find ourselves, therefore, in the order of the body and the theater. The body is that which comes, approaches a stage—and the theater is that which provides a place for the approach of a body.

This is what happens when I come to the world—everyday, every time. "I" do not come like the ever incorporeal punctuality of the subject of enunciation, of any subject for that matter. We could even say "I" never *comes*. It remains situated in the absolute anteriority of its punctuality. On the other hand, its eyes open and its mouth and ears, and its body stretches, moves away, arranges itself. Of course, it can be said that "I" exits from the mouth, from "its" mouth, and this is indeed true. But what comes, approaches, touches us, from the other, is the mouth, the voice, just as it is the eyes that approach, their gaze, their way of staring or foreseeing.

This is very much like the Creation according to Artaud—how could we not be in his company? Along at least one of his trajectories, it is through the Creation—with a capital "C"—that Artaud deduced, if I can put it this way, the theater. Without focusing on the alchemical symbolism that served as a prelude to this consideration, I simply note the following:

having posited that the theater forms the Double "not of this direct, everyday reality of which it is gradually being reduced to a mere inert replica" but "another typical and dangerous reality . . . [that] is not human but inhuman."[1]

It is then found that this reality is not another but that of Creation, in the sense that it does its work in two phases. The first is the act "of one Will alone—and *without conflict*."[2] During the second, "that of the difficulty and of the Double, that of matter and the materialization of the idea."[3]

It's easy to see that these two phases are logical rather than chronological. There is the moment of unity without conflict, which is, all things considered, simply the "idea," let's call it the principle and decision of the existence of the world, and there is the moment of actualization, which arises not so much as another phase but as the real opening of the world—of the "Cosmos in turmoil," as the text notes. The Cosmos is rife with conflict. This implies that the real is conflict laden and that it is—a detailed reading of the text would show this—precisely because of matter, that is, the "materialization of the idea," which we can also understand as the "solid and opaque expression of light itself, of rarity, and of irreducibility."[4] It is a question, therefore, of the material gold of the alchemical transmutation, itself a symbol of spiritual gold.

But—and this is a key point—a necessary symbol. I'm not examining the reasons for this necessity since I don't have to penetrate Artaud's logic. I'm simply stating, with him, that there is an opacity, a material density indispensable to the presentation of that which is in play in the Creation or in the Cosmos—as creation and cosmos—to the extent that the conflict belongs to whatever is in play. It is the cosmic conflict (metaphysical, he says elsewhere) that demands to be presented as "*drama*." Why must it be presented? Because of itself it is or it brings about the necessity of presentation.

A body does not consist simply of a particular concretion, an accumulation or local densification; the materialization Artaud speaks of obviously also implies the distinction and multiplicity of bodies. While the idea may appear to be whole, that of which it is the idea can only be plural. (I'll risk stating that this is exactly what Artaud expresses intuitively with his distinction between two "phases" of creation.) In truth, the idea of the cosmos is the idea of plurality and there is no creation that is not distinction, separation, spacing before all else.

But spacing itself is not a simple, inert interval. It is exposition. The void—to put it crudely—between bodies is not a negative thickness any more than other modes of spacing or incorporeality are. Here, the Stoic theory of incorporeals is relevant, which for them are four in number: the void, time, place, and *lekton*, the sayable or the expressible. The spacing I am speaking of combines the void and place, the first allowing for the distinction of places, and time is nothing other than the spacing of sense, the distension by which it tends toward itself (or, to put it differently, the signifier toward the signified).

Thus, bodies are exposed not by accident but by essence. The *disposition* is the nature of their position in being and the *dis-* carries with it the *ex-*: bodies are disposed *partes extra partes*, following the characteristic of extension in Descartes. But here as well exteriority is not the simple lack of interiority or presence-to-self; it is the condition of the co-presence of bodies, or their compearance, which is simply the rule and the effect of creation.

I might go so far as to say that the theater has already begun in the intersidereal spaces or even in the infinitesimal spacing of particles, for *drama* has already occurred there, as Artaud states, that is, action above all, the act of an accomplishment that responds to an expectation (service, religious worship, responsibility). The expectation is, in effect, already that of sense—of the "sayable" of the compearance of the things we call "cosmos."

But suffice it to say that the speaking body comes among bodies as the manifestation of this expectation. And this time, with the speaking body, the theater is already truly given or pre-given.

This body presents itself by opening itself up—this is called "sense." But while they are receiving sensory information, the senses are also transmitting information on their own behalf. Once again, the eye sees but also watches. By watching it exposes, it casts before itself something of what it is for it to see and be seen. And always, in addition to this, knows it is incapable of seeing itself. All this is given in a glance of the eyes, where, as Proust writes, "the flesh becomes the mirror and gives us the illusion that it allows us, more than through the other parts of the body, to approach the soul."[5]

Proust's sentence, all things considered, is not without strangeness, for while it is possible for me to see myself in another's eyes, it is not this optical mirror function that justifies the sentence. Rather, it expresses the fact that in the eyes of the other, I see myself gazing and, consequently, also gazed upon—and always in keeping with this fundamental extra-version that will never let me see myself and which, therefore, exposes me absolutely.

But "the other parts of the body" as Proust writes also provide approaches to the soul. My hands, my legs, my neck, my postures, my aspects, my gestures, my appearance or mannerisms, the timbre of my voice, everything we might call the pragmatics of the body, everything no doubt, everything without exception over the entire surface of my skin and everything with which I can cover it or ornament it, all of it exposes, announces, declares, addresses something: ways of coming toward or moving away, forces of attraction or repulsion, tensions for taking or releasing, for swallowing or rejecting.

"My skin thus becomes the theater of itself," writes Mohammed Khaïr-Eddine. He continues: "Which explains the fact that an actor or simple speaker can be moved by impulses whose original signification he himself is unaware of."[6]

*

In all the ways it has of opening and closing, of placing and displacing itself, of arranging itself, imposing itself, or being evasive, a body undertakes a drama that has nothing of the "personal" or "subjective" about it but which is, each time, the singular dramatization of its singular detachment amidst other bodies—cast along with them into the cosmos.

The affects are secondary here (love, hate, power, betrayal, rivalry, etc.), merely the modulations and transcriptions of the great primordial tension between bodies: how they are brought together and repelled, how they are caught and released. In other words, how they relate to one another, not "through" the incorporeal that distinguishes them—but like that incorporeal itself. Place, time, sense, and void ("void" should be understood as the absence of bodies that have disappeared or are not yet born) are the material and force of the relation. (It goes without saying that I am not making a distinction here between the relations of bodies among themselves and the relation of each body to itself—each of these relations passes through the other, such is the logic of compearance and (re)presentation.)

A scene is a place in which is engendered and is taken the inherent time of a presentation (of a body: this complement could be elided) as thrusts of sense between the voids of their fortuitous existences, a place where this fortuitousness itself assumes dramatic necessity and where the void assumes the compendial consistency of sense.

The *skene*, as we know, was initially a flimsy, temporary shelter in which to withdraw, sleep, drink, celebrate among friends, for example, on a boat. It's a place of intimacy and it is before this place, become the dark backdrop of the theater, the other side of the set, it is before the *proskenion* that the actors introduce themselves, leaving through one of the entrances to the set. (I don't want to linger over the "obscene," whose etymology is too

contested to provide anything other than the appeal of resonance. Nonetheless, it remains that, far from semantics, all exhibition tends toward the
obscene.)

Before the intimate shelter that, in a way, hovers outside space, in a
blind spot, there opens the space in which leaving is enacted, where the
body stands before itself—for its entire presence is there, in that outside
self that does not detach itself from an "inside" but that only evokes it as the
impossible, the void outside of place, time, and sense. "Self" thus becomes:
character, role, mask, manner, appearance, exhibition, presentation—that
is, singular variation of the dehiscence and distinction by which there is a
body, a presence.

In the poem entitled "The Theater of Cruelty," Artaud writes:

> There, where there is metaphysics,
> mysticism,
> implacable dialectics,
> I hear the great colon
> of my hunger
> writhing
> and exposed to the pulsing of its dark life
> I dictate to my hands
> > their dance,
> > to my feet
> > or to my arms.[7]

"My hunger" is my appetite, my desire, my impulse, the one that triggers the pulsing of that intimate, intestinal "dark life" that transmits
cadence, rhythm, all this "dance" that responds to the profound beating—
"metaphysical, mystical"—or to the "writhing" that responds to nothing
other—"implacable dialectic"—than birth itself, creation in its materialization, in coagulation, condensation, and distinction.

That this dance is not exclusively physical but belongs to the text as
well, to theatrical speech, and especially to the exchange of words, directed
speech, and that theatrical literature gets its most intrinsic traits from this,
I won't take the time to examine here. What is important is that, in the
theater, the text is bodied, it is body. And that is why we can say that in the
theater "something happens" really, as Claudel has one of his characters
(an actress) say:

> It's not worth going to the theater to see something that happens. You
> understand! That really happens! That begins and that ends![8]

What happens "really" and what begins and ends is what never happens for the subject whose birth and death, origin and escape are suspensions. But this is what happens to bodies that effectively arrive, that separate themselves and singularize themselves, then disappear into totality or into nothingness. What happens in this way, and what goes away—but this going away is also an arrival—is a presence. Which is to say, a sense. We could say: a "subject" is a lost goal of sense, a "body" is active sense. In the act of passage, between creation and de-creation.

This passage presents itself by presenting its arrival and departure, by introducing the beginning and end of sense: a sense that, consequently, cannot be fulfilled through signification but is the sense of passage, of the act of passing. Sense of the entire duration of a presence and, like that duration, highlighted by the rise and fall of the curtain, that is, the non-thickness of the truth that falls through sense.

What we don't know, then, this appearing-disappearing, happens there, in the space-time of the place where sense expresses itself between bodies—because sense can only take place "between" and from one to the other, can only be felt from one by the other. This space-time is what we call "scene," it is the *proskenion* on which bodies advance to present what every body does as body: present itself in its appearing and disappearing, present the action—the "drama"—of a sharing of sense.

There is beginning and end, there is—it is the scene itself, which opens itself and closes itself—the time characteristic of this (re)presentation. Time that is not succession but passage, brief dilation of a moment withdrawn from the passage of time (thus, we can imagine, in the classical rule of the three unities, something less formal than there appears to be).

Jean Magnan places the following words in the mouth of a character referred to as a "creature of the theater":

Here, between these three walls,
mirrorless that leads me to believe in
some kind of fourth,
time. Time. Time.

Fictive time. Personal time. Tangible
blend of the two. 50% Arabica.
Theater time. In its pure state.

Insomniac.
And sugar free.[9]

As in Proust, from whom the expression is taken, "pure time" is the time of (re)presentation, true presentation. Time withdrawn from the course of time, nighttime insomnia surrounding the theater, where actors, stage, and audience fall with the curtain.

Within the precise—as if instantaneous—duration of this time, bodies speak words to one another. The actors exchange them so that there might be directed at us, the audience, precisely that which involves directed speech. And it cannot involve anything else. Heiner Müller writes, "What is not said cannot be staged."[10]

A spoken word is a corporeal word. It is less signification than voice, and with the voice—or in silence—gesture, posture, bodily appeal. Here, speaking bodies maintain a bodily speech. In this way, they present themselves for what they are: presences whose spacing opens tensions—"conflicts" as Artaud put it—whose interplay informs the drama.

Play: here, the word refers collectively to articulation, the interconnectedness of directed speech, and the fact that it is interpreted. This dual meaning of play responds to the duality that in fact finds itself in play: presence must be presented because it is not simply given: it gives itself. Which is to say that it plays a role in the intensity—tension, intention—of the address. There is no neutral presence that could be intensified here and there. But presence calls for intensity—a body is an intensity.

Representation in the theatrical sense and in the sense—historically first—of bringing to presence is the intensive interplay of presence. My body is theater first of all because its very presence is double—it outside or before and me inside or behind (in fact, nowhere). All presence is doubled when presenting itself, and the theater is as ancient and, no doubt, very nearly as widespread as the speaking body.

*

Whether expressed by Artaud and his Double, Lacoue-Labarthe and his "originary *mimesis*," or François Regnault claiming, in Lacanian mode, that "the Theater presents the Discourse of the Other," theater is the duplication of presence as coming to presence of presents or as presentation of their being-present.[11] The body is itself, already, presentation: a body doesn't simply consist of a "being"—whatever we might pack into the word—it articulates that being in appearing or indexes it to a being-*there* that implies its copresence—distance, proximity, interaction—with other bodies. Theatricality proceeds from the declaration of existence—and existence itself is the being declared, presented, not withheld in itself. It is being giving sign of itself, allowing itself to feel not by simple perception but as a thickness and a tension.

That is why Hamlet can say, "The players cannot keep counsel; they tell all."[12] The specific sense of this statement within the theatrical scheming of the Prince of Denmark can only amplify its general scope. Theater is the cessation of the secret if the secret must be that of the being-in-itself or that of a soul withdrawn into intimacy. It is the in-itself itself or intimacy as such that steps out and exposes itself. Nothing less than the "world as theater" as we have known it ever since Calderon and Shakespeare, but one that our entire tradition—at least since Plato's cave—has brooded over, but this "world as theater" *as truth*, just as much as and because the body shows itself to be truth of the soul: truth that pushes itself onto the stage or, more accurately, truth that stages.

At this point, it is no longer possible to avoid returning to what underlies and, perhaps, has always supported a theater of any kind—namely, something like a form of worship.

Brecht said that it was out of religion that tragedy was born, and in this he wanted to emphasize the decisive character of that "exit."[13] Yet, this also meant overlooking what every exit brings with it. A religion is not simply a ritual in the sense of the formalism of the observance. It is, first and foremost, a form of behavior compatible with an encounter with something like a mystery, a secret, a reserved part that can be approached through the religious act (we approach it and it approaches us). It is the coming-to-presence of that which of itself remains hidden.

Religious belief is, thus, always organized around the expectation that something will arrive, that something will take place, be produced, and appear within some essential nonappearance. This is called "sacrifice"— we make sacred, we make the sacred. The theatrical body is the body that makes its own presence sacred—we could say its soul, its creation as well, its cosmic inscription, its glory, its enjoyment, its suffering, its dereliction; in a word, its compearance as sign among signs.

All religions involve theatricality, even if the theater is what it is only by abandoning all religions (including its own or their own, as it does all the time). But what remains religious in the theater, what, in a very specific sense, is sacrificed there (or is *ludified*, to refer once more to Roman comedy), is the speaking body—corporeal speech, not the story but the presentation, the signalization of bodies and, therefore, the gestural, as well, and all the physics, even the physiology, energetics and dynamics—the "biomechanics" to play with Meyerhold's term—that in fact *make* the scene.

It should also be said, not so much that religious worship precedes the theater and creates it but that the body-theater precedes all forms of religious worship and all scenes. Theatricality is neither religious nor artistic—even if religion and art stem from it. It is the condition of the body that is itself the condition of the world: the space of compearance of bodies, of their attractions and repulsions. "Every culture has given itself, in spectacle, the highest summits of the mastery of bodies in motion," writes Yves Lorelle in the beginning of his study of the body and the stage.[14] What we need to be concerned about is that a "culture" consists, precisely, in the possibility of assembling, of forming a mode for spectacle, that is, of presenting and signifying that once there is a world, there are bodies that encounter one another, that separate, that attract one another, repel one another, reveal themselves to one another while revealing behind and around themselves the incorporeal night of their provenance.

2011

After Tragedy

Here in America—perhaps not "in the U.S.," but in America, as Jacques Derrida states in "deconstruction is America," that is, the world we still have to discover— here, then, Philippe did have many friends. Many of them are here. Some have passed away, like Eugenio Donato, who was close to him, like Danielle Kormoz, who has been as well an American friend.

We never believe that one is dead. We know that he/she is, but we cannot believe it. Freud is wrong asserting that we cannot believe in our own death, for we believe in no death. This is beyond any belief, any sharing out, any mimesis and methexis.

But we are right. I believe Philippe is not dead, for I hear his voice within mine—like some other voices, the one of Jacques's own among them. Within what I will read for you, he is speaking, with and without me, for me, against me, apart from me, resounding forever in me.[1]

Five years ago, in Greece, I delivered the text I'm going to present to you today, which has, until now, been available only in Greek. Seven months ago, I presented it in German in Giessen, where the Institute for Theater Studies was honoring Philippe Lacoue-Labarthe. On the first occasion, I read it in Philippe's presence. The colloquium to which we had been invited was about tragedy "then and now" or "from the ancient Greeks until today," and it's this extension "until today" that made me decide to agree to speak about a subject I've rarely spoken about, generally leaving the field to Philippe. I had another reason to be in Stagire; we were also honoring a man who had recently passed away, Jean-Pierre Schobinger, a professor in Zurich, a long-time friend and great lover of Greece. Today, it is Philippe himself we are honoring—Philippe, whose disappearance is not exempt from the sense of the tragic that became the leading tonality of his thought and life—a life always painfully aware of its progression toward death. It was painful for him as well, as it is for any tradition whose tenacity or endurance continues to astonish me, to realize that he had arrived so long after tragedy, that is, after the moment we believe we were blessed to have been able to call—sing, play, interpret—the curse of mortals. That Greek moment when Homer had once been able to claim that the gods were plotting the destruction of mankind so it could then be recorded in poetry and song. In one mysterious and terrible sense, Philippe called down this will of the gods upon himself.

So here I am, six years later, in his absence as once before in his presence—I see him looking at me, a slight smile on his lips, thinking "yes, I know, Jean-Luc, I know what you're thinking about my nostalgia for the Greeks." We were in Stagire, the birthplace of Aristotle, chosen intentionally. Aristotle—whose theory of tragedy Philippe and I had so often discussed—arrived after tragedy itself. Long before us, of course, who appear at the end of this history, but already after the time of tragic song, which then had to be understood, reasoned, and justified. Aristotle is already a theoretician and historian of tragedy, but he is only the beginning of a very long history.

Yet this entire history—and the very concept of history as it came to be known long after Aristotle, consists essentially in coming *after*. The dimension of the *after* is constitutive and I might even go so far as to say congenital. The beginning or *arche*, the *proteron*, the *principium* or *initium*, by definition constitute that which escapes history or that which history can be sure of only by appropriating and deciding to be its own beginning, foundation, and origin. One or the other of these untenable postulates can be heard repeatedly throughout the history of philosophy, literature, and religion in the West. Either we are nostalgic for a forever-lost that, no doubt, never was; or we wish to bring about an absolutely-will-be that no form of presence could precede. In this way, memory and will are the two axes and the two figures of our relation to the impossible: to ourselves as aporia. Our aporia, our lack of a way out, is found in the birth that follows our absence without conveying us to anything other than the death that hollows out the *after*, until it erases even the possibility of considering a succession, posterity, or heritage. We all know how strong this belief was for Philippe, how *intense* it was, the way a wound can be.

It is in Greece that the fecund stomach, the *hystera*, took its name from what comes behind, after, as if to designate a perpetual ulteriority of provenance itself, an *after* for every *before*, or, to put it into the language of logicians, a permanent *hysteron-proteron*, in other words, a logical fault constitutive of our being. Just as this faulty reasoning consists in presenting as proof that which yet needs to be proven, the Western condition consists in assuming as being that which should have first been brought into being, and, thus, escape non-being. But we do not come from nothing and we do not lead (ourselves) to nothing. No provenance has been given to us, no destination, no exit is promised us. Thus, our condition or fundamental and intended constitution could be characterized as an *aporetic hysteria*. I wouldn't go so far as to say it's a pathology, which would assume I knew of a model of normality to compare it against. I will say that it is possibly less and possibly more than a pathology: for the West it may be opportunity itself, or its certain peril, and maybe, in both cases, it is now the entire world that goes with us into this aporetic hysteria, which writhes around and suffers, whether or not it manages to expose something like truth or sense there (unless aporetic hysteria is the last word of all our truth).

*

Under these conditions, the words "after tragedy" can assume an emblematic value, and for two reasons. Those two reasons are quite distinct, even contrary, but ultimately they converge.

The first reason is that among all the "afters" of the West (after the golden age, after the gods, after the pre-Socratic dawn, after myth, there are as many "afters" or "posts" each of which has been repeated several times throughout history, in the Late Greek mode, the Latin mode, Christian, re-emergent, progressive, romantic, and, finally, modern and postmodern, following the law of a generalized *post-x*), the "after" of tragedy occupies a particular and remarkable place. Our entire history has thought, and thought itself, "after tragedy," whether it was to dismiss said "tragedy" or, on the contrary, regret its passing and attempt to rediscover its truth. Certainly, we must also say that with tragedy the polis belongs to the same logic and the same chrono-logic of the "after." However, what we refer to as *democracy* still appears to us, no matter how minimally or badly, to represent a step forward following a bleak past and toward a promised future, whatever effort might still be required to render that democracy worthy of such a future.

On the other hand, tragedy appears to us as quintessential loss, whose return or replacement no longer seems possible. We can recite it, but not restore or reinvent it. Moreover, with tragedy it is theater as a whole that has wavered and grown concerned about itself for quite some time now. And we are well aware that the fates of both—of democracy and tragedy— are connected and that it wouldn't be impossible for the problems and fragility of the first to be expressed by the loss of the second. In that sense, whatever reform democracy might be capable of, it will find nothing and will not find itself if it continues to long for tragedy or for whatever it was that tragedy served as. (Wasn't this what Rousseau was talking about when he spoke of "civil religion"? The thing that democracy until today, and from the time of Rousseau, should have most obviously set aside or left fallow.)

According to this first reason, "after tragedy" would provide the formula of a threefold aporia—political, ethical, and aesthetic—that would require that we again consider, and once more with the associated costs, the risk in what we refer to as the loss of tragedy, that is, to conceive of that risk, if possible, other than as simple loss and aporetic hysteria without falling into the trap of resurrection (as Nietzsche, at one moment, wanted to believe in). Philippe kept all of this in mind simultaneously.

*

The second reason involves a very different use of words. "After tragedy" sounds to us like a familiar syntagm—terribly, tragically familiar—with two conjoint registers:

—On the one hand, it is a familiar expression for referring to the specific situation that follows a catastrophe (a drama, a tragedy—I'll return later to this confusion of words): an existence that drowns in the absurdity of accident or degradation, a love that tears itself apart, a ruined life, shattered dignity or loyalty; this situation is characterized by the lack of sense in every sense of the word, lack of direction and sensibility, apathy or hysteria, anxiety of aporia, the need for support and therapies that cannot get to the heart of the matter. To summarize, I would say that "after tragedy" evokes for us a situation in which grief itself is not possible or becomes manifestly and harshly infinite.

—On the other hand, the same formula haunts the history of the last century—if not already that of the late 19th century: at least since the first of the so-called world wars, the monstrosities of the camps, the gulags, genocide, "ethnic" cleansing, not to mention the increasingly less "natural" day-to-day catastrophes caused by fire, water, earth, cancers, or viruses—"after tragedy." The words "after Auschwitz" and "after Hiroshima," each with a different scope, have taken shape like two idiomatic emblems of this repetition, which did not end with them. To conclude, it is the entire twenty-first-century West that looks at itself and wonders what will happen "after the tragedy" that it itself has been, that it fomented and propagated throughout the world; but on this collective, political, and civilizational level, nothing occurs more consistently than it does on the level of the individual life. But here too, grief is impossible, here too, we are left with the need to retroactively confront a destruction that makes no sense, lacks provenance and truth. Let me point out the following: of all these dramas, representation (on stage, in memory, in interpretation) raises problems that no available form such as "tragedy" enables us to resolve, so that the question of their representation (their images, their stories) is continuously raised. It is also becoming increasingly clear that we cannot be satisfied with pointing out the guilty of history (here, a religion, there a policy, elsewhere, a people or an individual, an ideology, a technology); it is an entire history that is guilty of itself, and that is, therefore, beyond any assignable guilt. This is typical of the entire history of the West and, through it, the world, which shows itself to be a tragedy or a succession of tragedies, after each of which there is no "after" because there is certain to be another tragedy after the return, and the after turns into a before.

Here, we touch upon the point of contact between the two characteristic motives of the expression "after tragedy." For every history that appears as tragedy is also the history that represents itself as having bypassed tragedy. This contradiction between two uses of the term can only be explained by the incorrectness of one of them. This incorrectness, for that matter, is well known and when I previously neglected to focus on the necessary distinctions between "tragedy," "drama," and "catastrophe" (a word that is itself drawn from the tragic literary lexicon, but obviously given a different sense), to which I could have added "disaster" or "desolation," I knew that each of us, even those with a minimum of philological or philosophical knowledge, would refuse to remain deaf to these distinctions, because tragedy does not primarily represent a type of terrible event, even one of the worst, but names an entire structure of thought in the strongest sense of the word—the construction of sense, a system in the simplest sense of the word, or, if we prefer, a synergy and sympathy that form an inherent *ethos*. The tragic *ethos* cannot be reduced to the *pathos* of the one who is overcome by disaster or ruin.

But this points to the difficulty that results in the "tragedy" of our own history: if there is confusion or a misuse of meaning when we speak of the tragedy of the camps, of September 11, the tragedy of Rwanda or Nigeria, the hunger of children or their prostitution, it is because we are unable to connect our sloppy usage of the word to its core usage. And we are unable to do this because the inherent sense of the word escapes us. Our history is also the history of the various interpretations of tragedy itself, but as both an enrichment (no matter how contradictory) and a permanent return to a lost and uninterpretable secret. Whether we speak of Aristotelian *katharsis* and the successive values associated with it, of French classicism, German or English romanticism, Hegel, Schelling, Hölderlin, Nietzsche, Benjamin, Bataille, or Lacoue-Labarthe—to restrict myself to these names— regardless of the text, tragedy leaves behind a hard kernel, a simple dried castoff that bears at least this minimal signification: whatever the case with tragic truth, it is no longer ours, no matter how close to it, no matter how intimate anyone might be with it, and no *ethos*, no *techne poietike* can restore to us the possibility of experiencing it here and now, as a function of our life as a people or a polis.

Each and every one of us can share the pathetic and ethical issue found in Oedipus Rex, Antigone, or Medea (if it is even permitted to use "issue" in the singular, for we are confronted with a series of indefinitely varied accents modulated by so many different interpretive contexts). But we are not—to summarize with a word that couldn't be more appropriate—participating in a *liturgy* of tragedy: we do not participate in an institution or a service of shared culture and behavior, customs and structure, by which we might designate, indistinctly, syncretically, a politics and an ethics, a theology and aesthetics. But neither can we designate what tragedy might well have been for those who were not only its contemporaries but its actors, its authors, its spectators, together and in turn. That the figure of Oedipus has been able to make the transition from two plays by Sophocles to the position of signal and signifier for the personal investigations of psychoanalysis, that the son of Laius and interlocutor of the sphinx could be transformed from father into a point of reference, says a great deal (even if we don't know what it says) about fathers in general, about enigmas, about the polis, about knowledge, and about the power of our present cultural configurations.

*

There is, therefore, something like an unattainable exemplarity of tragedy. Its exemplarity signifies that we think (represent, imagine, dream possibly: it matters little compared to the ordeal being played out before us) we can or should relate everything to something associated with it; that is, we must think that within it the elementary knot of existence is tied, the one that attaches it to its own insignificance or misfortune. But that it is unattainable means that this knot can no longer be tied for us (except, as I've just mentioned, individually, which here means precisely nothing, for existence is essentially non-individual—another thing that tragic knowledge seems to have known).

Our situation is such, then, that when I read in the newspaper—to take an example at hand at the moment I am writing this—that the chief rabbi of England has said "I consider the current situation quite tragic," in a context in which he opposes Israel's policies in the name of Judaism, I say to myself that the "tragic" (in the sense of the disastrous and despairing) lies precisely in the fact that this word, "tragic," represents, for the rabbi, that there is no recourse, no truth other than that of a misfortune that will soon be irreparable. He has, we have no recourse to a higher (or more profound) truth upon which the "tragic" itself might unfold, as upon a possibility of making sense, in spite of everything, even if it were a question of making sense of the abandonment of sense.

Yet it is something like this that Greek (and perhaps classical) tragedy represents for us, even if we are unable to appropriate for ourselves this very specific mode—which we claim to have lost—of recourse, this mode we could refer to as one of recourse without safety. For, if tragedy is what it is for us (if not what it was for itself), it is so to the extent that, in it, ruin is conjoined to a truth rather than leading to truth in the wake of ruin, as is the case with disaster or modern dereliction.

How is this or was this possible? This is what we are unable to grasp and, yet, it is something we can at least approach from the outside. Such an approach is made necessary on the basis of the following: tragedy as well, already, comes *after*. It comes after religion, that is, after sacrifice. But coming after, it does not simply go elsewhere. For a moment, at least, the period of its existence between Thespis and Aristotle, it represents for us something like a delicate and unstable balance, yet maintained, between the after of sacrifice and the before of our desolation. It is with this double value that I would like to linger a moment, with a simple thought based on no philological or theoretical science of tragedy but simply on the consideration of the following, which I will condense into the following expression: for us, the "tragic" is no longer and can no longer be "a tragedy."

*

How can we characterize this moment of suspense, of uncertain balance, that tragedy represents for us? Berthold Brecht wrote, and I quote from memory, "When we say that tragedy arose from religious worship, we forget to say that it is by leaving it that it became tragedy." Brecht was right to reject a religious vision of tragedy, for nothing is clearer than the exit from the pre-Western religious world of which tragedy is one element, along with politics and philosophy. However, his sentence leaves open the question of what the "exit" from religious worship might be and, therefore, the way in which it introduces tragedy—or theater—in its specificity. In a sense, it's a particular case of a general reflection on the matter of "provenance," of a "results from" in which we always find, simultaneously, a break and a transmission. It is this double articulation that must be identified between religious worship and theater or, more specifically, between religious circumstance and theatrical event.[2]

By leaving worship, tragedy exited religion. Leaving religion signifies leaving a regime of social culture in which there is communication with the gods. This regime assumes the presence of gods and the possibility of establishing connections with them. Worship consists in implementing those connections. The gods with whom worshipers connect are not only present—they are *presences*, par excellence, active powers, tutelary or menacing, the Immortals to whom mortals confide their threatened fate, uneasy about propitiating their strength. The cult invokes these Presents, it convokes them, sometimes even provokes them while turning itself into the advocate of the mortal who, through the cult, enters into the presence of the Presents. The religious act is participation in ad-vocation or ad-oration: speech addressed to presence.

This speech is participatory: it takes part in the presence to which it speaks. It does so to the extent that it fulfills itself as sacrifice: a living mortal is consecrated to the immortals and his blood gathers or feeds their strength and their protection. In sacrifice, speech itself becomes act—it pronounces the formula that sanctifies the gesture of the sacrificer and immolates itself in the knife and in the blood. Presence annihilates speech.

But by leaving worship, tragedy also leaves presence. The gods withdrew, or mankind abandoned the gods, in making the transition from agrarian to urban life, from incantation to rhetoric, and from speech to writing. Maybe it should be said that the first difference between religious worship and theater is that the first is not, initially, written.

This farewell to presence (all writing says farewell to it, as Jean-Christophe Bailly has suggested) establishes theater—speech no longer has to be addressed to the gods and, even if we continue to name them, to invoke them, such traces of worship no longer have a sacrificial role. The speech of theater is addressed, precisely, to the absence of the gods, which is to say that it is no longer addressed to them at all but is exchanged among mortals, who are now alone among themselves.

It is in the theater, the first Greek theater, but already long after Thespis, in Sophocles's *Antigone*, that the voice speaks out to proclaim man as *terribly strange* and a *fearsome technician*, just as in *Oedipus* we are in the presence of the one who has answered the question about man. Between the conqueror of the world and the animal who grows old and dies, tragedy condenses everything that is in question: not tragic human stories but man himself as tragedy or comedy. But tragedy and comedy are woven around events: something happens, something occurs that makes man pitiful and that presents this pitiful individual with compassion or derision. It is not by accident that *Ecce Homo* is the expression, the utterance, the motto of religion deconstructing itself.

With the gods, nothing happens; they are the bearers or the spokesmen of what we call Destiny, Moira, Necessity, the general Arrival of all things. But now what happens is a destiny that is singular each time, and in which general Arrival is submerged, along with the worship we were once able to devote to it.

*

Tragedy, however, continues to share in worship or, rather—once again it is appropriate to point out—in liturgy, a word used by Christians and which initially referred to an action in the service of a people. It is even permissible to stray a little from the religious lexicon and speak of ceremony. Tragedy—and all subsequent theater retains a memory of it—forms a ceremonial. It is not simply a matter of social ceremony, although this, even shifted in terms of its sophistication, is not negligible. It is initially a question of that ceremony that is in itself tragedy (of which all theater has retained the memory, even if nothing more than memory). Where sacrificial worship brings about the invocation of the gods in the efficacy of the blood that is devoted to them, the theater brings about the invocation or mutual advocation among men (of characters among themselves and the

chorus with the characters). This mutual address and alternating chant—
wherein resides something essential to all literature after tragedy, even
non-theatrical—serves as the substitute for sacrifice. Regardless of the
sense of tragic action (we can say, simplifying greatly, that man there experiences the intimacy of irreconcilable gods or that he sets in motion the
responsibility of his own misfortune), and even if this sense expires in a
mortal wound of sense, tragedy ensures the nobility, the *ethos* of this *pathos*
of sense.

Hölderlin[3] in attempting to write another tragedy—a tragedy after the
tragedy, which was supposed to express this after and which, in fact, says as
much but by yielding to itself—has Empedocles say, "My tongue no longer serves/in the dialog of mortals, in empty words,"[4]—and I'll risk ven-
turing that he thereby states, at the same time as the forthcoming silence of
death, the nobility and essential tenor of the very tragedy we are reading.
In other words, tragedy retains, in the ceremonial of its speech, the trace of
sacrifice. I don't want to go further here into characterizing this ceremonial, but I will say that it belongs to the mode of direct discourse, addressed
discourse, not to its "imitation" (even though this might be *mimesis* in
contrast to *diegesis*), for it is not a matter of imitating day-to-day dialogue
but, on the contrary, of producing address as such. (Maybe this is how we
should understand the "*mimesis* without a model" Philippe spoke of.)

The "theatrical" character implies, in the best sense of the word, an
emphasis of address: speech directed to the other and thus directed beyond
the other and beyond itself. No longer addressed to the gods to offer them
victims, it is addressed by a man to an other to present him with that which
surpasses man and surpasses itself. In this sense, it is speech that is sacrificed. By this emphatic or ceremonial speech, tragedy preserves or invents,
it simultaneously preserves and invents the *ethos* through which, lacking
the help of the gods and any other assistance, a grandeur remains. The
grandeur of the mortal struck down by the gods who turn away from him,
is exposed in the nobility of tragic speech. When he has destroyed his eyes,
but not cut out his tongue, and while deploring his inability to deafen himself, Oedipus still speaks, he speaks even more, reciting the litany of his
crimes while he also states that he is as ashamed of speaking them as he is
of committing them, and the *nobility* of his discourse is identically the *nobility* of the only dignity that remains to him.

*

It is this grandeur that we represent as having lost, that we may, in fact,
have lost, or whose loss we may have already begun to grapple with during

the transition from worship to tragedy. It is this grandeur that is lacking in the modern "tragedy" of an entire civilization that is less able than any other to find holiness in its misery or no longer knows where to place what it calls the dignity of man, this absolute value that, ever since its invention, that is, specifically, ever since Kant, doesn't know what it is worth or allows that value to oscillate indefinitely between good and bad infinity. (This same Kant, I recall, and this Kant so well known to Hölderlin, wrote that the sublime in art assumes one of three forms: the didactic poem, the oratorio, or tragic verse. The specification of "verse," which gives the three modes the common feature of the poem or song, designates the regime of dignity. Philippe loved this enigmatic passage from Kant.)

By saying farewell to the world, the gods, and himself, Oedipus bestowed upon himself the dignity of this farewell. However, we need to recognize that "*after tragedy*" means "after the ceremony of farewells." Consequently, it also means, after this intensity and this moment of *nobility* whose loss, or the representation of whose loss, organizes what we can no longer call our tragedy but our drama or our desolation.

This merely establishes the terms of a problem, or a crisis, or an aporia even, and I'm not claiming to go any further than this at this time. But I want to conclude by clarifying certain terms. On the one hand, it should be clear to us that tragedy could no more respond to the end of sacrifice by returning to it, while shifting the totality of the sacred along with it, than we can return to tragedy—a return whose temptation has continued to haunt us. It is also up to us to find our own farewell to tragedy, just as we need to reinvent a grandeur, a dignity, or what might follow them—unless the worst becomes inevitable.

But our farewell must also consider that tragedy has retained the element from which it originated. What I have been referring to as the ceremony of tragic speech, is, when all is said and done, comparable to nothing other than what is indicated very approximately by the expression "civil religion," which I referred to earlier. The questions of tragedy, theater, politics, history, art, and everything we call "ethics," without distinction, no doubt share this determining characteristic of leading toward that deserted and seemingly unoccupiable place that the expression names. What do we do with this information in a time that is no longer only "after tragedy" but "after religion" and "after the polis," which, moreover, serves only to break down and highlight the first expression?

Thus, we must, we will have to, as my final point, recall that "after tragedy" also refers to the dual movement of philosophy and Christianity. Both have sought to call attention to sacrifice and tragedy at the same time, and both, through a movement that goes beyond—or, more specifically, seeks desperately to get beyond—the ceremonial of speech. Philosophy has sought this surpassing in a knowledge that is becoming identical with its very object, Christianity has sought it in a love that has become identical with existence.

Moreover, we represent both as offering a circumvention of death, a means of passage that is simply their most external and most ideological configuration, behind which there resides a much more severe challenge. But the force of mirroring these representations (death conquered through wisdom or resurrection) is nonetheless symptomatic of the desires of the West: with sacrifice and then with tragedy, it is the relationship to death that it has—or believed was—lost or broken.

But because death remains impassable, there has arisen, for both registers, a kind of silence whose last name is nihilism. Is there, will there be, or is there already an "after nihilism" that doesn't claim to offer an "after death" and yet assumes it is "after tragedy"? That is our "tragic" question. But if some chance of a response exists, it requires at least that we understand the following: for whatever reason we may invent another ceremony of speech, another liturgy of sense and truth, that too can advance only from within the very heart of our silence, providing that a throat continues to murmur in spite of everything.

And, as I said, I believe Philippe's throat is murmuring here and now.[5]

Stagire, September 2002; Giesen, October 2007;
New York, April 2008

Blanchot's Resurrection

The motif of resurrection does not seem, at least initially, to hold a major place in Blanchot's work. We find it, although infrequently, in his so-called "theoretical" works. Its presence may be greater in his fiction, but there the themes are necessarily more difficult to isolate as such. Yet resurrection is inseparable from this body of work of death and dying, which we are accustomed to associate with Blanchot's name. And if dying is not only inseparable from literature or writing but consubstantial with it, it is only to the extent that it is involved with resurrection and does nothing more than to follow its movement. The nature of this movement is what I want to try to approach, putting aside any attempt to reconstitute the economy found in Blanchot's work, which would be the subject of an entire book.

I would first like to introduce the major key: the resurrection in question does not escape death, does not arise from it, doesn't analyze it. On the contrary, it forms the extremity and truth of dying. It goes into death not to cross through it but, by burying itself within it inexorably, to resurrect it. To resurrect death is entirely different from resurrecting the dead. To resurrect the dead consists in returning them to life, to cause life to flow where death had stamped it out. A prodigious operation, miraculous, which substitutes a supernatural power for the laws of nature. To resurrect death is an entirely different operation, assuming it is an operation. Certainly, a work, an œuvre, is not far from this concept, or it's the business of the work, the work in its essential inoperability. Inoperability itself, in fact, can only be understood through the resurrection of death if, by the work, "speech gives voice to the intimacy of death."[1]

But for Blanchot, the "resurrection of death" constitutes a rare but decisive formulation. He may have mentioned it only once, but in such a decisive and striking way that this unique occurrence seemed sufficient to him—being at the same time too much of a risk not to become dangerous through repetition. For it is dangerous, of course, and it can lead to all sorts of ambiguity. Blanchot knows this; he is intent on avoiding the risk, not, however, without taking a carefully and, we could say even delicately calculated, share of it. That share is the one that preserves, at least in part, the monotheistic and, more specifically, Christian root of the thought of resurrection.

*

We should begin by lingering for a moment (which does not preclude returning to the question later in greater detail) on this Christian provenance. For Blanchot could have kept it silent, even suppressed it completely by substituting some other term for "resurrection," something along the lines of "inertia"—"an unfinished work"—or "madness," or "insomnia," or "overturn," or "reversal,"[2] or "recognition" as Christophe Bident used the term in identifying its movement, and "extravagance."[3] Up to a point, this substitution was conceivable and eliminated any religious assumption. However, it is clear that the immediate and manifest link with the death whose resurrection expressly implies deliverance and escape would have been lost. It seems as if it were not possible to do away with a term intended to function like a logical operator in relation to death presented as being essential to writing—no less than in relation to writing (speech, the cry, the poem) presented as being essential to dying or to mankind's mortality. Yet this is not quite it: we must address that which, by this very fact, can only function by also assuming a theological motif.

Here, we need to extend our investigation to the entirety of the theological or, if I can put it this way, theomorphological findings in Blanchot's text. But that will be for another day. Concerning resurrection, I merely note that this information is indicated in a highly unique manner in the vicinity of this motif. Namely, by a specifically evangelical reference to the character we might call the eponym of resurrection: Lazarus in the Gospel of St. John. In fact, Lazarus appears at the same time as the first, and perhaps only, occurrence of the expression "death resurrected." This occurs early in Blanchot's work, for it appears in 1941 in the first edition of *Thomas the Obscure*.[4] The text is the same in the second edition, but the two sentences before and after the one in which Lazarus is named have been modified. That is, the attention the author gives to the sentence whose subject is Thomas: "He walked, the only true Lazarus whose very death was resurrected."[5]

We immediately note that two lines earlier, the text contains these words: "he appeared at the narrow gate of his sepulcher, not risen but dead, and with the certainty of being snatched at once from death and from life."[6] This last sentence slightly transforms, mitigates, the expression in the first edition in which the order of the words is reversed—"from life and from death." This mitigation consists in modifying the embedded clause: "having suddenly, with the most pitiless awareness, the feeling that he had been snatched." These micrological features are instructive. Although the gate of the sepulcher continues to recall the biblical episode and preface the name of Lazarus, Thomas's awareness has shifted from "feeling" to "certainty," and this certainty is stripped of any "sudden" and spectacular qualification. From a type of commotion we have moved to the affirmation of a certainty—which is never, in general, very far from the domain of the Cartesian *ego sum*. From an overwhelming impression, Thomas has made the transition to a form of dead *cogito*, in death or of death. He knows he has been "snatched" from death as well as life (thus the importance of the alteration of the order of the terms). Although dead, he has not been plunged into the "dead" thing: he becomes the dead subject of a snatching from death itself. That is why he is not resurrected; he doesn't recover life after having passed through death—while dead he advances through death ("he walked") and it is death itself that is resurrected in this "only true Lazarus."

*

Death is the subject; the subject is not or is no longer its own subject. This is the challenge of resurrection: neither subjectivation nor objectivation. Neither the "resurrected" nor the cadaver—but "resurrected death," as if lying upon the cadaver and thus laying it out without raising it up. Nothing else. *Wo ich war soll es auferstehen.*[7]

The other Lazarus, the man of the gospel, is, therefore, not true: he is a character in a miraculous story, a transgression of death by the most unlikely return to life. Truth cannot be found in a return such as this: it resides in the concomitance of death and a life in death that does not return to life but which brings death back to life as such. Or we could say that the true Lazarus lives his dying as he dies his living. It is in this way that he "walks." The text continues, concluding the chapter (and also transforming, mitigating the first version, in which, moreover, the chapter was far from its end): "He went forward, passing beyond the last shadows of night without losing any of his glory, covered with grass and earth, walking at an even pace beneath the falling stars, the same pace which, for those men who are not wrapped in a winding-sheet, marks the ascent toward the most precious point in life."[8] This glorious, subterranean advance in the midst of the *disaster* proceeds at the same pace with which we make our way toward death. Thomas is wrapped in a winding-sheet, as well as Lazarus, while the movement of men is that of an "ascension," another Christian term that designates, this time, the advance of the Resurrected par excellence. Thus, the separation in John's Gospel occurs through a renewed reminder of its reference. The true Lazarus requires that there remain something of the Lazarus resurrected by Christ (by the one who says, in this same episode of John's Gospel, "I am the resurrection"): there remains in him something of this miraculousness.

But it's not exactly a miracle. Rather, it's the sense that Thomas's story gives to the miraculous story: this sense, or this truth, is not a crossing of death but death itself as crossing, as transport, and as transformation of itself into itself withdrawn from its thingness, its objective positivity as death to reveal itself—"the most precious point of life"—as the extremity to which returns, and is disclosed, life's access to that which is neither its contrary, nor its beyond, nor its sublimation, but only and, at the same time, infinitely its opposite and its illumination by its darkest face, Thomas's face, the face that receives the light of shadows and is, therefore, able to relinquish the sole light of possible significations.

Need it be pointed out? *Thomas the Obscure* proposes nothing other than the history of a resurrection and, more than this, the history of the resurrection. For Thomas himself *is* the resurrection, just as this Christ for whom Anne's death calls to mind another word; whereas Anne is the resurrected one, the dead woman whose "body without consolation"[9] is, at the same time, the presence that "bestowed on death all the reality and all the existence which constituted the proof of her own nothingness."[10] And Thomas, watching over her, continues his monologue: "neither impalpable nor dissolved in the shadows, she imposed herself ever more strongly on the senses."[11] Yet this last sentence, which presents the affirmation of the strong tangible presence of the body, should also be read in terms of the narrator's express indication, noting that Thomas speaks "as if his thoughts had a chance of being heard,"[12] and from that point on, according to this orality, the plural found in "on the senses"—an expression that is, moreover, somewhat unusual in this context—becomes inaudible and is elided into a singular calculated to make itself heard without formally imposing its concept.

In every way possible Blanchot confirms this: resurrection refers to the access to the beyond of sense, the advance into this beyond with a step that goes nowhere other than toward the repetition of its equality. We know that writing is the trace or mark of this step. But it is so only to the extent that it opens onto "a space where, strictly speaking, nothing yet has sense, toward which, however, everything that has sense rises as toward its origin."[13] I'm overlooking the fact that this text from 1950 speaks a language slightly different from the one Blanchot would speak later on. This shift is certainly not without significance, and Blanchot pointed it out, although this did not prevent, quite the contrary, the impressive repetition, the remarkable obstinacy of thinking expressed through necessary variations. Nonetheless, it remains that the space of resurrection, the space that defines it and makes it possible, is the space outside the sense that precedes and follows sense—it being understood that anteriority and posteriority have no chronological value here but designate an out-of-time that is as interminable as it is instantaneous, eternity in its essential value of subtraction. (But the remark made concerning the displacement of terms in Blanchot after the period of *The Space of Literature*, should unfold into another kind of questioning: up to a certain point, Blanchot was engaging in a suspension or interruption of the mythic register. However, aside from the interruption, what is it that, perhaps, even undoubtedly, insists and can only insist? This insistence coincides, in Blanchot, with the insistence on the name of "God," which will have to be addressed elsewhere.)

*

Life devoid of sense, the dying of life that makes its writing—not that of the writer alone but that of the reader and, more distant still, of one who neither writes nor reads, whether illiterate or whether he has abandoned all intellectual commerce, writing finally defined by the "dying of a book in all books"[14] to which this definition also applies: "To write, 'to form,' where no form holds sway, an absent meaning"[15]—this life is life withdrawn from sense, which does not resurrect as life but which resurrects death: it withdraws death from its advent and its event, it withdraws from the death of mortality the dying of immortality through which, incessantly, I know this radical withdrawal of sense and, therefore, truth itself. I know it, I share it, which is to say that I withdraw my death, my expiration, from all propriety, all proper presence. It is, thus, from myself that I am released, and I transform "the fact of death"[16] in two ways: death no longer occurs as a break inflicted upon "me" but becomes the common and anonymous fate it can only be, and, as a corollary, resurrected death, withdrawing me from myself and from sense, exposes me not only to truth but finally as the truth—the tenebrous glory of enacted truth.

Subtly, Blanchot's life, whose intimate withdrawal will have enabled the affirmation and exposition of an altogether different life, whose declared absence will have engaged the most insistent public presence of a life withdrawn from the death of objectivized existence identified in the person and in the work, this life of Blanchot, not hidden but, on the contrary, the most published of all, was a life resurrected during its lifetime by the very publication of his death, which was always at work. No doubt there is some ambivalence in this attitude. But its coherence and nobility still cause us to wonder. At least there is consistency in the fact that Blanchot was never guided by reviviscence or by the miraculous, but was able to comprehend his life as dead from the outset and thus returned in resurrection.

That there is no reviviscence, no miracle, here is described in the text "*Lazare, Veni Foras*" in *The Space of Literature*. Here, Blanchot describes reading as an act of access to the work of art, "absent, perhaps radically so; in any case it is concealed, obfuscated by the evidence of the book."[17] He identifies the "liberating decision"[18] of reading in the "*Lazare, Veni Foras*" of the Gospel. This identification discloses a considerable displacement, by which it is no longer a matter of a corpse rising from a tomb but of identifying the very stone of the sepulcher as "the presence" that is not something to be dissolved but whose "opacity" should be recognized and affirmed as the truth of the expected transparency, or "obscurity" (that of Thomas, once again) as true "clarity." But while the operation of reading, to the extent that it is revelatory, can be considered a "miracle" (a word that Blanchot presents in quotes, indicating both a commonplace way of speaking—"the miracle of reading"—and the operation of Christ on Lazarus), it is only by understanding its revelation through this stony opacity that we too might be enlightened "about the sense of all thaumaturgies."[19] Blanchot makes or slips in this remark quite incidentally. Yet it indicates nothing other than a clarification of what the miracle implies. "Thaumaturgy" serves to distance and push the evangelical miracle to the side of a scene of magic or the marvellous (this last word occurs a few lines below, it too with a slightly deprecatory edge). Note, however, that for all intents and purposes, he declines the name of *Thomas*, which, sometimes treated as a common noun rather than a proper name in this eponymous book, continues to make a sign to a "marvel" more marvelous, because less illuminating, than all the marvels of the Gospels or even . . . the literature of marvels, of fables. In any event, we find that "the sense of any" miracle is given by the sense of reading, which is to say, not by any operation that challenges a given nature, but by this "dance with an invisible partner" that characterizes—to conclude the "trivial," unintellectual reading, which is also, he goes on to say, a reading that is not "penetrated by devotion and quasi-religious"—only that reading that doesn't turn the book into a "cult" object and that might even be "ignorant," thereby opening itself up to the withdrawal of the work of art. The sense of the miracle is to give rise to no sense that exceeds or distorts common sense but only to the uncertainty of sense in a *pas de danse*.

This image may itself cause discomfort. There is something too immediately seductive about it for it not to be too simple. But, nonetheless, it does indicate the relation between levity and gravity around which it is drawn by Blanchot. For he concludes "for where levity is given us, gravity does not lack."[20] This gravity that does not lack but which remains discreet is contrasted with the portentous gravity that fixes thought to the thing, the being, the substance, and, therefore, to the thought fixed to the substance of death and which hopes to mitigate it, consoling itself with the thaumaturgy of a weighty return to life. This dancing gravity executes no entrechats before the tomb, it experiences the stone as something insubstantial, it places or senses in the heavy stone the infinite lightness of sense. Such is the opposition between resurrected death and the resurrection of the dead.

*

Thus, as it appears in another text of Blanchot's, it is "as if, in us alone, death could purify, could interiorize itself and apply to its own reality that power of metamorphosis, that force of invisibility whose original profundity it is."[21] *In us alone*: the context allows us to specify that, here, it's not only a question of us as humans but as the dead. "Us alone" is also us in our solitude and in our desolation as the dead, and as mortals, "us . . . of all beings the most fragile."[22] In this text devoted to Rilke, it is to the poem and its song that the lighthearted gravity of the resurrection of death is confided. "Speech," he writes, "gives voice to death's intimacy." This occurs "at the moment of separation," at the moment when speech dies. The swan's song will always be the basso continuo of Blanchot's text. This signifies two things whose union forms the difficult, strange, and obstinately fleeting thought of resurrection.

On the one hand, this song doesn't sing or, perhaps, this step dances only at the instant of its self destruction, in so far as it breaks itself, and in doing so can only assign to its own death the care of maintaining its harmony, of dancing its step. And this must be the case throughout writing, it must be the case that at each point there is inscribed what is exscribed: that there is nothing more to say, nothing unspeakable nor the return of any word of truth other than the cessation of speaking. But there is no relaxation of this exscription, and poetry—*sive philosophia*—is a vain word only up to the point when it too dies. At that point, dance or song pursue no further arabesque and, in a sense, are no longer even present. Their only contour is one of dexterity, a strained dexterity assigned to that purpose, to the one, him or her, who can no longer be reached. As Lacoue-Labarthe wrote concerning a text by Blanchot: "a kind of confidence or—it amounts to the same thing—confession. This text is quite simply *entrusted*, it appeals to faith and fidelity."[23] We must return to this "faith" that appears to presume everything that "resurrection," or however it may be called, implies, "poetry" or perhaps the leveling of all names. For the moment, we can simply say that dying *discloses* that which death, in fact, snatches and buries without appeal. Dying is the appeal.

On the other hand, resurrection is not simply borrowed from the lexicon of the miracle for the convenience or provocation of its imagery. It also presents itself as a rewriting of Holy Scripture: a holiness withdrawn from religious fantasy but also withdrawing from that very fantasy an access neither credulous nor pious to that which it is no longer appropriate to call "death"—reality of the unreal—but "consent," the reality of a correspondence to the real itself of dying. The word recurs on several occasions in the texts discussed and elsewhere in Blanchot. Later referred to as the "patience of passivity"[24] by which it is possible to "answer to the impossible and for the impossible,"[25] consent neither submits nor resigns itself: it grants a sense or a feeling. It agrees precisely with the sense and the feeling of the insensible and of sense in absence. It is nothing other than the infinitely simple—and indefinitely renewed, indefinitely rewritable—experience in us of being without essence and, thus, of dying. Resurrection—or, in Greek, *anastasis*—dresses death like the thick, heavy stone of the tomb, like the stele on which is inscribed, until its final erasure, the name of an inalienable and uninscribable identity always exscribed. This stele erected in the presence of the void and with nothing beyond, without consolation, strengthens, with its entire mass, a desolation already distanced from it and from lamentation. An infinitesimal, discrete, and insistent levity that results in the consent of this consentment to the insensible. Who causes it or writes it, if writing is the name—as lacking in substance as any other but inevitable, as much as "poetry," as much as "holiness"—of the refusal of any belief in a substantiality foreign to the world. Consent to resurrection consents, above all, to the refusal of belief, just as faith challenges and forecloses that same belief. But in reality belief is never believable and, within us, something or someone obscure has always known this for us. This presentiment of the absolutely unbelievable, unwaveringly defying all credulity, relying only on itself, absolutely, has always spared us the dead end of consent.

If consent, or resurrection—the surrection that erects death in death as a living death—occurs in writing or in literature, this means that literature supports the cessation or dissipation of sense. "Literature," here, doesn't mean "literary genre" but every type of speech, cry, prayer, laugh, or sob that holds—as one holds a note, a chord—the infinite suspension of sense. One can understand that this holding is associated with ethics more than it is with aesthetics but in the end it frustrates and undoes those categories. We could put it differently: to the extent that these categories belong to philosophy, they also indicate that philosophical ontotheology practices embalming, or metempsychosis, or the escape of the soul—but never resurrection. Metaphysical practices always refer to a going-forward, the future of a renaissance, a type of possible and power, whereas literature only writes the present of that which has always already happened to us, that is, the impossible in which our being consists in disappearing.

January 2004

The Neutral, Neutralization
of the Neutral

The motif of the neutral occupies a significant place in Blanchot's thought. It would be no exaggeration to say that everything in his thinking is related to the "neutral" as its point of condensation, incandesecence, and vanishing, all at the same time.

With Blanchot, we must begin with writing: with literature to the extent that it forms the ever renewed play and continual dwelling on *"the need to write."*[1] This need means that what "does not take place"[2] is repeated, that the non-place or non-presence of all origin, substance, subject is affirmed in the only way possible: in a *"nomadic affirmation."*[3] This last term should not only be understood as the perpetual displacement of affirmation, which would never settle upon a presumably "full" or "living" presence, but also (at least, this is the gloss that it seems necessary to introduce) as the regime of affirmation (literary, scriptural) itself: it affirms in nomadic mode, that is, it affirms without settling (itself) on its affirmation—or, if you prefer, on the affirmed of the affirmation—as if it sealed the truth within an acquired sense. Nomadic affirmation asserts that what it affirms has neither the form nor the nature of the "acquired," of the "established," or of the "foundational."

In short, nomadic affirmation is that for which there can be no fulfillment of sense and for which all affirmation always implies this other affirmation, "God is dead," which is to say, "God" is "*a surplus word*,"[4] an excess
word, a word displaced from its status as word, as signifier, a word that is
lost for and by language. Moreover, a word that is lost "without another
announcing itself there: absolute slip."[5]

To that extent, Blanchot's major concern is to confront, without concession or avoidance, the need to recognize that there may be "a surplus
word"—and several versions, several figures, or several names of the "surplus word": that is, we must acknowledge a closure of signification. Whether
we give to a governing idea of Sense the name God, Mankind, or History,
we are saying too much, saying that which, specifically, should not be
said—but *written* in the sense that he gives to this word.

*

What Blanchot is asking is essentially the following: to unreservedly satisfy
the beyond of sense, a beyond that is precisely *the step not beyond*, which is
the transition, here and now, at every moment, in every place, toward the
non-place or out-of-place (he also names this "dying," but the transition
doesn't need this image to convey the idea that it's a matter, quite simply,
of the mortal condition, a singular condition, one exposed by its finitude to
the infinitude of its singularity, which nothing can absorb).

Writing is devoted to the interminable contour of this passage that
doesn't pass. But which passes without passing. Which passes if not *to*
(much less *until*), then at least *toward* the non- and out-of-place of this
"outside" to which there is no question of "arriving"—but which comes to
us. In this sense, writing obeys the fundamental ethical requirement of not
lying about this "arriving."

The problem of the death of God—or "nihilism"—is, therefore, perfectly delineated: not a word in excess but the movement that maintains the
opening beyond words.

The neutral is the name given to that which magnetizes this movement:
it qualifies its destination as being *ne uter*—"neither one nor the other"[6]—
and, more specifically, as Blanchot himself notes: "Neither one nor the
other, nothing more precise." That is: neither anything at all, nor any
"one" at all, nor the other, nor any other one than the first, whoever that
might be. Here, Blanchot insists on the analysis that he then begins (and
which I won't follow in detail): even more than the deposition of the "one,"
it is the displacement of the "other" that forms the effect of the neutral.
Unable to be the other of the one, as, for example, the negative of a positive,

the other also cannot be "an" other, much less "the Other." The neutral asserts "the other of the other, the un-known of the other."[7]

But this alterity of the other that sets it apart—and setting apart with it every "one," whether same or other—also sets apart the non-place of all possibility of location, even negative. The non-place or out-of-place toward which the need to write moves is nothing, no place *toward* which one could make a move.

Therefore, if it is legitimate to say that "writing" signifies tirelessly approaching the limit of speech, this limit that speech alone designates and whose designation unlimits us, us, the speakers, who are thus opened beyond ourselves and beyond sense, it is nonetheless necessary—strictly necessary—to at the same time recall that no "approach" makes sense if the proximity with the beyond is not proximity of the absolutely distant. "The near promises that it will never take hold. Praise for the approach of that which escapes: the next death, the distance of the next death."[8]

Thus, the neutral cannot, strictly speaking, be approached or can only if there is an infinite distancing inscribed in the approach itself. That is why, like "God,"[9] the neutral is a word in excess. "*The neutral: a word* too many *that withdraws*."[10] It is withdrawn from language, it "barely speaks,"[11] it is "the name without name."[12]

*

No one knew the extreme difficulty of the situation thus described better than Blanchot: if the neutral is the nameless name, how then can it be named? And yet, it is, it must be if it is not possible to give up trying to approach—distancing oneself at the same time—the limit to which we are opened, exposed. That this must indeed be is shown by the fact that Blanchot sometimes writes it with a capital, here, for example: "The Neutral does not have the ancient mythological names that any night carries with it."[13]

The sentence signifies that night, any night, registers its mythological assets by being itself—who it is or who makes the opening—opened by the neutral and so, in some way, neutralized as nocturnal power (for example, like Victor Hugo's "hideous black sun from which radiates the night"). The neutral dissipates mythical powers, those that were capable of providing a proximity of distances.

But the difficulty increases when we realize the power this dissipation assumes in spite of everything. As long as "the Neutral" or "the neuter" function in a discourse that provides its predicates and describes it, a secret recourse to a supranominal power can be suspected. What happens, for example, when the neutral in a sense authorizes an "experience" of that very thing whose approach is separation? Blanchot writes "writing is a break with thought when thought gives itself as an immediate proximity; it is also a break with all *empirical* experience of the world. In this sense, writing also entails a rupture with all present consciousness, it being always already engaged in the experience of the non-manifest or the unknown (understood as a grammatical neuter)."[14]

How can he write that it is "engaged" in this non-empirical experience—in this experience that, according to the entire philosophical tradition, is experience bound up with a transcendental (that is, involving a pure subject) or transcendent (experience of the beyond itself) necessity? It can only be "engaged" in a way that, at the same time, disengages it from any transcendental or transcendent formation of the experience it makes or is.

Thus, the recourse to the conceptual instrumentation underlying the use of the word "empirical" must be set aside, as must the use of the nomination—also precisely transcendtal or transcendent—of any "excess word" such as "the neutral." Neither *a priori* condition of a subject nor divine instance, the "neutral" must erase itself from the discourse by and about it. It is literally obligated to do so.

And isn't this what the use of the "neuter" in an adverbial sense is already doing in the sentence quoted above? "Neuter" displaces the nomination *of the* neutral. *The* neutral finds itself neutralized.

This expression is not Blanchot's and he himself would have been suspicious of the risk of dialectical contortion. In fact, he writes "The Neuter . . . neutralizes, neutralizes (itself), thus evokes (does nothing but evoke) the movement of *Aufhebung*."[15] If it does nothing more than evoke the Hegelian negation of the negation and with it the power of the negative, it is because it does not neutralize *itself* by itself or only appears to do so (which is indicated by the parentheses around "itself"). The Hegelian negative is itself negated: it already possesses the power of self-enactment. And it is specifically this power that Blanchot denies to the neutral. He can only do so, however, by indicating, in passing, a disturbing proximity to *Aufhebung*—and thus to the very power of support outside the self.

What then inscribes the impossibility of stopping at this proximity? What is it that takes into account that "the neutral" is not supported in nor as the "outside" or the "night" whose fundamental inappropriability it references?

At this point it is possible to go somewhat further with Blanchot or move slightly away from what he himself states (without claiming to have cleared up the very complex and dense tangle of his thought).

   Blanchot continues to point out that which takes into account (if we can put it that way) the (non-autarchic) neutralization of the neutral. In other words, it is writing, or literature, that takes responsibility for the "step not beyond." Yet it is literature, precisely, that does not name "the Neutral," any more than "God" or "madness," or any excess word at all. Literature doesn't make use of excess words; on the contrary, it consists in mobilizing all words, all their resources, from their "mythological titles" to their insignificances, in the assumed conviction that there cannot be an excess of words or any excess word.

   That is why literature narrates, recites, and fictionalizes: fiction—which can be understood here rather broadly to encompass poetry, recitation with the narrative, even . . . the music of the recitatif—can be understood as the only effective neutralization of every "one/other," of every presence/absence, represented as given, stable, substantial, and approachable. Literary fiction specifically consists in distancing presumably constituted, or constitutable, truth and through this distancing to "engage" itself in the "experience" of "neither one nor the other"—neither, nor, no name, but the infinite that goes before and tirelessly follows all names.

                                                                        2011

Exclamations

Introductory note. This entry doesn't have precisely the encyclopedic character of a dictionary article in the sense that its subject is not available in advance and susceptible to being treated as one of the givens within the general scope of this work. It is, rather, a subject awaiting construction, as shown by the difficulty that accompanied the choice of the title of this essay and which exists only to the extent that the context of this dictionary could provide the precise sense given to the term "exclamations." It involves a consideration of the signification or pornographic use of the word in the context of sexual relations. (We also find the word used in some general descriptions, such as "orgasm can be accompanied by verbal exclamations or trembling." But there is no term that could be said to be unique to this signification, nor any suggestive connotation, as is the case with the term "position." Among several possible reasons, we can put forward the fact that it entails a very broad register that can encompass whole sentences, even speeches, as well as such things as interjections, cries, and whimpers—we are in a zone of indeterminacy, variable and situated at the limit of language.)

*

"Heavens! if mighty Lucifer were to take it upon himself to discharge, methinks he'd unloose his seed less thunderously, would not foam so much at the mouth nor so gnash his teeth, at the gods would not hurl blasphemies and imprecations so fearful."[1] This comparison serves to characterize the behavior of one of Sade's characters (in *Juliette*). As we know, for Sade, as is often the case in erotic literature, exclamations accompany the sexual act and, especially, its supreme moment. The same holds for cinema (pornographic or not), even for popular song (for example, Serge Gainsbourg's *Je t'aime moi non plus* or Johnny Hallyday's *Que je t'aime*).

The register of the words uttered as well as their tonality can vary from the cry or eructation to the murmur or groan—as between two limits where language begins to fade away. It is in this way that for the obscene and blasphematory utterings of the Sadean hero can be substituted short emissions of approval or imploration, as in the series of "Please" and "Yes" in a very complex scene in *Everything Is Illuminated* by Jonathan Safran Foer. This may call to mind the religious expression, "ejaculatory orison," referring to a very short prayer, monological, repeated with fervor, an expression whose unwillingly obscene resonance often leads its hearers to smile. The ejaculatory orison is at the heart of the hesychastic tradition, whose name refers to the sense of calm brought about by the repetition of the impassioned exclamation.

It is not by chance that a film title—*Cries and Whispers*—summarizes the amplitude that runs from one extreme of exclamatory, or exclamative, possibilities to the other. Although the film's title is not provided specifically with this in mind, it remains that the title has been intentionally appropriated by pornography.

Even if the deviation between the two extreme possibilities is absolute and contrasts one with the other as the epitome of hedonic cruelty versus the epitome of amorous joy, a slender and almost imperceptible thread connects all the registers of the exclamation (whether it be the fact and expression, to refer to the Greek, of an *erastes* [male or female] in the ardor of possession or an *eromenos* [male or female] overcome by the fervor of being possessed), within the various possible combinations of the four elementary declarations "I possess you / I'm coming / You possess me / you're coming." This continuous thread corresponds to a character that might be referred to as fundamentally pornographic, even if it is so only virtually or tendentiously: something of an at least possible, latent, or asymptotic pornography appears to belong to the very fact of the utterance in the act of lovemaking. That is the reason why this dictionary entry was first proposed.

If we define pornography as an exposition of the unexposable, the latter being understood not only in the sense of the indecent but literally as the un-showable, such as, and precisely, the emission of sexual fluids, female or male, and the emotion of orgasm (here, everything turns on these two concepts: emission and emotion), we can then understand how exclamations, whether their sense is directly sexual or amorous ("I love you" *also* belongs to one of the registers evoked: it's all a matter of intonation), are in themselves already part of lived reality, an inchoate form of pornography, and why pornography as such has to make use of them. Here, speech shows that which is not shown, it emphasizes the fact that there is something in excess of what can be shown—like a paradoxical excess of sensuality itself and like a supplementary admission of the inadmissible.

That this usage is much more common in literature than it is in film or the various possible kinds of pornographic production (at least, the author of the article ventures to conjecture on the basis of limited experience) may no doubt be the result of technical difficulties (requirements of the interplay among the participants, sound recording, etc.), but it is also associated with the fact that the sexual exclamation can be considered a kind of poetry *in nuce* as well as a second-degree pornographic exhibition, doubling the visual on the plane of language.

Indeed, the exclamation—especially in its somewhat paradigmatic form of "I'm coming!"—or "Fuck! I can't go on . . . !" as well as "Yes!" (which brings to mind the final line of Joyce's *Ulysses*)—in this form, therefore, where the French language enables us to gather essence in assonance, "*Oui, je (tu) jouis!*"—offers nothing other than a form of evidence: it enunciates what has taken place and which, of itself, has no need to be enunciated. It enacts a tautology of the act for which the use of language provides few equivalents (except, and not by chance, the complaint "I don't feel well . . . ," although this can easily also contain some piece of information).

This use of speech refers both to tautology (or, better, to "tautegory," to use Schelling's term in speaking of myth) and performativity: it is as if "I'm (you're) coming" effectively resulted in ejaculation and, as if, as a result, coming resulted in saying, or being said, just as saying and "the" saying (saying "that") resulted in coming. Based on which, we would, of course, have to risk also understanding that "saying" itself and absolutely, is jouissance.

Likewise, and little by little, we must understand the designations of the obscene and the "shameful" (gestures, parts of the body, tastes) as desperate attempts to rediscover the hidden heart of jouissance, even to display its very concealment. Here, the "despair" belongs to the knowledge of the impossible—but at the same time it goes beyond this overly simple designation of an "impossible": for it designates and shapes the possibility itself. Moreover, that is also why, whereas pornography consists in remaining riveted to the fantasy of exhibition (and to exclamation as overexhibition), love, on the other hand (or however we choose to call it), releases itself from fantasy by turning away from the cry to murmurs and silence.

Thus, the exclamation touches the center of the enigma of pornography. On the one hand, it says nothing: it doubles the act by an assumed naming (as if "fuck!" could name what it entailed . . .) but in reality is merely one more shudder of that act. Yet there is, in fact, nothing to say or show. But, at the same time, the impasse is spoken, whether in the unsaid that is yet exclaimed, or in the wrongly said, the "blasphemy" and "imprecation" that index the exclamation less to religious transgression than to the anger of speech that rails against itself, to the point where it can only say too much or too little. We might then point out to Lacan that although the sexual relation "cannot be written" (that is, if there is no "relation," no recorded and signifying relation), it can be spoken and it is spoken as far as—or even from—the extremity of its exclamation.

Bibliography

Christian Prigent, "Un gros fil rouge ciré," in *L'Intenable* (Paris: P.O.L., 2004); Jean-Luc Nancy, "The 'There Is' of Sexual Relation," in *Corpus II: Writings on Sexuality*, trans. Anne O'Byrne (New York: Fordham University Press, 2013); Jonathan Safran Foer, *Everything Is Illuminated* (New York: Harper Perennial, 2003). Concerning the quotation from page 177 of the Foer book, which, like the last page of *Ulysses*, is merely one reference among a million others possible in literature, this is not by chance the actual place where a word can be given to the exclamation that is capable of carrying it momentarily. Consequently, in this case, the literary bibliography is, in principle, impossible to delimit. I prefer, therefore, to sidestep the bibliography and simply quote Apollinaire in one of his *Poems to Madeleine*:

> This is what the symphonic song of love heard in the conch shell of
>   Venus is made of
> There is the song of the love of times gone by
> The sound of the wild kisses of famous lovers
> The love-cries of mortal women raped by gods

The male members of fabled heroes erect as church candles come and go
    like obscene murmurs
There are also the demented cries of the Bacchantes made with love from
    eating the hippomanes secreted in the vulva of mares in heat
The love-cries of felines in the jungle
The dull sound of sap rising in tropical plants
The racket of the tides
The thunder of artillery batteries' obscenely shaped canons enacting the
    terrible love of peoples
The waves of the sea birthplace of life and beauty
And the song of victory that the first rays of sunshine caused Memnon the
    unmoving to sing
There is the cry of the Sabines at the moment of their ravishment
The wedding song of the Sulamite
        I am black but beautiful
And Jason's priceless cry
At finding the Fleece
And the swan's mortal song as its down snuggled between Leda's blue-
    tinged thighs
There is the song of all the love in the world
And between your beloved thighs
        Madeleine
May be heard the murmur of all love just as the sacred song of the entire
    ocean resounds in the seashell[2]

        2005

The Only Reading

For me there is no single reading and it would be difficult to provide the general form of such an activity.

There is the informative reading: I read to learn what the text can provide. This reading is not unlike other types of data recording (recording a lecture, for example). It predominates in the reading of the work of students and candidates for publication.

There is onboard reading: we climb on board, let ourselves be carried away, float toward unknown shores; we move to the rhythm of the waves, at the whim of currents. We do not necessarily identify with a hero but with the movement of writing. This kind of reading is not unlike other forms of letting go: listening to music, watching a movie. It relates mostly to literature, including philosophy, but is limited to the amount of time available. After a while, I'm in a hurry to write.

We can also read for research: we read to find something, we follow a path. We may, for example, read to identify the presence or operation of a concept, an image; we read to identify a structure, a latent meaning, revelatory associations. Such reading is not unlike other kinds of analytic, interpretative, or selective quests.

No doubt, all of my reading combines something of these three forms in variable proportions. The third assumes greater importance with time, but it is the closest to writing. The tracks I follow are intended for my own use. They will become materials, quotations, allusions. In reality, I continuously coax reading toward writing.

I should conclude where I began: reading escapes me as form, essence, or definite property.

But this tentative approach has revealed a very simple truth. The only form of reading that is truly unlike these insufficient modes is reading aloud. It alone keeps at a distance information, and identification, and interpretation. It confides the text to our lips, our throat, and our tongue: these take over from the head. Our voice takes over from the letter, that is, sense finds itself pushed aside, not suppressed but distracted, pushed to the margin, postponed until later, maybe never. Or sense becomes sensible, sensitive, sensual, which is another way of not ending as intelligible sense.

Reading aloud—not too loud, we need to carefully adjust the volume— is the only kind that directs the text from mouth to ear, even if it's my own ear. The ear opens upon an interminable resonance, within me and without, from within me to without, from you to me. Nothing is closer to the essence of language: the echo of the murmur of things.

August 2005

PART IV

Parodos

Unlike the previous essays, the texts gathered in this section are not presented as theoretical texts about literature. Should they then be called "literary"? Far be it from me to claim as much. They do not arise from the spontaneous movement of a voice that narrates or sings (even though the word "spontaneous" might require certain commentaries and reservations). They arise, in all cases, from a specific request inviting me, directly or indirectly, to engage with literature. Or to act as if I had.

An expectation—I wrote, forgetting the title I gave to this collection. Language is called back to itself and leads me to say that these expectations arrived, knowingly or not, ahead of any such expectation of mine . . .

The Greek word parodos referred to the song sung by the members of the choir as they made their way to the stage (the first sense of the word is "passage"). If we detect any homophony with parōdia, from which the word "parody" is derived, it is because we have erased the difference between short "o" and long "ō." Parōdia referred to an overblown, comic song. I'll leave the homophony where it is . . . Parodos making its slow entry, obliquely, upon the stage—parōdia so that I do not presume to be there—that is, believe myself to be in a place threatened by the temptation of the Ode and the sacred song.

Psyche

"Psyche ist ausgedehnt, weiss nicht davon." This is a posthumous note of Freud's. The psyche is outstretched, without knowing it. Everything ends, thus, with this brief melody:

Psyche ist ausgedehnt, weiss nicht davon.

Psyche is outstretched, *partes extra partes*; she is but a dispersion of infinitely parceled out places in locations that divide themselves and never penetrate each other. No encasement, no overlap; everything is outside another outside—anyone can calculate their order and demonstrate their relationships. Psyche alone knows nothing of this; for her, there is no relationship between these places, these locations, these bits of a plane.

Psyche is outstretched in the shade of a walnut tree, as evening falls. She is resting; the slight movements of sleep have partly uncovered her chest. Eros contemplates her, with both emotion and malice. Psyche knows nothing of this. Her sleep is so deep that it has taken from her even the abandon of her pose.

Psyche is outstretched in her coffin. Soon it will be closed. Among those present, some hide their faces, others keep their eyes desperately fixed on Psyche's body. She knows nothing of this—and that is what everyone around her knows, with such exact and cruel knowledge.

Translated by Emily McVarish
1978

The Young Carp

To Philippe Lacoue-Labarthe
Always predisposed
to extravagant speech
for which your prose is too
primitive,
I have made this arabesque,
which I dedicate to you.

Introductory Note

In a sense, I would prefer that this preface not be read. I fear that one might think it contains either a guide , or a theory, or a justification of the text that follows. Aside from this fear, it is reasonable to believe that I am reluctant to *present* this text, in any way at all. Perhaps it's a matter of love and hate. However, it can't present itself, as if it were self-evident. So, I can briefly state the following:

This text derived (I use the word purposely, for this movement was not entirely planned) from a project for a study of Valéry's *La Jeune Parque*. Alain[1] had already provided a commentary to the poem. This would not, in itself, indicate recidivism but there is another factor to consider: Valéry himself provided a commentary to Alain's commentary in his fable, *Le Philosophe et la Jeune Parque*. It is not so surprising that Valéry wrote—not without irony—this commentary on his own poem and did so by instructing us with a philosophical lesson about poetry itself. His entire poetics is didactic, a didactics of poetry to the extent that it forms a didactics of thought (one might reread, for example, *L'Amateur de poèmes*).—Should this be commented on or (therefore) written in verse? What is a didactic poem?

But at the same time: what is parody? It isn't a pastiche. Nor is it simply a caustic imitation or burlesque travesty of a noble genre. And if it were not *only* that? (And what is "that," exactly?) If it were, at the same time—*para-ôdè*—the discrepant moment of song, the moment of access to the poem (a fit of poetry, crisis of verse) that cannot be accessed (out of refusal or impotence), and which *marks time*[2] upon this threshold. To mark the time of poetry: a parodic Blanchot would have dictated those words to us.

But what is it here about the rivalry between speech and the poem, and the philosopher and the poet (this case is primarily that of Valéry)? Could this rivalry turn into a *competition*, simultaneously assault and encounter? Parody plays with competition first and foremost, but what is a parodic competition?

And lastly, shouldn't we stop to consider that parody is already at work in Valéry? Couldn't his entire poetic enterprise (or that of Monsieur Teste, as well) be defined in this way? In that sense, we would have here not a parody of parody but the repetition of *time marked*, the shuffling feet of poetry. As if, necessarily, the ground found itself deformed, or reformed. Wouldn't there at least be a conviction in this that poetry is not the infinite power of a language (one of the most curious characteristics of modernity is to have reactivated this romantic claim) but obeys the laws of the finitude of speech (parody, a question of closure, my lyric neighbor tells me), and that the *competition* between the two may find itself singularly displaced?

What follows has no doubt been written to leave all these questions pending for a while—somewhere.

The number of verses, their meter and arrangement, the choice of rhymes on every page are exactly those of *La Jeune Parque* (in the edition of 1942). However, it is not always a question of prosody, which here mixes with other models: if this weren't so, the genre would be that of a pastiche. As for the rest, "a silence is the strange source of poems" Valéry writes in *Le Philosophe et la Jeune Parque*, and, in the *Notebooks*: "here, the reader will find a meaning."

February 1979

I listen, and in my pensive mind compare
That which speaks with that which murmurs.

VICTOR HUGO, *Paroles sur la dune.*

Who sings this song, so simple, who imitates it,
Unconcerned with being lost within? . . . But who sings
Without laughter, smiling at the edge of speech?

Yet no offering could restore, belatedly,
For us, the fervor of the poem.
Wars have cast it into the pallid disaster
Our peoples demanded for this imperial age
With mouths torn by litanies of horror,
Moaning, raging, cursing, uncadenced exhalations,
Mournful fevers shrilly voiced . . .
And we, ever since, gossips plagued by boredom,
Chanting the irony of your frozen charms,
We share more of you than your departure, poet,
Whose silent farewell resonates and is repeated
In millions of damp whispers and images
Void of exile upon the barren islands of your home . . .
A century hangs on our inanity.

Who, then, would pass us on the way to this eternity
Of albums, ancient verses, submerged in your binding,
White shroud with its sharp crease readied?
Oh, the fingernail beneath the sheet of paper, the number absolute
That follows, on every page resolved,
By the wistful ceremony of a reader
Sacrificing the immense absence of the author
To the pure meter by which all thought thinks itself.
Who will dare to abolish this rite, violence
Without name? if not ourselves, anonymous, we
Who never kiss the ivory knees
Of any idol, and with our worn eyelids,
Skeptical spectators of museum splendors.
Civilized at last by knowing we are mortal
Our genius decorates its altars with prose,

Fragile liturgy, biblical memorial
Drunk with histories whose perishable essence,
Beneath the ink that constellates a pallid firmament,
Ferments in the bitter odor of the novel.

Our stories are filled with this absence of order.

Which Fate has refused to spin for us
The thread from which the ideal poem is wound,
Idea itself, into the candid and sidereal fabric?

What Destiny, nourishing the spinner's fright,
Suspends her religious hand with a gesture?
Her spindle rolls along the ground and her voice is silent,
Which recited the cantilena of a pure
Spirit, absorbed with reflecting
the first spark of its own light upon itself,
Soul of a body formed of fragments of mica.

Transparency, you are shattered in this silent
Struggle that deconstructs the arch of saliva.

Long ago, to the sound of an allusive strophe,
A science dreamt its beginning and its end,
Moved by clear numbers and at last calculating
The code, frequency, and exact amplitude
Of the blind discourse that reveals the pact
By which Mankind takes pride in the first utterance
Of the massive turmoil forever renounced.
Dizzyingly rising from no space
Such knowledge tightens rapacious claws
Around the violent articulation of a cry,
Exhausting the flanks of the proscribed animal.
. . . And the calm, gentle, indolent tongue,
Which, delighted, delivers its bloodless speech:
Too demanding poem! impatient monument
Whose nacreous stele is illuminated from moment
To successive moment by an innumerable glyph,
Engraved, fierce and fertile tool, by a claw
Torn live from a supplicant's flesh,
You splash with your sigil an oracle begun
At every mortal moment in the deep throated
Being whose impure mouth consumes a world.
For him you would burn, with manifold perfumes,
Muses, the sacred wood of your abandoned temples,
That now, in a flutter of powder,
Is resigned to the odor warm and impalpable.
Scent! . . . column of air above an obscure plinth,
Motionless emotion of this pure motive
That vibrates in the exalted breath of your leaf . . .
The earth trembles where a vapor forms . . . a wave
For which no form, no gleam, no color
Is offered to reveal, insidious, the disseminated
Scope . . . All presence concludes
In the effusion with which a nostril is fecundated,

Essential trace and pure vestige of spirit
Whose breeze captures surprised delight.
Word for word, if his atom must be declined,
The nascent thought is exhaled in a sublime
Aroma, unsuspected by its own gaze,
Which a cold sun immolates and consecrates, haggard,
In the heart of its hearth, luminous dross,
Blinding oblivion laden with theory.
But that sure eye is blind to the slow ascension;
In the barely labile air, barely a scansion,
The young odor brings forth new insolence,
The serene and soft inspiration of a proof
More absolute because issuing from no source
Other than the vague incantation of its pride.

Thus you celebrated your delightful origin
In the furtive respiration that illuminates,
With the rhythm of its breast, the grace to discern it
Cloaked in a perfumed veil of things.

Such SILENCE, you say, pulls my soul back from the dream . . .

What SILENCE, exhaled by a body extended,
Flatters more than perfume the folds of desire,
And wears itself away in pleasure's bright wake?
O Fate! . . . your intimate fragrance enthralls me
When, within your ambit, I detect the furtive presence
Of Man, incessantly shaped by your fingers
From a branch of hemp in which his destiny slept,
Fine frail fiber and too precocious cord.

Your grace offers him a singular bargain,
Wrapped in its own embrace, ever covetous
of its own self-pleasure, and through its own vigor
always eager for the energetic avowal of sap
In love with its confusion! . . . Violent truce
By the Unique brought forth against all his equals:
"No people, no commerce! and the only devices
Of my glory are those that my shadow conceives,
Obscure procession of a numberless crowd,
That summarizes and accompanies me, and reproduces,
Silently and with my voice, the call that seduces.
In the company of this insignificance
I can hear my self-destruction before my omnipotence.

Innocent, dismembered by a blade of flesh
On my own altars . . . The great disorder
Of sacrifice exalts the victim's soul,
Who now prepared, his makeup applied, drowns slowly
In his own blood . . . I myself, shameless voyeur,
have let this limpid blood flow and this elsewhere
That it pleases me to slowly mix with the same
Imperishable mortal in me, desert that loves me.

And this rape releases an immense repose
In which the happy memory of a sister cries.

Too precious nostalgia of my complicit race,
To you I dedicate my name! Incestuous Narcissus,
I must forget the flowering stucco
from which my bee's dream distilled the sap.
No honey! No abundance that retreats,
If the ring of blood leaves no more than a glaze,
Intact fugitive bitten by repentance!
It is to me alone, here, that my hand must be joined.
Offering without music fulfilled in calmness,
My reason yields to the cool breeze of an infinite
Palm that the wise adoration, slow creation,
Of my astonishment, balances.
Pure element of thought! I imagine you,
Tenebrous, rising from the shores of the Sign."
. . . Everywhere the same menace introduces
Your festival, Dear Poem . . .

An angel trembles at the end
Of each of these words, which an implacable margin
Causes to resonate in another likeness,
Double, double rival, too cutting echo
That grants to the only *aoidos* his due,
Golden offering given to the festival of language
Torn by the thousand styles of a lengthy
Orgy that swallows it alive and vomits it
Into your changed throat, Dear Reader! . . . for you whimper
With the gift of this illustrious nourishment,
Fruit of a mouth . . . noise . . . the rustle of writing
Upon the decorated lips of the musical drawing
Traced by a vocal portent in its arcanum . . .
Your tympanum is touched and shaken by a rhythm
That breaks through your narrow chest and crosses the uncertain
Isthmus of a strange pleasure . . . And I can hear
Rise in you the temptation of the narrator.
I know that beneath your closed eyelids a swarm
Of syllables grows, certain of their pauses,
And with a familiar cry is recognized
One like the other in their regular flight . . .
The word is made flesh the moment it is mimed
In the docile repetition of a rhyme
From which, upon its insolent simulacrum, is suspended
The extraordinary promise to utter nothingness.

Enduring memory of Troy's ruin!

These ashes preserve for my piety the prey
That escapes into the more virgin air of a Greek miracle,
The gift of saying and the desire that probes with
Anger a naked captive of its speech.
From sudden antiquity is born the symbol
Of a terrible and tender oath:
I offer my throat to the glow of your passion,
Goddess so long caressed, solemn breath,
You rise, charged with subterranean shadow
Cloaked in subtle vapor and the unlaced sky,
Black flash, frozen by my oracular voice!

What monster, what living thing is torn from my mouth
Touched by a blinding frost
In the faint respiration of this ether,
That grows emptier as your breath is lost,
Helen, and more sonorous with the distinction of your shame?

Murmur ever close to my ready ear,
I listen to myself . . . Saga of my own return
Made many by the breeze and the day's ruses,
In the language of gods myself imperishable,
Abandoning my trace to its destiny of sand
For nothing other than a song . . . the impalpable paean
Obstinately beating on the yawning drum
Of my pleura, long enamored of my shock . . .
Strike again, drummer! Yes! Force my surprise
To dance! Chase in the hollows of my body
The confused movement that will snatch me from my deaths.
. . . For I am leaving you at last, tutelary poets
Whose larvae populated my studious graveyards.

What vow will be formed from your heavens past?
No charming theater will now provide
The long whispered offering of doves
Between your gold laden lips, between your tombs . . .
And I . . . the pure forgetfulness of a dawn that was
Yours disorders my unruly plans.

"May the one who observes you perish in his turn,
Wrapped in the Occident of your example!"

Prophesizes a voice more muted than mine
More insinuating and yet nearby,
Delicate viper, captive to my tongue's fold.
Yours, without rest, remains attentive
To my disaster . . . And who plans his pleasure?
My own heart in me wants to destroy itself
In the abyss overflowing with a bestial absence . . .

Venerable asp, I scorn the trivial tongue
That yours has licked. Please, Go! then,
Gather in my mouth the trembling maze
Of venomous vessels woven beneath your fragile skin;
Beneath my gums open this cruel wound
Infected by your silent, burning poison;
Mingle with my laden breath your pestilent breath,
Ruin in my flesh the most secret sources
Of this long human cry without resource
Through which I speak . . . And lastly, make me like
Those glaucous depths ignored by the sun . . .
Blind, and on my tongue a block of cold lava,
I will still the waters upon my wreckage.
The beating waves, laden with large animals,
Will scatter in shadows a disorder of words,
Whose ink is loosed from an octopus
Legendary and enormous . . . Oh, what suspicion of the Work,
Among the storms and shattered archipelagos,
Leads to the abyss the memory of the drowned!
The hard coral on which their bodies reproduce
Scatters their hopes upon my flanks, which it tears

With such nonchalance . . . A trickle of blood
Briefly signals the impotent swimmer
Deafened by the cries of the proud ocean,
Foaming clamor . . . a million shards of language.

But have I destroyed this order among us,
This speech?
            Again I find you on your knees,
Imploring me always and I always granting,
Too subtle vapor, faithful and false strophe,
Psalm engendered in the flaw of my throat,
Such simple shiver in an ashen sigh
Of an absent flame . . . Oh, penetrating Phrase!
With my lip fearful of your band of gauze,
I bless you, I kiss the air through which you fly,
And the grass trampled by your twists and turns,
Deeply I breathe their peaceful bitterness . . .
Your flight reveals the audacious volume
In which silence itself inscribes its black number,
And notes the uneasy imminence of duty:

Speak! . . . but keep hidden the mouth to say it!

Phrase whose damp coolness is torn,
Unfolds with the dawn, and like it enthralled
With dissolving the sterile humor of night,
You are an immense birth for me, another stomach
Larger and maternal . . . darker in my center
Where the impossible division reigns . . . I write
That you have birthed in me a legion of cries,
Screamers of exile from the shattered depths of my memory . . .
The ravaged faces of fairground animals!
Unhearing harmonies of the setting sun . . . Distant chords,
Strident and sorrowful, heavier than any remorse . . .
And you, cold moans! . . . music of eclipses . . .
Apocalyptic murmurs and burns . . .
Speak! . . . I beg you! . . . I'll abandon my voice
If yours renew at last the emotion
Of that brief agony, which was my origin!

An ancient terror worn by childbirth
Revives in you the fever of being, and the worry
Smuggler on uncertain rivers . . . It is you I thank
For the sobs surprised on the banks of my genesis,
And this pain in you that soothes me against your will . . .

Such disorder on my tongue . . . Oh, the very first noise!

A shock grazes this emptiness and offers me the fruit,
The cymbal of flesh. Behold, the unexpected
Term of the obscure sacrifice of sperm:
Large lips drink the water that contains me,
A body bares itself and that body belongs
To the pure fire of the air that penetrates it . . .
The delicate motion of the wind deflowers my entire being
And the same, unchanging, before the slender shudders
That bruise the frail soul and its rare fragments
Scattered among the distant glimmers of a dawn . . .
Plunges into the broad shadow a long resonant ribbon,
And rocks me—Oh day—with your very first verse!
In your sudden throat my heart is riven
By difficult laughter and with a strange cry
The old ether whimpers . . . On my tongue a bitter
Mix of broken voices and buried groans,
Of barbarous dictions and joyful calls,
Offers me, beyond me, the same mouth,
The same that once around my bed
Wove a long cloth of absolute silence.
Sleep! What lasting pain was needed
To arouse the severe games of your dream,
And this ample lesson whose relentless speech
Each night instructs the unmoving terror
Of the one who awakens at the moment of his death . . .
I dare, in the intact navel that speaks me,

To expose myself at last, distorted by a protracted desire
To hear myself embrace my pure invocation!
Prayer abandoned in its supplication,
The weak flesh is silent . . . its anguish shapes me . . .

No presence here . . . no monster who sleeps
In an eternal thickness of forgetfulness.
But this unique cry tears the virgin
And already bloody folds of a throat foreign
To the melodious larynx of this weightless soul . . .
Yes! by the torn skin of an odious contour
An absence of noise struggles toward the day,
And composes the slow movement of a thing
Unnamable and that yet calls to me and forces upon me
The dismantled horror of the specter of my voice . . .
Deafened by my own lethargy, I see myself
Repeating the echo that no rock conceals.

Nothing goes before you, silence that splits you!
Nothing more than fright and harsh disorder . . .

Language, mine, and you, my mouth, speak to me!

A calm, self-adoring monument by your side,
Long but vain beat that dreams of containing me
In the all-powerful interval . . .
                                        But this pale gullet
Resists . . . unable to quench itself with your water
Mixed with the acid humor of my spit
Whose solvent liquefies this naïve attempt
In me of a silent thought upon its threshold.
A foul, green algae consumes mourning . . .
A word's memory grows confused and mixes
With the slow stifling of the depths . . .
                                        Oh, mire

Untouched by silent memories,
You putrefy so many graceful memories!
From their first limpid moment, you soil them
With the ferment of peat and rust
That eats away their knees with an aborted idiom . . .
Form is abolished in your opacity.

Born of the intense rot of the poem,
A foul crowd spumes blasphemed verses
And profanes the issue of the maternal womb
Where a savage and solemn child trembled.
The attenuated flame of its desire fails,
Its ravaged curls flow across my shell . . .
Its terrified face bears a cruel circle.

Hail! Absolute breath of the sole azure as such,
In a mouth knotted by its own gaping
In the fierce interdict of non-birth.
Child! . . . you shall keep the idol of your name,
The voiceless fetish whose mask says: No!
No! In the calm commotion of your tongue
No speech shall divide this seam
In which the past's fleeting cry grows hard,
Unchanging chance forever retraced.
Child, I myself, though wet, am your idol,
And in luxuriant depths escape your reflection, which I sacrifice
In the morose glimmer of my frozen flanks.
I cradle the obscure delirium of your excess.

In the waters in which a smoky wave dissolves,
Vestige of the mud worn by my shadow,
Your lips will bathe my piscine bath,
Without even a murmur, impassive shudder . . .
With my pale and ancient body I graze
The miniscule debris of bitter speech
That was spoken once . . . The silent prodigy
That I complete bends before the duty to transform
Each scattered word in its unique pause.

In the secret sharing of the restful water,
The air stands apart from its sterility
In the multiple sonority of birds.
The liquid order harbors a thought more tender . . .
Volume that a white crystal infinitely engenders,
When no atom vibrates or resonates with song,
The lake to which I draw you in your youthful penchant
To suit a lucid voice to your own measure
Will offer nothing but the naked angle of a caesura . . .

There the speaker declares before his pale future
The unchangeable moment . . . What can be said? . . . and what pleasure?

This mouth that opens and chooses its torture
Did it ask that its epoch end
In the moment that the tongue begins its flight?
Should it, from the delicate arc of this neck,
So violently offer the virginal cord
And break in blood this rival force
Whose rapid alterations are song?
. . . But I ask in vain, if my self-seeking voice
Already precipitates its useless cadence,
And strangles itself, obstinately hostile to itself . . .
Will I have modulated no more than a suspended rest?
Soon everything will take offence at my desperate breath . . .
The mud gathers me, avid and solitary,
And presses its mass against my side, to silence it.
A thickness weighs on me, exhausts me . . . Oh, the insolent
Fate of those who take flight!
The peaceful altitude that blooms on their grazed lip
Convokes the kisses of a tongue frightened
By the sovereign suaveness of the sky
In the effusion of its honeyed signs . . .
And I, there . . . below . . . on a brow that takes refuge
Forever sharing the stilled avalanche,
I dream . . . and it isn't a dream, it is nothing,
Nothing but the stupid, empty envy that sustains
The dull confusion that my languor cuts away.

What sinister decor the asylum of a carp
Slips beneath the oblique procession of my days!
And what forbidden laugh is revealed by the contours
Of this fleeting and sluggish life that limits itself
With a monotone skin and a dismal rule . . .
Every moment abandons me to the detailed pattern
Of the number of the scale with the scale entwined.

Thus, always garbed in inflexible writing
I advance masked by a pure maxim!
But here, in the swollen abyss, no gaze
Will read or resolve this harmonious maze . . .

Alone I pursue myself and alone I inform myself
A gnosis of impoverished fear disdains me . . .
I do not die, I forget . . . I deliver from oblivion
This great speech of expected silence,
This long beginning that never begins,
This fold worn by more than one futile absence
At the bottom of the waters, distracted baptism of spirit.
Surprised by the deformity of my desire.

Unbound torment of birth, blinded by tenderness,
In liquid repetition, an incredulous vivacity
Fades and flees along its self;
And I, so contrary to my new emotion,
Voluble without voice, though faint I offer myself
To the declamations of an unheard throat . . .

Speech! . . . the stricken air that breaks upon the waters!
For which my sandy shelter calculates a grave,
My listless mouth opens to the waves that stifle
The secret event, the imperceptible gale
Of a sign, in the absolute infancy of its fate
Whose name reveals imponderable strife.

This name . . . already mine! . . . is suddenly undone
And suddenly grinds in minutes of sand
The star unsettled by its advent.
Vain silent tumult that misleads and deceives me,
Why conceal from me the obscure deliberations
Of an open mouth that gently nullifies itself?
An intent to coax me toward some adulation
Of my submerged swimming? What speculation?

In the middle of the path taken by our life,
What is repeated and what renews the desire
To receive, with grace, the first gift of the gods,
Sonorous origin, melodious preface
Of this very pure love of speech for itself,
That gently fails in its own poem
And prefers itself to its message?

                                        Nothing spreads
The shadow of this lake over me more certainly
Than the confused torment of your presence on its bank
To again cleave the ancient image of a virgin,

Whose dreamy charm would guide to Hell,
Superannuated prophet, the footfall of your verses.
But so beautiful a resurrection is concealed;
The heart, my heart fails me . . . suffering enfolds me . . .

My proverb instructs me of my mournful clarity,
Wordless legend, insulted symbol!

(That which wounds your foul throat . . . is an ash-filled
urn . . . The grave was always taciturn . . .
If the wave multiplies the glaucous monstrances . . .
No longer can you pray . . . Depopulate their mirrors . . .)

My long noiseless night, which you say is a cure
Too powerful, whose sap within overwhelms me.
The water grows cloudy around my nacreous rings
As if to celebrate sacred storms!
I see . . . I believe I see again a distant icon
Raise the outline of its throne upon these waters!
Unfurled seaweed, churning sands,
Tremble all around me and rouse my silent domain!
Who speaks? . . . Spoken by a marine splendor,
A sign is suspended from my vesuvianite race . . .
Tongues loosen . . . What prodigious hiatus
Mixes my damp skin with Venus's loins!
A history . . . an accident perhaps . . . replaces me . . .
And the one who is silent is found to have spoken
With a voice of divine and expansive luxury,
That reveals a name, gleaming nudity.
True goddess! accent of love, and fable
Of a pure outrush of ineffable presence,
In whose convulsion I would grow weak
When the wave bent its swell to take pleasure
In your birth . . . Moment of the frailest cadence
Barely measured on the wave that buoys you,
Hollow sound of thirst, stuttering desire
Of a sound that pierces me, and the unconscious rite
Of this prodigal poetry of a language
In me that rejects itself and defeats its work.
How can you compare me, vulgar as I am, to this honor
Without breaking on my heavy lip a fury
That your kisses can never contain?
I fear the obscene word that gives birth to you . . .
Derisive swelter! . . . On your swooning throat,
Myth retains a rhythm declaimed,
Its tenderness flows at your feet in the foam

On which the bubble of my bitterness has burst.
You say nothing, allowing my fear to worsen,
But your slender breast exhales a favor,
Candid, dedicated parody of a word,
Barely a beat, the fold that consoles me
And divides the heart of an infinitesimal pulse
In the laceration of time . . . Profound percussion
Of your meter beating on my rebellious ear . . .
Open mouthed . . . salvation . . . original wound!
Imperceptibly I offer my cheek to the tacit and
Divided rigor of a holy modesty
Whose ill-fated virtue in which my luck takes pleasure
Observes my secret, mother of my silence . . .
Daughter of the distinguished sacrifice of my blood,
Which spreads across the waters of your indecent charm.

1979

"Within my breast, alas, two souls . . ."

To accompany L'Isola del silenzio

by Claudio Parmiggiani

Faust 1

Labor lost, philosophy,
jurisprudence, and medicine,
other labor lost, theology, physiology, and you,
learned disciplines of every kind,
all your efforts lost, as well as mine.[1]

Take care, for in a short while nothing of you shall remain, knowledge, wisdom, venerable deposits of nights of study and lives of contemplation. Nothing will remain but my closed fist on your torn pages, which I will toss into the fire.

The bell strikes (the bell in the bell tower)

I have sounded the alarm of a fire that spreads through you, your pages, your volumes, and your shelves, your images, and your ideas. Oh, memory of Alexandria, Sarajevo, of the emperor Chi Hoang Ti! But here an unstable substance has spontaneously burst into flame without any external cause to bring its spark. No arsonist, no torchbearer or flamethrower, no shells of phosphorous or napalm. But your writings and symbols are scorched, and the incandescence has effortlessly spread through words and sentences, through images and maps, equations and diagrams.

And, of course, through the grimoires of the inventors of fire, of tow and tar, of saltpeter and black powder, of the alchemists of consumption and consummation: they too, their volumes burn.

Faust 2

Labor lost, thoughts, meditations and reflections, and you, as well, inquiries and treaties, manuals, almagests, antiphonaries and bestiaries, missals, breviaries and compendiums, Bibles and Korans, sutras, Psalters and song books, albums and atlases. Take care, for I shall not allow you to remain. I warn you, but leave you no chance to escape my fury. In fact, nothing will save you, and nowhere will you find safety. I bring forth within you, against you, an unparalleled rage, an exasperation that releases the burning desire to consume all knowledge and all speech.

What I want is your charred spirit, your reasons scorched and singed within your bindings changed into coal and that coal into slag and dense ash.

The bell speaks (the bell in the campanile)

I sound the alarm but it serves no purpose. There is nowhere for you to flee: nowhere you can run to or seek shelter. You reside only in yourselves and bent over yourselves. You are like a walled city everywhere in flames, whose ramparts prevent your escape. There you lie, books abandoned to your own flame, and who has ever saved himself from the destruction within his own heart? It is not an autodafé that destroys you, for they too, the pyre makers, the pyromaniacs of the mind, their books burn as well, along with their incendiary doctrines.

Faust 3

A large pyramid of cold, calcified books, like stones in a mausoleum, is what I desire and what I obtain. A pile, a mass of burned volumes, all legibility buried between their pages, which the heat has welded shut, blurring the distinction between ink and paper, and with it the separation of signifier and signified, and finally, the distinction between sense and cinder. That is what I want: to incinerate sign and sense.

The bell speaks (the golden bell)

He will speak no more of sense. He will no longer decipher it. No longer interpret it. Quite simply, he will no longer understand it. It will no longer be there. But squeezed in his fist like an overripe fruit that is crushed and whose juice drips between his fingers, what was once learning will, in the end, be absolved of all relations, all perspective, and everything shall be ruined or exalted in the pure act.

He wants no part of it now, he wants his death and announces it. He rejects the unbearable distance between knowledge known and knowing knowledge, between the savant and science, between science and itself, this unbearable and non-reducible detour that returns his self-consciousness to him like the necessary guarantee of his assurance: the evidence of a knowledge of the self that underlies all knowledge of the other, the object, the thing, the world, language as well, and, finally, thought itself, its noesis, its notion, its judgment.

I ring the extinction of knowledge and speech, the proposition and the sentence, categories and syncategoremes, copulas and commas. I ring a monotonous carillon interminable in its silent resonance, for extinction itself is interminable. Thought is not abolished in this violent movement for it imprints itself to wed the thing and the idea itself, to melt one into the other and their compact mass into a paste of black glass. A crystal forms, which reverberates in rhythmical frequencies of the beating of its own funeral service. Thought still thinks.

Faust 4

What I want is to make thought identical to the being whose thought it is. Not similar, or like, or analogous, but identical. Being and thought, one and the same thing. An old poem said this, but I no longer want a poem to say this. That poem too will burn; besides, it has already lost more than one papyrus and more than one verse.

But to do this, to arrive at the same thing, we must clearly understand verbs: to think and to be, not thought and being. For thought can certainly take being for its object and being can certainly have thought as one of its species, as one thing among others. But if to think is to be, then there is no longer any object nor any thing. Everything becomes identical: to think is to weigh, but it should be obvious that in an identical manner, to be is still to weigh. Nothing is without weight, there is nothing that does not press upon the soil or upon itself. That which does not bear down, nor weigh upon, no matter how minimally, dissolves into vapor, into smoke, and, ultimately, into pure dissipation.

My books; now you know why I am burning you. I am giving you back your weightlessness. I retain nothing of you. I want only the weight, the weighing of things on the scale of justice. The gravity of a just weighing of things, without the interposition of meaning or value.

The bell speaks (the bell jar, the bell of despair)

He loved books, following their lines with his finger, turning their pages slowly to accompany the unbroken passage between one word and another, between recto and verso, the two sides of the same thinness. It is only the remaining thickness of this thinness that irritates him and angers him so. And consequently, even more so the stacked thinnesses of the book, their unwelcome volume between him and the world, between him and the thing itself, between him and the act. For he wanted the act, wanted it from start to finish and in such a way that there would no longer be a beginning or an end but only a single action present to itself everywhere and gathered in itself with such energy, such intensity that its entire duration is equal to a moment and its spectacle is that of a dream in which everything is simultaneous and the order of reason has no place because, there, the chain of reasoning does not take place but everything is presented together, cause and effect, conception and execution, himself, finally, and that which is not himself, that which he wishes to become and in which he wants to exist, as man wants to become child, animal, or woman. Unfortunately, everyone can see that man has disappeared and it is no longer him that we find outside himself but his loss, his confusion, and his madness. Everyone but him.

He sees nothing but sinks deeper into the solemn and compact heaviness of being.

Faust 5

I see extension dissolved to a point and duration contracted to a moment in which that point is formed, at the intersection of my act and efficacy. No dimension, no delay, no waiting. Tomorrow comes today and stays there. We are tired of waiting and transforming into waiting that which consists of nothing other than motionless intervals between the same and its repetition. We must make a fist, I mean, my fist, *"meine Faust,"* my fingers tightly folded over the palm and turning the hand into a club, a vice, a massive weapon of destruction that first crushes the world's exteriority within it, all its excrescences and protuberances, the tumors of being. I have stopped expecting a future, a savior, a chance. If I am not already what I am, how could I become it? That, myself, will not be given to me from anywhere or anyone if my already tightened fist does not already contain it as its very clenching, and its oath. In my fist, cognition and history are turned to ash, consumed without flame by the terrible constriction of my fingers alone, which weld themselves together to form a shard of silex held at arm's length, my extended arm now directed toward nothing other than that very silex to which everything conforms as it is crushed.

The bell speaks (bell jar in the vegetable garden)

It is growth that he suppresses. Not the growth that reproduces the identical and the equivalent by always recapitalizing it in new programs, but that which follows a birth, that develops a conception, *cresco, creo*, the care and ripening of a being that exists. The growth that arises from almost nothing, an encounter, a chance, a *clinamen* of atoms, an inclination of passions. That which delivers not to expectation but to this availability that does not even expect and that is only arranged, lets itself be arranged. The ripening of fruit, but also the fruit as it is detached and falls, shriveled, to the grass, where it is eaten by insects and worms and birds. How could he have forgotten that? He wanted hothouses and imperishable fruits, never shriveled but never ripe either. Because he wants the fruit at once, he also wants knowledge without books and history without narratives. He wants man without flaws, without openings, the clenched fist that infinity or the improbable no longer releases.

Faust 6

The unnamable is the only name that, in the end, I can accept. Not the name that surpasses all names and names them all by nicknaming itself, but the unnamable whose very name corrupts and wears away all names, the unnamable as a disgust of names, nausea, and revulsion.

The bell speaks (bell moved by the wind among
the prayer flags at the mountain pass)

To understand the name, one must first listen to the sound. One must allow the simple effect of a rustling, of a beat to resonate. What a bell wants to say is, above all, the oscillation of its clapper against the swell of its walls. It strikes its own wall, returning to itself from the other side of its opening. It turns to the ground a mouth of shadow in which the heavy tongue beats, this finger or iron plectrum. We may see in this a form of terrible suffering, but we may also understand it as the foreshadowing of all language, as the appeal to all language and all naming—that is, to the desire of an embrace, to the exasperated desire to be wrapped in things by their names. The bell calls to the word, the *Glockenspiel* to the games and prayers of the word that brings peace.

Faust 7

No longer to decipher but to tear apart. To undo the fabric of signs that wraps the world for us only to unwrap it later, embittered, poorly preserved. To go toward things themselves: Oh! Let me split apart! Just as we pour the metal of a bell to cast a canon, likewise . . .

But I know this: at my approach things themselves shy away. That which made them *selves*, themselves, changes and rots. Their beautiful selfness withdraws as soon as, reaching out, I disturb and disrupt it.

Just one more reason to shed myself of signs and any means of approach. I must even leave behind the senses that inform me. It is no longer a question of seeing, or hearing, not even of smelling, tasting, or stroking. Not even touching, no, for touch keeps the thing a skin's thickness away and that is not what I want. It is not what we want, Oh, my fellow man! No skin, no membrane, we want only to be one with the thing in such a way that our arrival does not alter anything about it.

I will lose myself within it so that no sign, no trace of me will ever be found. I will open a world without traces, without the slightest scratch, or the least flexion. No trace, no modification of the surface on which circulate only kernels of energy energetically displaced, exchanged, permuted and combined. A moment suffices, an instant suffices, a simple click—an onomatopoeia, a dull noise, a bell fixed in its reverberation—not the moment that remains but the one that cracks like a whip. Not the moment that lingers and enjoys but the one that flashes and sparks, setting alight a trail of powder.

Molded and coated at the heart of the thing, I disperse signs and no longer act other than by signals transmitted from one end to the other of my apparatus, of my great tentacular station from which I measure in real time the velocities of separation of all worlds together, their indefinite expansion originating in a swarm of particles in reciprocal motion. Throughout the community of propagation, the network of conductors, the charge and discharge of their voltages, I cause an unprecedented increase in the frequency of exchanges and connections. I myself am here, in impeccable and self-transparent nowness, devoid of sense, pure truth finally capable of vanishing into its own manifestation.

The bell speaks (the bourdon)

He doesn't realize how signs around him insist. He doesn't perceive their sliding. He can't hear them hiss. He cannot guess their rustling. One cannot be free of their intrigues in this way. They weave nets, they lay cables in the void, they plot, they scheme, they knot and unknot.

He himself, when he speaks, doesn't he hear himself? Isn't he the first to receive, in the echo of his voice within his skull, the trace of another voice that has been sent into his own from afar, far ahead of him? Yes, he hears that. He hears in his rapid and muffled world a few breaths from a very old world, filled with slowness and tumult.

He cannot act unless he merges with the thing, for things themselves do not merge with one another and their principle older than any principle, their reason prior to any reason, so far back in the ages of the world that its backward motion is painful to consider, their primordial reason deprived of reason has no energy other than that of an ever renewed separation whose origin is itself already separated from the self, open orifice, gap and yawning gulf of places in which births, origins, and excrescences occur. That he is so far removed, to the point that he feels distant from all things, that is how the world allows itself to be felt, opens itself to its feeling. Within his breast, alas, two souls separate, become recognizable, and break apart while pulling forcefully on their slender integuments. But he, poor man, he takes this tension between his two souls to be the schism and expulsion of sense. A liquidation and annihilation.

He is and is not correct. I move without stopping between the two, between himself and himself. He is right to reject separation. He is wrong not to accept it. We are separate, and sense is made of our separation. We are separated into rocks and fish, foam and clouds, wolves and citizens, *I* and *you*, man and woman, seeing and touching. We are separate, this makes sense, that is, an insurmountable and fragile distance, bearer of itself and nothing more—but bearer, yes, an open door to enter/detain us.

Faust 8

I wanted the world to stop being silent, as it has become and has been for a long time now. I wanted the world to speak and, to that end, that a word truly speaking lodge its power in the hollow of things themselves. I wanted a silence overcome with passion for the immediacy of our actions, our calculations, our prodigious operations. I wanted language to give way to an unspeakable amazement and to extravagant transformations and revolutions. Yes the extravagant has continued to guide me, yet how could it direct?

It cannot guide but conscientiously and obstinately leads astray. Yet, the extravagant is nothing other than the blood brother and foster brother of everything that asks for reason and final cause, justification and redemption. How difficult it is to tell them apart! How impossible to detach with one sharp blow the moment that is fixed and the one that passes, the one that holds back and the one that offers itself. How unlikely it is to sort out sense and non-sense, sign and touch, speech and silence.

To you, burned books, I see return a silent procession of ash that coats you with the traces of a flight that is always yet to come.

To say nothing and say everything, to keep silent and gather sense in a sovereign word, is the same ambition, the same disappointment. Holy book and book of ash have the same text the color of soot, the color of night.

But you remain, partly burned books, fragments fallen away from the flames or buried in the still intact thickness of thick volumes. You survive still, blackened pages on which one can decipher the remains of a poem and be moved by its beauty as a ruin. You insist, soiled pages that reveal half-formed thoughts, truncated conclusions, but with them the movement of an uneasiness, the suspension of an impulse, so many invitations to return to.

Maybe it is necessary and desirable that books burn and that there remain charred signs for feverish, uneasy decipherment, lacking sense and truth. But maybe there is nothing more there than a desire to justify myself?

The bell speaks (the cymbal, the gong)

To say nothing, to say everything, to say the thing itself and embed the word in its pure thinglike presence amounts to the same thing, to the same fury. It always overlooks the caress of the sign, the gentle touch of always swerving, never completed meanings. Neither the explicit nor the implicit attest to anything other than unfolding or folding, always halfway. Not to say everything but let something be said of everything.

The poverty of knowledge is great, no less great is that of the narrative, to the extent that we wait for the ending and anticipate the gain. But in doing so, this poverty recognizes and takes pity on itself. In doing so it does justice to itself. Knowledge unburdens itself of things known and the narrative of things told. However, there remains the wound of sense that a cold and singed truth does not extinguish.

Such are the remains of books that will have burned themselves—but he knew nothing of this, thinking he was the one who had set them on fire. What remains is a wound that cannot heal. Words constantly fail us, in love and in horror, but their loss continues to bear witness on their behalf, attests to their clumsy insistence. For words to have failed him in ecstasy or fainting, it would have first been necessary that they be written and of their writing there will have remained, on the blackened sheets, illegible traces that we must transcribe into a language yet to be invented.

It is true that our knowledge no longer knows what to know, and our tales what to tell. But we continue to speak with ashen words, we continue to trace signs only to signal our presence. We can forget all the incantations and evocations of the unnamable, but before us, continuing to make a sign to us, a new unnamed advances every time, which makes a sign without signifying.

Faust 9

The bells have gone silent. There is no alarm, no announcement now. The minarets themselves are silent and in the temples the little bells are too shrill. The fire is permanent even as it is extinguished everywhere. Ash covers the signs and the new signs are themselves incinerated. Everything has turned into cold lava and smoke stains on the walls of libraries.

The inkwell that I threw in the face of the devil has blackened the pages of the sacred books like black and burning bile. Books, I no longer want to read you but want you to decipher me. But I know very well, only too well, the extent to which I am illegible and how little your blind signs can interpret me!

It is no longer a question of interpreting, it is only a question of tasting the burned ink and its cold ash. There is no longer an alarm or an announcement, for the worst is certain just as the best and the indifferent—but above all the real is certain. There is no future for there is no longer a past. Nothing more occurs and everything is suspended in a terrible hesitation that embraces the present moment. The present no longer presents itself, it settles itself.

And yet, yes, a new unnamed advances, or we advance toward it. And, yes, at any moment I can open a book of blank pages and trace the first word of a language yet to be invented. Another wound can begin without our awareness, for our unawareness is the exact knowledge of the unnamed.

City Moments

a cobblestone street
among the asphalt pavements
the fawn colored stones gleaming
on the back of the great lizard
a hint of grass between the scales

*

worksite ditch barrier
crane shovel pothole
jackhammer compressor
protective grating
on all those hoses
electric gas hydraulic digital

*

entrails cables conduits
sewers basements catacombs

shelters foundations underground
subway

                                   *

rue rupture *via rupta*
from one side to the other
shadow and sun odd and even
pedestrian crossing

                                   *

teeming with others with sames
with nearness and distance
and neighborhoods
assembly without wholeness
gathering of appearances
likenesses brushing past

                                   *

in the old cities
the city-cities
there is the moment of the monument
the glory of gods or men
warning of the spirit
among contemporaries
there are moments of expectation
a monument will arise
or a large building
without warning

                                   *

streetcar subway bus
convenient mass transit
inconvenient crowds
stolen glances
sleeping standing sitting and stiff necks
scattered papers

                                   *

how surprising
to contemplate everyone

in their apartment
separate turned inward
monad world in itself
the city remains outside
humming distant other world

*

river ribbon waterway strip of water
banks on either side islands and bridges
water black and deep diving
as the city's rationale

*

urbanity uncertain meandering
country houses
we'll work in town
commercial craft industrial areas
zones belts layers expansions
as far as the borders of other zones

*

pleasure of the empty city
vacations great migrations
mass transport
sight of empty avenues

*

city civilization
where the city
was sign emblem blazon
neither fortress nor sanctuary
nor royal domain
city

*

bourgeois town
false town real people
outskirt hangout decivilized
without signs emblems blazons
signals without signage concrete

*

town center downtown below
ringroad rolled around what's below
bypass loop non-penetrating
what's below remains impenetrable
the city is there below very low
beneath the powerful arches of freeways

*

metropolis megalopolis
origin city large city
police politics politeness
city citizen outskirts banished
civil byroads
incivility of proximity
urban conurbation
tentacles pseudopods pseudopoles

*

in town or at home
in the city or on stage
in town or in the village

*

instantaneous city
without cityscape
without landscape
without geography
contiguous moments
abutted places
uncertain joinings

*

neither substance nor subject
encounter passage crossing
of bodies calls indices gestures
marks markdowns countermarks
bank court market
hotel parking cathedral
newsstand drugstore pharmacy

fast-food junk food
kebab hotdog quiche pizza

*

without duration only moments
appearances disappearances
balcony coffee plane tree
sidewalk hairdresser florist
palisade pastry
alley door bell
antennas relays sign-bearers
posters films sales concerts
people crossing colliding hurrying
people squeezed people absorbed
scoundrels and scoundrelletes
anodynes and anodettes
countrymen and countrywomen
citizens and citizenettes all
like cousins and their *cousines*

2010

La *Selva*

for Jacqueline Risset

Multitudinous she remains
On the border of our lives
A lair of panthers
Of enigmas of sky circles

This clearing that stands
Before us indecisive as to
Whether we will penetrate its paths
Their tracks devoid of signs

One so sylvan and leafy
Where branches barely part
Taloned and biting torsos
Only good for wild boars

This murmuring wood
Busy sylphs and fauns
Nymphs beneath the rough bark
Wet with arboreal juices

Sap of the very highest virtue
Slender delicious naked
Graceful lady of the forest
Tasting of moss and earth

Copse enclosed in memory
Opens by the beautiful force
Of a poem the other caller
Bristling from tree to tree

2012

Simple Sonnet

Notes beads broken necklace
Or my glass a burst of laughter
Yours
Notes leaves blond and rust
In a thick layer beneath the trees
Notes tossed into the forest
The panther's intermingled spots
Clear voice keyboard notes
Slender crystal hint of foam
Suddenly your blood unbinds you.

2014

Dem Sprung hatt ich Leib und Leben zu danken

To the leap I owe my life, the leap out of my mother, the leap
out of myself.
How would I be here without that leap beyond?
How would I have gotten out if not for that leap,
that force, haste, thrust?
How, since there is no passage,
not the slightest continuity
between the enclosed within
and the unfurled without?
between immanence and transcendence?
between visceral life submerged
and breath, cry, glance, shock?

Yes the step begins with the leap,
the passage without law,
the jetty in the midst of things
of this other sudden thing
that leaves, jumps, rushes

head forward, head down,
head that leaps in order to think

Es wär ein Sprung gewesen, wie man von einem Gedanken auf einen
  andern und schönern hüpft[1]

leaping from thought to thought
thinking of a leap, a *sprung*, a spring,
sperkos, salto, hopsala,
of dice rolled or tossed,
even one well thrown,
pirouette and cabriole,
skip, burst, jolt,
lacking conclusion or premise
logic leaps and dizzies

Natur nimmt den kürzesten weg (lex parsimoniae); sie thut gleichwohl keinen
  sprung, weder in der folge ihrer veränderungen, noch der zusammenstellung
  specifisch verschiedener formen (lex continui in natura).[2]

But nature spurts and surges
primum aurora novo cum spargit lumine terras
  . . . quam subito soleat sol.[3]
Oh, how the sun leaps and all the celestial bodies,
and how the new shoots of grass push up
green suddenly pointed
and the chick bursts its shell
and the man dances,
the man, the woman
and the god dances
the fire
and the dust and spark

and leap one two three
numbers and atoms
quanta ultrashort pulses
real-time dazzling time

Oh! the leap
it is life's duty to be
and thought
the thing in itself

Oh! the very leap though
salto mortale
the jump over
the insurmountable still
belongs to it
Der ein grossen sprung wil thun, gehet zuvor hinder sich.[4]

2012

"Let him kiss me
with his mouth's kisses"

Let him kiss me with his mouth's kisses
Thus sings the song of songs
Thus his mouth sings and enchants itself
As his demand so his expectation
Not kisses from another mouth
Except from the one she calls

The mouth of the other who loves her
She alone who knows
How to kiss with the kiss of her desire
For in her mouth is held
Completely breath soul perfume
And from her mouth exhaled
The thought the soft weight
Of clinging of joining of
Drinking eating believing oneself

Osculum the little mouth
That advances and arranges the gathered border of two lips

Perhaps quickly on another's cheek or lips
Kiss kissed surprise surprised
Stolen stolen in this furtive kiss
So soft from the being so light
Pulp airborne puff
And touch mouth

Visus Allocutio Tactus Osculum
Traced from the *linea amoris*
Later coming to *Coitus*
Gift of mercy
Where all mouths are joined
Kiss and kiss one another
Touch and touch one another
Put to bed and put one another to bed

Kisses come in several kinds
Osculum, Basium, Suavium
Kiss of a friend, child, parent
Kiss of peace, of decorum
Or foamy caress
That swells beneath the tongue

Kisses by the thousand like sand
In Libya or grains of wheat
Scattered to the lines of Catullus.

They resonate in several tongues
Their clicks go *Kuss, kiss, kyssa*
Κυνεω was the Greek name
Sounds like an adoration
Προσκυνεω
Almost a silent φιλεω
But always mouth addressed
Exclamation of lip and fever
Breath always scent aroma
Breath moved by the soul
That tastes and breathes your own—
Oh, kiss me with your mouth's kisses.

2014

NOTES

EXPECTATION: PREFACE TO THE ENGLISH-LANGUAGE EDITION
1. [In English by the author. Trans.]
2. [See Jacques Lacan, "The Signification of the Phallus," in *Écrits*, translated by Bruce Fink (New York: Norton, 2006), 583. Trans.]

"WET THE ROPES!": POETICS OF SENSE,
FROM PAUL VALÉRY TO JEAN-LUC NANCY
1. The French text has "une idée mit la pierre debout." See Paul Valéry, "Le Prince et la Jeune Parque," *Variété*, *Œuvres* I, ed. Jean Hytier (Paris: Gallimard, La Pléiade), 1495. See also Paul Valéry, *The Art of Poetry*, trans. Denise Folliot (Princeton: Bollingen Series, Princeton University Press, 1958), 138.
2. Hans Blumenberg, *The Laughter of the Thracian Woman: A Protohistory of Theory*, trans. Spencer Hawkins (New York: Bloomsbury, 2015).
3. See Sigmund Freud, *Three Essays on Sexuality*, in *The Psychology of Love*, edited by Shaun Whiteside (London: Penguin, 2006), 160.
4. Louis Labé, *Œuvres Complètes* (Paris, Garnier-Flammarion, 1986), 131.
5. Philippe Lacoue-Labarthe and Jean-Luc Nancy, *The Literary Absolute: The Theory of Literature in German Romanticism*, trans. Philip Barnard and Cheryl Lester (Albany: SUNY Press, 1988). The original book was published in Paris (Le Seuil, 1978), in the "Poétique" series. Further references to this book will appear parenthetically as *LA*.
6. Jacques Derrida, "Qual Quelle: Valéry's Sources," *Margins of Philosophy*, trans. Alan Bass (Chicago: University of Chicago Press, 1982), 291.
7. Quoted in Michel Jarrety, *Paul Valéry* (Paris: Hachette, 1992), 49.
8. Alain (Émile Chartier), "Qu'est-ce que la Jeune Parque?" in *Propos de littérature* (Paris: Paul Hartmann, 1934), 31.
9. See Jean-Luc Nancy, "Vox clamans in deserto," in *Demande* (Paris, Galilée, 2015), 333.
10. Paul Valéry, "Agathe," in *Œuvres* II, ed. Jean Hytier (Paris, Gallimard, Pléiade, 1966), 1392.
11. Paul Valéry, "Tel Quel," in *Œuvres* II, 473–781
12. Paul Valéry, *Œuvres* I, 1438.

13. Ibid., 1440.

14. Ibid., 1441.

15. Valéry, *Œuvres* I, 1442, and *Oeuvres* II, 478.

16. Even though Derrida voices important objections concerning Nancy's "sense" of touch as self-touching. See Jacques Derrida, *On Touching: Jean-Luc Nancy*, trans. Christine Irizarry (Stanford: Stanford University Press, 2005).

A KIND OF PROLOGUE

1. [Immanuel Kant, *Anthropology from a Pragmatic Point of View*, translated and edited by Robert B. Louden with an introduction by Manfred Kuehn (Cambridge: Cambridge University Press, 2006), 120.—Trans.]

2. [Laurence Sterne, *The Life and Opinions of Tristram Shandy, Gent.* (London: Routledge and Sons, 1893), 5.—Trans.]

3. [John Locke, *An Essay Concerning Human Understanding*, edited with an introduction by Peter H. Nidditch (Oxford: Clarendon Press Oxford, 1988), Book II, Chap. XI, 156.—Trans.]

"ONE DAY, THE GODS WITHDRAW . . .":
(LITERATURE/PHILOSOPHY: IN-BETWEEN)

1. Friedrich Nietzsche, *Thus Spake Zarathustra: A Book for None and All*, trans. Walter Kaufmann (London: Penguin Books, 1978), 237. Translation modified by Jean-Luc Nancy. Nietzsche only italicizes "work" (Ed.). [In Kaufmann's English translation, neither word is italicized.—Trans.]

2. Lucretius, *On the Nature of Things*, VI, 1283–86, trans. Ronald Melville (London: Oxford World Classics, 1999), 217.

3. A response to a proposal to write "whatever you like."

4. [Lucius Annaeus Seneca. *Moral Epistles*, trans. Richard M. Gummere. The Loeb Classical Library (Cambridge: Harvard University Press, 1917–25), vol. I, epistle XXXVII.—Trans.]

5. Georg Wilhelm Friedrich Hegel, *La Science de la logique. Encyclopédie des sciences philosophiques I*, 1830 ed., trans. B. Bourgeois (Paris: Vrin, 1988), §17, p. 183 (translation modified by J.-L. Nancy). (Ed.). [See: Hegel, *The Encyclopaedia: Logic; Part 1 of the Encyclopedia of Philosophical Sciences with the Zusätze*; trans. T. F. Geraets, W. A. Suchting, H. S. Harris (Indianapolis: Hackett, 1991), 41.—Trans.]

6. [Artaud, *Oeuvres complètes, tome 14: Suppôts et supplications* (Paris: Gallimard, 1978), 44.—Trans.]

REASONS TO WRITE

1. Jacques Derrida, *Writing and Difference*, trans. Alan Bass (London: Routledge, 2001).

2. [In English in Nancy's text.—Trans.]

3. [Dante Alighieri, *The Divine Comedy, Paradise*: Canto XXXIII, 85–87 trans. C. H. Sisson (Oxford: Oxford University Press, 2008), 498.—Trans.]

4. [Georges Bataille, *The Impossible*, trans. Robert Hurley (San Francisco: City Lights Books, 1991), 25.—Trans.]

5. [Stéphane Mallarmé, *Divagations*, trans. Barbara Johnson (Cambridge: Harvard University Press, 2007), 229.—Trans.]

6. [Michel de Montaigne, "Of Giving the Lie," II, 18, in *The Complete Works*, trans. Donald Frame (New York: Everyman's Library, 2003), 612.—Trans.]

7. [Ibid., 611.—Trans.]

8. [Jacques Derrida, *Margins of Philosophy*, "Signature Event Context," trans. Alan Bass (Chicago: University of Chicago Press, 1985), 328.—Trans.]

9. [Jacques Derrida, *Writing and Difference*, trans. Alan Bass (London: Routledge Classics, 2001), 95–96. The complete quote reads "The question about the origin of the book, the absolute interrogation, the interrogation of all possible interrogations, the 'interrogation of God' will never belong to a book."—Trans.]

10. [Dante Alighieri, *The Divine Comedy*, Inferno: Canto II, 8–9, trans. C. H. Sisson (Oxford: Oxford University Press, 2008), 51.—Trans.]

11. [Alain Robbe-Grillet, "New Novel, New Man" in *For a New Novel* (Evanston, Ill.: Northwestern University Press, 1992), 139.—Trans.]

12. [Joseph Joubert, *The Notebooks of Joseph Joubert*, trans. and with an introduction by Paul Auster (New York: New York Review Books, 2005), 32.—Trans.]

13. [Ibid., 70.—Trans.]

14. [Michel de Montaigne, "Of Vanity," III, 9, in *The Complete Works*, trans. Donald Frame (New York: Everyman's Library, 2003), 876.—Trans.]

15. [Michel de Montaigne, "Of Books," II, 10, in *The Complete Works*, trans. Donald Frame (New York: Everyman's Library, 2003), 359.—Trans.]

16. [Ibid., "Of Vanity," III, 9, 877.—Trans.]

17. [Edmund Husserl, *Cartesian Meditations: An Introduction to Phenomenology*, trans. Dorion Cairns (Boston: Kluwer Academic Publications, 1999), 136.—Trans.]

18. [Franz Kafka, "The Penal Colony," in *Metamorphosis and Other Stories*, trans. Michael Hofmann (London: Penguin Classics, 2008), 157 and 159.—Trans.]

19. [Maurice Blanchot, "The Limit-Experience," in *The Infinite Conversation*, trans. Susan Hanson (Minneapolis: University of Minnesota Press, 1992), 261–62.—Trans.]

20. ["The Revelation of St. John the Divine," 2.1. *The New Testament*, King James Version (New York: Everyman's Library, 1998).—Trans.]

21. [James Joyce, *Finnegans Wake* (London: Penguin Classics, 1999), 598.—Trans.]

22. [My translation. The published translation reads: "Come, and give back to us the becomingness of [la convenance de] what disappears, the movement of a heart." See: Jacques Derrida, *"Pace* Not(s)" in *Parages*, trans. by John P. Leavey (Stanford: Stanford University Press, 2011), 37.—Trans.]

23. [My translation. The published translation reads: "To you to take the (non)page of (no)sense [le pas de sens]. There is no chance to decide, no chance to be decided, in whatever language it may be, what comes in come." See: Jacques Derrida, *"Pace* Not(s)" in *Parages*, trans. by John P. Leavey (Stanford: Stanford University Press, 2011), 58.—Trans.]

24. [Stéphane Mallarmé, *Divagations*, trans. Barbara Johnson (Cambridge: Harvard University Press, 2007), 246.—Trans.]

25. ["The Revelation of St. John the Divine," 10.9. *The New Testament*, King James Version (New York: Everyman's Library, 1998).—Trans.]

26. [James Joyce, *Finnegans Wake* (London: Penguin Classics, 1999), 628.—Trans.]

NARRATIVE, NARRATION, RECITATIVE

1. Philippe Lacoue-Labarthe, *Portrait de l'artiste, en général* (Paris: Christian Bourgois, 1979), 90; and *L'« Allégorie »*, *suivi de Un commencement* by Jean-Luc Nancy (Paris: Galilée, 2005), 19. Here, I want to speak of narrative and Philippe Lacoue-Labarthe. Of one by the other and one for the other. Of the narrative he made of his life, of the life—the thought—he derived from narrative.

2. [The French title of the essay is *"Récit, récitation, récitatif."* Given the complicated history of these terms in literary theory and their inherent polysemy, they have been subject to multiple and conflicting translations. The French demonstrates the close interrelation among them, with the lexeme *récit-* embedded in them all. Unfortunately, there is no equivalent English cognate for these terms. Possibly, "narrative-narration-narrating," but Nancy is using *récitatif* here in a way that is closest to the musicological sense of recitative. There is an echo of Gérard Genette in this, too, and in translating the terms I have followed the example found in *Narrative Discourse* (*Discours du récit*), where the term *récit* is consistently translated as "narrative." There is a footnote to that effect. See *Narrative Discourse: An Essay on Method*, trans. Jane E. Lewin (Ithaca: Cornell University Press, 1983), 25 and 27.—Trans.]

3. William Faulkner, "Old Man," in *If I Forget Thee, Jerusalem* [*The Wild Palms*] (New York: Vintage International, 1995), 20.

4. Philippe Lacoue-Labarthe, *Poetry as Experience*, trans. Andrea Tarnowski (Stanford: Stanford University Press, 1999), 89. [Translation modified.—Trans.]

5. [Nancy's French text reads: "*Il arrive que* 'Il' *arrive.*" There is no way to fully disambiguate the author's use of the French pronoun "*il*," which can be either masculine or neuter, "he" or "it," although he does distinguish between the personal and the impersonal in this passage. Nancy is also taking advantage of a feature of the French language by which the verb "*arriver*," "to arrive," can also mean "it happens" or "it occurs" when used in the form "*il arrive que*" or "*il s'arrive que*." (In translation, the expression is frequently eliminated entirely and the phrase reworked.) Here, there is a constant inter-play between the idea of something occurring and the occurrence of someone arriving.—Trans.]

6. Lacoue-Labarthe, *Poetry as Experience*, 89.[Translation modified. The published translation reads: "But from where do we begin to think if not the starting point of 'terror,' the threat that 'It happens that' will stop happening."—Trans.]

7. G. W. F. Hegel, *Encyclopédie des sciences philosophiques III*, trans. Bernard Bourgeois (Paris: Vrin, 1990), §17, 183.

8. At the same time, philosophy also assumes its own narrative: it too has already begun before beginning. Either there have been preexisting, imper-fect forms of the *logos* or the *muthos* must be considered both as illusory knowledge and as crude knowledge, in expectation of "logical" emergence. In one mode or another, there was antecedence, either of philosophy to itself or of something other than itself . . . More broadly speaking, no philosophical text is exempt from narrative. This can easily be demonstrated. So, it is inac-curate but nonetheless illuminating to simplify, as I've done here, by reducing philosophers' texts to their intentions.

9. See Philippe Lacoue-Labarthe, *Musica-Ficta* (*Figures of Wagner*), trans. Felicia McCarren (Stanford: Stanford University Press, 1995), 84, where this failure is imputed to the art that wants to be "*itself.*" The shortcomings of the subject thus turn out to form the intimate spring of art (like religion, accord-ing to the passage in question—but that is another matter, if art is itself the "caesura of religion" as the conclusion of the book claims).

10. Philippe Lacoue-Labarthe, *Phrase* (Paris: Christian Bourgois, 2000), 45–46.

11. Philippe Lacoue-Labarthe, *Le Sujet de la philosophie. Typographie I* (Paris: Flammarion, 1979), 261. See: "The Echo of the Subject," in *Typogra-phy: Mimesis, Philosophy, Politics*, ed. Christopher Fynsk (Cambridge: Harvard University Press, 1989), 175.

12. Italo Calvino, *If on a Winter's Night a Traveler*, trans. William Weaver (New York: Everyman's Library, 1993), 149.

13. William Faulkner, *As I Lay Dying* (New York: Vintage International, 1990), 3.

14. Ibid., 261. [However, the French translation of Faulkner's text reads "'Je vous présente Mrs Bundren,' qu'il dit *comme ça*." "'This is Mrs. Bundren,' he says, *without further comment*."—Trans. My emphasis.]

15. Malcom Lowry, *Under the Volcano* (New York: Harper Perennial, 2007), 391.

16. Philippe Lacoue-Labarthe, *Le chant des muses: Petite conférence sur la musique* (Paris: Bayard, 2005), 29–30.

17. Philippe Lacoue-Labarthe, "The Echo of the Subject," 145.

18. Concerning musical romanticism, it would be appropriate here to introduce an examination of the *lied*—a form loved by Philippe as by an entire spectrum of contemporary taste, whose deep motives are certainly tied to the fact that the *lied*, often a short narrative, attempts to achieve a delicate balance between melody and rhythm or, anticipating what will be presented later, between *aria* and *recitativo*. It is capable of a singsong effusiveness as well as a vocalized beat, one bordering the other. When it is successful, this can be heard.

19. Concerning the uppercase Subject as distinguished from the lowercase subject, see *Musica ficta*, 149.

20. The quotation [from Heraclitus], "One differing in himself," has been modified by Nancy (Ed.).

21. Nor is it easy to separate rhythm from melody without an overlap. That, however, is a separate question.

22. We should analyze how, within music's contemporary destiny, beginning with Wagner and Debussy, and including Schönberg, Berio, the blues, Miles Davis, certain aspects of pop and rock, even electronic music and rap, something of the recitative has penetrated to a place where we were previously familiar only with "melody," and, in fact, perhaps overly familiar with some "precious melody." Far from being in the service of action to allow greater space for the arias, as was true of classical opera, the recitative no doubt rediscovers, in contrast with the ornamental aria, a value less associated with language than with the pulsation of speech, psalmody, chant, the antiphon—that is, the response and, thus, through another kind of echo, the religious past of the recitative. No doubt, the narrative has always been partly connected, if not with religion, at least with a sacrality associated with the alterity that goes before us and will follow us. The "caesura of religion" Lacoue-Labarthe called it.

23. Philippe Lacoue-Labarthe, *Phrase*, 130.

24. Philippe Lacoue-Labarthe, *L'« Allégorie »*, 17 ("Récitatif").

. . . WOULD HAVE TO BE A NOVEL . . .

1. In "Letter About the Novel," Schlegel writes that it would be good to create "a theory of the novel which would be a theory in the original sense of

the word; a spiritual viewing of the subject with calm and serene feeling, as it is proper to view in solemn joy the meaningful play of divine images. Such a theory of the novel would have to be in itself a novel which would reflect imaginatively every eternal tone of the imagination and would again confound the chaos of the world of the knights." See Friedrich Schlegel, "Letter About the Novel" in *Classic and Romantic German Aesthetics*, ed. J. M. Bernstein (Cambridge: Cambridge University Press, 2003), 294.

2. [*Archi-écriture*, literally, "arche-writing" or "primal-writing" is a term coined by Jacques Derrida to "connote those aspects of writing shared with speech which are denied and repressed in theories that have an investment in maintaining the natural and unmediated nature of the spoken word." See Christina Howells, *Derrida: Deconstruction from Phenomenology to Ethics* (Cambridge: Polity Press, 1998), 49.—Trans.]

3. Philippe Grand, *Tas II* (Marseille, Éric Pesty, 2006), 126.

4. "Monsieur mon Passé" is the name of a song by Léo Ferré in which the past is asked to pass on by, to no longer prey on the present.

5. This is the final strophe of Verlaine's "L'Art Poétique": "Que ton vers soit la bonne aventure/Éparse au vent crispé du matin/Qui va fleurant la menthe et le thym . . ./Et tout le reste est littérature."

6. "Étourdissons-nous avec le bruit de la plume et buvons de l'encre. Cela grise mieux que le vin," letter to Ernest Feydeau, July 15, 1861.

7. Roland Barthes, *New Critical Essays*, trans. Richard Howard (Evanston, Ill.: Northwestern University Press, 2009), 51. [My translation. The published text reads as follows: "casts a certain enchantment on the intentional meaning, returns speech to a kind of *asymptote* of meaning."—Trans.]

8. James Joyce, *Ulysses* (New York: Modern Library, 1961), 423.

9. [Homer, *The Iliad*, trans. Robert Fitzgerald (Oxford: Oxford World Classics, 2008), 1. Homer, *The Odyssey*, trans. Robert Fitzgerald (New York: Farrar, Strauss and Giroux, 1998), 1.—Trans.]

10. Even when Virgil, in a decisive shift, begins in the first person— *Arma virorum cano* . . . Wars and a man I sing—this person knows himself to be inspired—inspirated—by the song. The literary *I*, even that of Rousseau, always knows itself to be the fiction of a subject of speech but as the truth of and within this speech. It knows it has come from nowhere but is, all the same, exposed.

ON THE WORK AND WORKS

1. [Generally translated as *The Masterpiece*. See Émile Zola, *The Masterpiece*, ed. Roger Pearson, trans. Thomas Walton (Oxford: Oxford World Classics, 2008).—Trans.]

2. [The French expressions are *"vous avez une oeuvre"* and *"vous aurez bientôt une oeuvre."* There is no "standard" English equivalent that translates these expressions and also marks the difference with the term "travaux" later in this sentence. French "travaux" is used for far more mundane (although arguably more utilitarian) accomplishments—the construction of a building or road repair, for example.—Trans.]

3. Marcel Proust, *Remembrance of Things Past*, vol. 3, *The Captive*, trans. C. K. Scott Moncrieff, revised by Terence Kilmartin (New York: Vintage, 1982), 382.

4. Juan-Manuel Garrido, *Chances de la pensée* (Paris: Galilée, 2011), 38.

5. Proust, *Remembrance of Things Past*, vol. 3, 182.

6. Maurice Blanchot, *The Writing of the Disaster*, trans. Ann Smock (University of Nebraska Press, 1995), 80. [Translation modified.—Trans.]

7. Michel Foucault, "Madness, the Absence of Work," in *Foucault and His Interlocutors*, ed. Arnold I. Davidson (Chicago: University of Chicago Press, 1998). [My translation.—Trans.]

TO OPEN THE BOOK

1. Maurice Merleau-Ponty, *The Phenomenology of Perception*, trans. Donald A. Landes (London: Routledge, 2013), 182.

2. Ibid., 182.

3. See Philippe Lacoue-Labarthe, *Phrase* (Paris: Christian Bourgois, 2000), 173.

4. Didier Cahen, *À livre ouvert* (Paris: Hermann, 2013).

EXERGUES

[Georges Bataille wrote *La Haine de la poésie*; Norman Mailer, *The Executioner's Song*. XXX stands as the title for a book yet to be written . . .—Trans.]

1. [See Johan Wolfgang Goethe, *The Autobiography of Goethe: Truth and Poetry: From My Own Life*, vol. 2, trans. John Oxenford (London: George Bell, 1894), 84.—Trans.]

2. [See Georges Bataille, *The Impossible*, trans. Robert Hurley (San Francisco: City Lights Books, 2001).—Trans.]

THE POET'S CALCULATION

1. I'm intentionally bypassing the Heideggerian interpretation of Hölderlin. I would simply note that such an interpretation, considered independently of its themes, always overlooks Hölderlin's poetics, even when it—rarely—makes allusion to them (for example, in Heidegger's *Approche de Hölderlin*, trans. from the German by H. Corbin, M. Deguy, Fr. Fédier, and J. Launay [Paris: Gallimard, 1973], 242–43). [See *Elucidations of Holderlin's*

Poetry (Contemporary Studies in Philosophy and the Human Sciences), trans. Keith Hoeller (Amherst, N.Y.: Humanity Books, 2000).—Trans.], and even when it takes precautions with respect to the poetic nature of the texts it interprets philosophically (for example, in the introduction to the hymn "Germany"). Elsewhere, I return to Heidegger's relation, or non-relation, to the *ars poetica* as such. Moreover, I put forward this brief essay as a maverick with respect to (that is, by ignoring) the technical studies of Hölderlin's poetics, for example, that of Lawrence Ryan, which was pointed out to me by Alexandre Garcia-Düttman (*Hölderlins Lehre vom Wechsel der Töne* [Stuttgart: Metzler, 1960]). I would also like to point out my debt to the work of Éliane Escoubas, François Fédier, and Rainer Nägele, published in *Cahier de L'Herne Hölderlin*, edited by Jean-François Courtine (Paris, 1989). In general, I do not claim to offer a true "interpretation of Hölderlin," for I intentionally overlook too many aspects of his thought. Here, Hölderlin is midway between theme and pretext.

2. Page 662 of the Pléiade edition, under the direction of Philippe Jaccottet (F. Hölderlin, *Œuvres* [Paris: Gallimard, 1967]). I have used this source for all quotations, for the sake of convenience, sometimes modifying the translation whenever it was absolutely necessary. Unless otherwise noted, all emphasis is by Hölderlin.

3. French translation by J.-L. Nancy.

4. This is obviously the point of intersection between this analysis and that of the tragic in Hölderlin provided by Philippe Lacoue-Labarthe in "La césure du spéculatif," which appears in *L'Antigone de Hölderlin* (Paris: Christian Bourgois, 1978). We also find an extension of this by Arnaud Villani in *Cahier de L'Herne* and "Courage de la poésie" (Paris: Les Conférences de Perroquet, 1993), and in the study by Jean-François Courtine of Hölderlin's diversion from speculative idealism, "Hölderlin au seuil de l'idéalisme allemand," in *Extase de la raison. Essais sur Schelling* (Paris: Galilée, 1990).

5. French translation by J.-L. Nancy.

6. Emphasis by J.-L. Nancy.

7. [See *Friedrich Hölderlin: Essays and Letters on Theory*, trans. and edited by Thomas Pfau (Albany: SUNY Press, 1988), 62–82.—Trans.]

8. Ibid., 66.

9. Ibid., 70.

10. Ibid., 83.

11. [Friedrich Hölderlin, *Selected Poems and Fragments*, ed. Jeremy Adler, trans. Michael Hamburger (London: Penguin Classics, 1998), 171 and 302, respectively.—Trans.]

12. [Ibid., 179. The published French translation (page 841 of the Pléiade edition) reads as follows:

Une étrangère s'en vient à nous, celle qui rompt
Le sommeil, la
Voix façonneuse d'hommes.

The second English translation is my own and based on Nancy's French translation from the German, which reads as follows:

Vient une d'ailleurs
À nous, la réveilleuse,
La voix faiseuse d'hommes.—Trans.]

13. Ibid., 209.
14. Ibid., 211.
15. Ibid., 137, 139.
16. Ibid., 139.
17. French translation by J.-L. Nancy.
18. Friedrich Hölderlin, *Selected Poems*, trans. David Constantine (Newcastle upon Tyne: Bloodaxe Books, 1996), 37.
19. French translation modified by J.-L. Nancy.
20. *Selected Poems and Fragments*, 141.
21. Ibid., 137.
22. Ibid.
23. Ibid., 159.
24. Ibid.
25. Ibid., 163.
26. Ibid., 153.
27. French translation modified by J.-L. Nancy. [Hölderlin's German reads *"Dorther kommt und zurük deutet der kommende Gott."* In Hamburger's translation: "Thence has come and back there points the god who's to come." See page 153.—Trans.]
28. Ibid., 133.
29. F. Hölderlin, *Œuvres* (Paris: Gallimard, La Pléiade, 1967), 939.
30. F. Hölderlin, *Hymns and Fragments*, trans. Richard Sieburth (Princeton: Princeton University Press, 1984), 241.
31. Translation of lines 5–8 modified by J.-L. Nancy. [The translation, from the French as modified by Nancy, is my own. Michael Hamburger's translation reads as follows:

Silence often behooves us: deficient in names that are holy,
Hearts may beat high, while the lips hesitate, wary of speech?
Yes a lyre to each hour lends the right mode, the right music,

And, it may be, delights heavenly ones who draw near.
This makes ready, and almost nothing remains of the care that
Darkened our festive day, troubled the promise of joy.
Whether he like it or not, and often, a singer must harbor
Cares like these in his soul; not, though, the wrong sort of cares.

> See "Homecoming" in *Selected Poems and Fragments*,
> pages 166–67.—Trans.]

32. *Selected Poems and Fragments*, 181.

33. Ibid., 155.

34. French translation by J.-L. Nancy.

35. *Selected Poems and Fragments*, 159.

36. [My translation from Nancy's French. There is an alternate reading from Hölderlin's German by David Constantine in his *Selected Poems*: "In the Alps it is still bright night and in there cloud, / Dreaming up joyful things, covers the valley mouth." See Friedrich Hölderlin, *Selected Poems*, trans. David Constantine (Newcastle upon Tyne: Bloodaxe Books, 1996), 41.—Trans.]

37. [*Selected Poems and Fragments*, 161.—Trans.]

38. Ibid., 83.

39. French translation by J.-L. Nancy. [The Hamburger translation from the German reads:

So rivers plunge—not movement, but rest they seek—
Drawn on, pulled down against their will from
Boulder to boulder—abandoned, helmless—
By that mysterious yearning toward the chasm. —Trans.]

40. See, Hölderlin, *Selected Poems and Fragments*, 87: "So their descendants heard, and no doubt such lore / Is good, because it serves to remind us of / The Highest; yet there's also need of / One to interpret these holy legends."

41. [French] translation by J.-L. Nancy. [The Hamburger translation from the German reads: "And as the stream must follow the river's course, / Where his thought goes I'm drawn, impelled to / Follow the sure one through devious orbits." *Selected Poems and Fragments*, 89.—Trans.]

42. [French] translation by J.-L. Nancy.

43. Hölderlin, *Selected Poems and Fragments*, 183.

44. French translation by J.-L. Nancy. [The Hamburger translation from the German reads: "A mystery are those of pure origin. / Even song may hardly unveil it." *Selected Poems and Fragments*, 199.—Trans.]

45. French translation by J.-L. Nancy. [The Constantine translation reads: "people / Want presence." See "The Journey," *Selected Poems*, trans. David Constantine (Newcastle upon Tyne: Bloodaxe Books, 1996), 46.—Trans.]

46. French translation by J.-L. Nancy. [The Hamburger translation reads: "Yet each of us has his measure." See "The Rhine," in *Selected Poems and Fragments*, 207.—Trans.]

47. French translation by J.-L. Nancy.

48. Hölderlin, *Selected Poems and Fragments*, 223.

49. Ibid., 285.

50. Ibid., 311.

51. [See *Friedrich Hölderlin: Essays and Letters on Theory*, trans. and edited by Thomas Pfau (Albany: SUNY Press, 1988), 71.—Trans.]

52. Friedrich Hölderlin, "In a Lovely Blue," in *Selected Poems*, trans. David Constantine (Newcastle upon Tyne: Bloodaxe Books, 1996), 103. [Translation modified.—Trans.]

53. [This is given in the Hamburger translation as "the attentive man." See Hölderlin, "Patmos" and "Patmos (Fragments of the later version)," in *Selected Poems and Fragments*, 235 and 249.—Trans.]

54. Friedrich Hölderlin, *Empedocles* (1st version), Act 2, Scene 4.

55. Friedrich Hölderlin, letter to Neuffer, June 4, 1799.

REASON DEMANDS POETRY: AN INTERVIEW WITH EMMANUEL LAUGIER

1. Jean-Luc Nancy, *Résistance de la poésie* (Bordeaux, William Blake & Col, 1997). Ed.

2. Jean-Luc Nancy, *Haine de la poésie* (Paris: Christian Bourgois, 1979). Ed. ["La Jeune Parque" ("The Young Fate"), reputed to be Paul Valéry's masterpiece, is a 512-line poem composed in alexandrines. It is spoken in the first person by Clotho, the youngest of the three Roman deities known as the Parcae, or Fates, as she stands by the seashore. Nancy's "La Jeune Carpe" ("The Young Carp") is an obvious play on words.—Trans.]

3. See "The Poet's Calculation" in this volume.

4. [The French "saut" (from the verb "sauter"), which Nancy uses, has several related senses. These include: a jump, leap, or hop; a quick visit ("faire un saut à . . ."); or a jump in the sense of jumping or skipping over something ("saut de page").—Trans.]

5. Seneca, *Ad Lucilium—Epistulae Morales*, Book IV, Epistles 1–65, trans. Richard H. Gummere (Cambridge: Harvard University Press, "Loeb Classical Library," 1979), 257.

6. See "The Poet's Calculation" in this volume.

7. [Laugier employs a reversal of the expression "once and for all" ("une fois pour toutes"). The expression ("toutes fois pour une") can be traced to Gilles Deleuze but it's unclear if it began with him.—Trans.]

8. [A play on words. French "*vers*" (verse) and "*ver*" (worm) have identical pronunciations.—Trans.]

9. Philippe Lacoue-Labarthe and Jean-Luc Nancy, *The Literary Absolute*, trans. Philip Barnard and Cheryl Leser (Albany: SUNY Press, 1988). Jean-Luc Nancy, *Résistance de la poésie* (Paris: William Blake & Co., 1997).

10. René Char, *Hypnos*, trans. Mark Hutchinson (Seagull Books, 2014).

11. Jean Améry, "Dans quelle mesure a-t-on besoin de sa terre natale?" in *Par-delà le crime et le châtiment. Essai pour surmonter l'insurmontable*, trans. Fr. Wuilmart (Arles: Actes Sud, 1995 [1996]), 81–110. Ed.

12. J.-L. Nancy, "Vers endurci," afterward to Philippe Beck, *Dernière mode familiale* (Paris: Flammarion, 2000). Ed.

13. Preface to Gérard Haller, *Météoriques* (Paris: Seghers, 2001). Ed.

14. Jean-Christophe Bailly, "Poème de l'adieu au poème: Bailly," *Poésie 89* (Paris: Belin, 1999), 59–63. Ed.

15. See "Taking Account of Poetry" in this volume. Ed.

16. Ryoko Sekiguchi, *Calque* (Paris: P.O.L., 2001), quoted by J.-L. Nancy in "L'oscillation distincte," *in Sans commune mesure (image et texte dans l'art actuel)* (Paris: Léo Scheer, 2002); reprinted in *Au fond des images* (Paris: Galilée, 2003), 145. See *The Ground of the Image*, trans. Jeff Fort (New York: Fordham University Press, 2009).

WOZU DICHTER

1. In this short essay, I translate without examining the existing translations—numerous and, for the most part, authoritative—and without providing, except intermittently, the necessary justifications from the German. I'm not writing as a philologist any more than I am as a philosopher of Hölderlin: I'm doing nothing more than providing a marginal note inviting readers to continue the investigation.

2. [The words "wozu Dichter" are from Hölderlin's poem "Bread and Wine." They appear near the end of the seventh strophe, which reads, in Michael Hamburger's translation:

> But, my friend, we have come too late. Though the gods are living,
> Over our heads they live, up in a different world.
> Endlessly there they act and, such is their kind wish to spare us,
> Little they seem to care whether we live or do not.
> For not always a frail, a delicate vessel can hold them,
> Only at times can our kind bear the full impact of gods.
> Ever after our life is dream about them. But frenzy,
> Wandering, helps, like sleep; Night and distress make us strong
> Till in that cradle of steel heroes enough have been fostered,
> Hearts in strength can match heavenly strength as before.
> Thundering then they come. But meanwhile too often I think it's
> Better to sleep than to be friendless as we are, alone,

Always waiting, and what to do or to say in the meantime
I don't know, and who wants poets at all in lean years?
But they are, you say, like those holy ones, priests of the wine-god
Who in holy Night roamed from one place to the next.

See Friedrich Hölderlin, *Selected Poems and Fragments*, trans. Michael
Hamburger, 157. The quoted lines that appear in the essay are translated
directly from Nancy's French translations of Hölderlin. Twice removed from
the German, they display the inevitable slippage of translating from secondary sources.—Trans.]

3. Used at least by Jean-Pierre Faye—based on an inventory of all the
existing [French] translations.

4. [Hamburger's translation from the German reads:

"But they are, you say, like those holy ones, priests of the wine-god
Who in holy Night roamed from one place to the next."—Trans.]

5. I should point out that Philippe Lacoue-Labarthe, whose close attention to Hölderlin is well known, chose to translate the sixth version—and,
unless I'm mistaken, introducing it for the first time to the French public—
when he presented five translations of "Bread and Wine" to illustrate the different ways in which Hölderlin's text has been approached over time. He did
so without commentary, letting the reader evaluate, among the many other
differences, the considerable divergence that marked this strophe. I'm
inclined to believe that he was not displeased to distance himself from what
had already been done with *Wozu Dichter*.

6. Including the word *Mitternacht* (midnight).

7. *Heilige Nacht* are the last words of the strophe. One might be tempted
to hear in this the well-known Christmas canticle originating in Germany
(*Stille Nacht, heilege Nacht*—Silent night, holy night), but it was composed
later than "Brot und Wein," in 1818. This doesn't prevent us from thinking
that the expression might already have been in use as a way of referring to
Christmas night.

8. We would have to begin by acknowledging the recent work of
Wolfram Groddeck, *Hölderlins Elegie Brod und Wein oder Die Nacht*
(Frankfurt-am-Main: Stroemfeld Verlag, 2012). (It should be pointed out
that Brod is the spelling used during Hölderlin's lifetime for what is now
written *Brot* [bread].)

NOLI ME FRANGERE

1. [René François Armand (Sully) Prudhomme (1839–1907) was a
French poet and essayist and the first to win the Nobel Prize for literature
(1901). He published over a dozen volumes of poetry and several books of

essays. While his early work was personal in nature, later in life it assumed a more abstract, formal quality, largely based on his interest in philosophy and science.—Trans.]

2. [An obvious play on homophony. In French, the word forms *émoi* (agitation, confusion, turmoil), *é-moi*, and *Et moi!* (And me!) are pronounced identically.—Trans.]

RESPONDING FOR SENSE

1. Emmanuel Loi, *D'ordinaire* (Romainville: Al Dante, 2000), 7. The book consists of the letters and journals of a prisoner.

2. Philippe Lacoue-Labarthe, *Phrase* (Paris: Christian Bourgois, 2000), 17.

3. [In contemporary usage, French "*entente*" is commonly translated as "harmony," "understanding," "agreement," "arrangement." The word is said to be derived from the Latin verb *intendere* and its participle *intenta*. However, hovering behind and around all these senses of the word, is the reference to *entendre*—to hear, to understand, to comprehend. *Entente* has been used to refer to the act of hearing, but such usage is rare and appears to have fallen into disuse in the nineteenth century.—Trans.]

4. See J.-L. Nancy, *La Partage des voix* (Paris: Galilée, 1982). See "Sharing Voices" in *Transforming the Hermeneutic Context: From Nietzsche to Nancy*, edited and with an introduction by Gayle L Ormiston and Alan D. Schrift (Albany: SUNY Press, 1990).

5. Arthur Rimbaud, "Bad Blood," in *A Season in Hell*, trans. Louise Varese (New York: New Directions, 2011), 11.

6. [There are at least four primary senses of the French "sens," namely, "sense," "meaning," "direction of movement," and the physical senses. The two "senses" referred to here are sense/meaning and the physical senses.—Trans.]

BODY—THEATER

1. Antonin Artaud, *The Theater and Its Double*, trans. Mary Caroline Richards (New York: Grove Press, 1958), 48. [Translation modified.—Trans.]

2. Ibid., 51. Artaud's emphasis.

3. Ibid.

4. Ibid.

5. Marcel Proust, *Within a Budding Grove*, trans. C. K. Scott Moncrieff (New York: Random House, 1934), 708.

6. Mohammed Khaïr-Eddine, *Soleil arachnide et autres poèmes*, new edition, introduced by Jean-Paul Michel (Paris: Gallimard, 2009), 120.

7. Antonin Artaud, *Oeuvres* (Paris: Gallimard, 2004), 1662.

8. Paul Claudel, *L'Échange* (Paris: Mercure de France, 1964), 166.

9. Jean Magnan, *Un peu de temps à l'état pur* (Geneva: Philippe Macasdar, 1987), 71.

10. Heiner Müller, "Adieu à la pièce dialectique," *Hamlet-machine*, trans. J. Jourdheuil and H. Schwarzinger (Paris: Éditions de Minuit, 1985), 67.

11. François Regnault, *Petite éthique pour le comédien* (Paris: Les Conférences du Perroquet, vol. 34, March 1992).

12. Hamlet, Act 3, Scene 2, line 144.

13. Florence Dupont insists upon the religious origin—in the rites of the *ludi*—of Latin comedy. For her this comedy continued an authentic ritual whose celebration consisted in enacting—in every sense of the expression— the circumstances and codes of the ordinary seriousness of life. She sees Aristotle, on the contrary, as someone who is forced, by detaching himself completely from Dionysian ritual, to consider the theater from the viewpoint of *muthos*, that is, of the narrative in which, through *mimesis* and *catharsis*, the function of the theater is enacted (see *Aristote ou le vampire du théâtre occidental* [Paris: Flammarion, 2007]). I don't wish to participate in this debate but will simply point out that, in Aristotle, *mimesis* and *catharsis* also represent, but without his awareness of the fact, the transformations and extensions of ritual celebration.

14. Yves Lorelle, *Le corps, les rites et la scène, des origines au XXe siècle* (Paris: Éditions de l'Amandier, 2003), 19.

AFTER TRAGEDY

1. [English Translation by Jean-Luc Nancy.—Trans.] This paragraph, together with the following two texts, was delivered in English by Jean-Luc Nancy during a reading in New York for the colloquium "Honoring the Work and Person(s) of Philippe Lacoue-Labarthe (1940–2007)," organized by Avital Ronell and Denis Hollier, New York University and Cardozo Law School, which took place in April 2008. [Ed.]

2. It is worth noting, in passing, that this is also what is involved in the broader notion that bears the confused or obscure name of "secularization."

3. I remember Philippe saying to me one day, "I know what needs to be done for there to be a new Hölderlin today, but it's too difficult . . ."

4. Empédocle (third version), trans. R. Rovini, in *Oeuvres* (Paris: Gallimard, "Bibliothèque de la Pléiade," 1967), 573.

5. [In English in Nancy's text.—Trans.]

BLANCHOT'S RESURRECTION

1. Maurice Blanchot, *The Space of Literature*, trans. Ann Smock (University of Nebraska Press, 1989). [Translation modified.—Trans.]

2. Without adding further detail, I'll quickly add five references to the five terms, all taken from *The Space of Literature*, on pages 45, 116, 130, 216, 29.

3. See Christophe Bident, *Reconnaissances—Antelme, Blanchot, Deleuze* (Paris: Calmann-Lévy, 2003).

4. Maurice Blanchot, *Thomas the Obscure*, trans. Robert Lamberton (New York: Station Hill Press, c1988). [This English translation is based on the text of the second edition of Blanchot's French text.—Trans.]

5. Ibid., 38.

6. Ibid., 37.

7. [A reversal by Nancy of Freud's well-known maxim "Wo es war soll ich werden"—"Where id was there ego shall be." The expression appears in Freud's *New Introductory Lectures on Psychoanalysis*, vol. 22 of the *Standard Edition of the Works of Sigmund Freud*. Nancy's reversal would read "Where ego was, it shall rise again."—Trans.]

8. Ibid., 38.

9. Ibid., 89.

10. Ibid., 90.

11. Ibid.

12. Ibid., 89. [Translation modified.—Trans.]

13. See "Reading," in *The Space of Literature*.

14. Maurice Blanchot, *The Writing of the Disaster*, trans. Ann Smock (University of Nebraska Press, 1995), 124.

15. Ibid., 41.

16. Maurice Blanchot, *The Space of Literature*, trans. Ann Smock, 190.

17. Ibid., 194. [Translation modified.—Trans.]

18. Ibid.

19. Ibid.

20. Ibid., 197.

21. Ibid., 147.

22. Ibid.

23. Philippe Lacoue-Labarthe, *Agonie terminée, agonie interminable. Sur Maurice Blanchot*, followed by *L'émoi* (Paris: Galilée, 2011), 149. See *Ending and Unending Agony: On Maurice Blanchot*, trans. by Hannes Opelz (New York: Fordham University Press, 2015).

24. Blanchot, *The Writing of the Disaster*, 18.

25. Ibid., 20.

THE NEUTRAL, NEUTRALIZATION OF THE NEUTRAL

1. Maurice Blanchot, *The Step Not Beyond*, trans. Lycette Nelson (Albany: SUNY Press, 1992), 32.

2. Ibid.

3. Ibid., 33.

4. Ibid., 59.

5. Ibid., 60.

6. Ibid., 74.

7. Ibid., 75.

8. Ibid., 71.

9. And other words: "fear," "madness" (ibid., 59).

10. Maurice Blanchot, *The Infinite Conversation*, trans. Susan Hanson (Minneapolis: University of Minnesota Press, 1992), 312.

11. Blanchot, *The Step Not Beyond*, 75.

12. Ibid., 118.

13. Ibid., 74. We find in these pages a constant alternation of "Neutral" and "neuter," which cannot be entirely explained by the assumption that the second would have its current grammatical value. [I have modified the translation (and Nancy's note) to comply with the author's wishes and the remainder of this essay. However, throughout *The Step Not Beyond*, the translation of French "neutre" is given as "neuter." Indeed, "neutral" and "neuter" are treated as equivalent by the translator.—Trans.]

14. Blanchot, *The Infinite Conversation*, 261. [Translation modified.—Trans.] (Strictly speaking, we would need to consider the respective dates of the texts referenced and take into consideration the displacements and modifications of Blanchot's thought; but that is not my purpose here.)

15. Blanchot, *The Step Not Beyond*, 75.

EXCLAMATIONS

1. Marquis de Sade, Juliette, translated by Austryn Wainhouse (New York: Grove Press, 1968 [1994]), 333.

2. Guillaume Apollinaire, Letters to Madeleine, trans. Donald Nicholson-Smith (London: Seagull Books, 2010), 471.

THE YOUNG CARP

1. Alain, born Émile-Auguste Chartier, was a French philosopher, teacher, and prolific author. In 1936, he wrote a commentary for a new French edition of Valéry's *La Jeune Parque*.

2. [In Nancy's French, "marque le pas," literally "indicate the not" or negation of poetry. The French term is ordinarily translated as "to mark time"; however, Nancy is playing upon the inherent ambiguity of "pas," which, as a noun, can mean a "step," "tread," and so on but is also used to signify negation. It is, as well, an echo of Blanchot's *Le Pas au-delà*, *The Step Not Beyond*.—Trans.]

"WITHIN MY BREAST, ALAS, TWO SOULS . . ."

1. [Taken from the opening lines of Goethe's *Faust*, Scene 1. My English translation is based on a French paraphrase of Goethe's German by Nancy. The opening lines from the German read:

FAUST:

> Habe nun, ach! Philosophie,
> Juristerei und Medizin,
> Und leider auch Theologie
> Durchaus studiert, mit heißem Bemühn.
> Da steh ich nun, ich armer Tor!
—Trans.]

DEM SPRUNG HATT ICH LEIB UND LEBEN ZU DANKEN

About the German title: Friedrich Schiller, "*Die Räuber*," Act 1, Scene 2.
"To that jump I owe my body and my life." [My translation from Nancy's
French translation of the German. Taken from "The Robbers," Schiller's first
dramatic work, published in 1781. See Friedrich Schiller, *The Robbers/Wallen-
stein*, trans. with an introduction by F. J. Lamport (London: Penguin Books,
1979), 39 and 63. Lamport's published translation reads, "That jump saved
my skin; the brute would have torn me to pieces."—Trans.]

1. Ibid., Act 2, Scene 2. "That would have been a jump, as when one
jumps from one thought to another, and then some."

2. Immanuel Kant, *Kritik der Urteilskraft, Erste Einleintung*, V. "Nature
takes the shortest path (*lex parsimoniae*); it makes no leap, either in the succession of its changes or in the composition of specifically different forms (*lex
continui in natura*)."

["Nature takes the shortest way (*lex parsimoniae*); yet it makes no leap, either
in the sequence of its changes, or in the juxtaposition of specifically different
forms (*lex continui in natura*); its vast variety in empirical laws is for all that,
unity under a few principles (*principia praeter necessitatem non sunt multipli-
canda*)." See, *The Critique of Judgment (Part One: The Critique of Aesthetic
Judgment)*, trans. James Creed Meredith (Oxford: Oxford World's Classics,
2008), 15.—Trans.]

3. Lucretius, *De Rerum Natura*, II, v. 144–47.

["Now what the speed to matter's atoms given
Thou mayest in few, my Memmius, learn from this:
**When first the dawn is sprinkling with new light
The lands**, and all the breed of birds abroad
Flit round the trackless forests, with liquid notes
Filling the regions along the mellow air,
We see 'tis forthwith manifest to man
How suddenly the risen sun is wont
At such an hour to overspread and clothe
The whole with its own splendour . . .

See *On the Nature of Things*, trans. William Ellery Leonard (New York: E. P. Dutton, 1916), Book II, 142–47.—Trans.]

4. Christian Egenolff, *Sprichwoerter*, 237a, 1565. "He who wants to jump far must back up behind himself."

"MENSTRUUM UNIVERSALE: LITERARY DISSOLUTION"

First appeared in *Aléa*, no. 1, Jean-Christophe Bailly (ed.) (Paris: Christian Bourgois, 1981). [First English translation, by Paula Moddel in *SubStance* 21 (1978): 21–35, and reprinted in *The Birth to Presence* (Stanford: Stanford University Press, 1993).]

"ONE DAY THE GODS WITHDRAW . . ."

Originally published as "*Un jour, les dieux se retirent . . .*" (Bordeaux: William Blake & Co., 2001). The first version of the text, "Entre-deux," was published in *Le Magazine littéraire* (Paris), no. 392, November 2000; the second version appeared as "À votre guise" in *La Quinzaine littéraire* (Paris), no. 793, Oct. 1–15, 2000; Spanish translation, J. Barja, *Sileno* (Madrid: Edicion Identificacion y Desarrollo), vol. 9, 2000; first English translation, F. Manjali, "Between story and truth," *The Little Magazine* (Delhi), vol. 2, no. 4, July–August 2001; Danish translation, J. Lohmann, *Passe partout* (Aarhus: Aarhus Universitet), no. 22, 2003.

"REASONS TO WRITE"

Written in April 1977, this text first appeared as "Les raisons d'écrire" in Maurice Blanchot, Michel Deutsch, Emmanuel Hocquard, Roger Laporte, Jean-Luc Nancy, Jean Louis Schefer, Mathieu Bénézet, Philippe Lacoue-Labarthe, *Misère de la littérature* (Paris: Christian Bourgois, 1979).

"NARRATIVE, NARRATION, RECITATIVE"

First published as "Récit, récitation, récitatif" in *Europe*, "Philippe Lacoue-Labarthe," no. 973, May 2010.

". . . WOULD HAVE TO BE A NOVEL . . ."

First appeared as ". . . devrait être un roman . . ." in *Contemporary French and Francophone Studies* (London: Routledge), vol. 16, no. 2, March 2012; Portuguese trans. F. Walace Rodrigues and P. Eyben in *Revista Cerrados : "Acontecimento e Experiências Limites"* (Brazil), vol. 21, no. 33, 2012.

"ON THE WORK AND WORKS"

"De l'œuvre et des œuvres" is an unpublished text first presented at a conference held at the Musée Rodin, Paris, June 2011.

"TO OPEN THE BOOK"

First published as "Pour ouvrir le livre," the preface to Didier Cahen, *À livre ouvert* (Paris: Hermann, 2013).

"EXERGUES"

First appeared as "Exergues" in *Aléa*, no. 5, edited by Jean-Christophe Bailly (Paris: Christian Bourgois, 1984). [The current translation, by Emily McVarish, was previously published in English in *The Birth to Presence* (Stanford: Stanford University Press, 1993).]

"THE POET'S CALCULATION"

First appeared as "Calcul du poète" in *Des lieux divins* followed by *Calcul du poète* (Mauvezin: Éditions Trans-Europ-Repress, 1997 [1987]); German trans., G. Febel and J. Legueil, *Kalkül des Dichters nach Hölderlins Mass* (Stuttgart: Jutta Legueil, 1997); Italian trans., A. Moscati, "Calcolo del poeta," in *Micromega. Almanacco di filosofia*, 2/1998; Italian trans. [with *Luoghi divini*] with an afterward by Luisa Bonesio ["*Luoghi desertati*"] (Padua, Il Poligrafo, 1999); Japanese trans., M. Onishi, *Shoraisha*, Tokyo, 2001.

"REASON DEMANDS POETRY:
AN INTERVIEW WITH EMMANUEL LAUGIER"

"La raison demande la poésie." This interview with Emmanuel Laugier first appeared in "Cahier Jean-Luc Nancy," in *L'Animal* (Metz), no. 14–15, Summer 2003.

"WOZU DICHTER"

Previously unpublished in French.

"NOLI ME FRANGERE" (WITH PHILIPPE LACOUE-LABARTHE)

This text, initially intended to be published in German (German trans. E. Jacoby), in *Fragment und Totalität*, Lucien Dallenbach and Christian L. Hart Nibbrig (eds.) (Frankfurt-am-Main: Suhrkamp, 1984), appeared in French as "La littérature et la philosophie" in *La Revue des sciences humaines* (Lille: Université de Lille III), no. 185, 1982, and in *Europe*, "Philippe Lacoue-Labarthe," no. 193, May 2010. [The current translation, by Brian Holmes, was previously published in English in *The Birth to Presence* (Stanford: Stanford University Press, 1993).]

"RESPONDING FOR SENSE"

"Répondre du sens" first appeared in *Po&sie* (Paris: Belin), no. 92, 2000; reissued in *La Pensée dérobée* (Paris: Galilée, 2001) 167–77; Spanish trans. I. D.

Entrabasaguas and J.-M. Garrido, *Vertebra* (Santiago da Chile: RIL Editores), no. 6, November 2000; Italian trans., F. Garitano and M. Machi, *Ou. Riflessioni e provocazioni* (Cosenza: *Edizioni Scientifiche Italiana*), v. X, 2, 2000; German trans., J. Wolf, *Singularitäten*, Marianne Schuller and Elisabeth Strowick (eds.) (Fribourg-en-Brisgau: Rombach Verlag, 2001); first English trans., J.-Ch. Cloutier, *A Time for the Humanities, Futurity and the Limits of Autonomy*, ed. J. J. Bono, T. Dean, and E. P. Ziarek (New York: Fordham University Press, 2008).

"body—theater"
First published as "Corps-théâtre" in *Passions du corps dans les dramaturgies contemporaines*, ed. Alexandra Poulain (Villeneuve-d'Ascq: Presses universitaires du Septentrion, 2011).

"After Tragedy"
"Après la tragédie," unpublished in French, was presented at a symposium entitled "Honoring the Work and Person(s) of Philippe Lacoue-Labarthe (1940–2007)," organized by Avital Ronell and Denis Hollier, New York University and Cardozo Law School, April 2008; Italian trans., A. Moscati, *Corpo teatro* (Naples: Cronopio, 2010); published in Greek (Athens: J. Kastaniotis, 2006) and German (Stuttgart: Jutta Legueil, 2010).

"blanchot's resurrection"
"Résurrection de Blanchot" is based on a talk given in January 2004 for the opening of a series of symposia on Maurice Blanchot held at the Centre Georges-Pompidou under the direction of Christophe Bident; appeared in *La Déclosion (Déconstruction du christianisme 1)* (Paris: Galilée, 2005). First English translation by Michael B. Smith in *Dis-Enclosure: Deconstruction of Christianity* (New York: Fordham University Press, 2008).

"the neutral, neutralization of the neutral"
First appeared as "Le neutre, la neutralisation du neutre" in *Cahiers Maurice Blanchot* (Paris: Les Presses du Réel), no. 1, 2011.

"exclamations"
First published as "Exclamations" in *Dictionnaire de la pornographie*, ed. Philippe Di Folco, preface by Jean-Claude Carrière (Paris: PUF, 2005), and as "Il y a du rapport sexuel—et après," *Littérature* (Paris: Larousse), no. 142(2):30, January 2006.

"the only reading"
First appeared as "La seule lecture" in *La Quinzaine littéraire* (Paris), no. 905, August 1–31, 2005.

"PSYCHE"

First published as "Psychè" in *Première Livraison* (Paris), no. 16, 1978. This text was quoted in its entirety, with a commentary by Jacques Derrida in *Le Toucher, Jean-Luc Nancy* (Paris: Galilée, 2010). [The current translation, by Emily McVarish, was previously published in English in *The Birth to Presence* (Stanford: Stanford University Press, 1993).]

"THE YOUNG CARP"

First appeared as "La Jeune Carpe" in Mathieu Bénézet, Michel Deutsch, Emmanuel Hocquard, Philippe Lacoue-Labarthe, Jean-Luc Nancy, Bernard Noël, Alain Veinstein, and Franck Venaille, *Haine de la poésie* (Paris: Christian Bourgois, 1979).

" 'WITHIN MY BREAST, ALAS, TWO SOULS . . .' "

Italian trans., A. Panaro, *"Nel mio petto, ahimé, due anime . . .,"* in Claudio Parmiggiani, *L'Isola del silenzio* (Turin: Umberto Allemandi & C., 2006); first English trans. *Topoi*, v. 25, nos. 1–2, Spring 2006; Italian trans., A. Panaro, in J.-L. Nancy, *Narrazioni del fervore. Il desiderio, il sapere, il fuoco*, with an essay by Flavio Ermini (Bergamo: Moretti & Vitali Editori, 2007). [The French version of the text is available in Claudio Parmiggiani, *L'Isola del silenzio* (Turin: Umberto Allemandi & C., 2006), together with a version in Flemish and an essay by Elena La Spina.—Trans.]

"CITY MOMENTS"

First published as "Instants de ville" in *E-rea* (an electronic review of Anglophone studies), 7.2, Nathalie Cochoy (ed.), 2010. See: https://erea.revues.org/?lang=en.

"LA SELVA"

First appeared in *I pensieri dell'istante. Scritti per Jacqueline Risset* (Rome: Editori Internazionali Riuniti, 2012).

"SIMPLE SONNET"

First published as "Sonate facile" in *Lignes*, no. 45, 2014, "À la mémoire de Jacqueline Risset."

"*DEM SPRUNG HATT ICH LEIB AND LEBEN ZU DANKEN*"

First published in French and German in *Brink Magazin zwischen Kultur und Wissenschaft*, no. 2, June 2012.

" 'LET HIM KISS ME WITH HIS MOUTH'S KISSES' "

Previously unpublished, 2014.